Globalization, Industrialization and Labour Markets in East and South Asia

Among the key debates fought in developing economies is whether globalization through liberalization is the means by which economies can industrialize and provide their labour forces with tangible improvements in the material conditions of living. This book addresses this issue head on, using empirical evidence from some of the fastest growing and transition economies from East and South Asia. Countries such as the Philippines and Malaysia have already started to deindustrialize before enjoying industrial maturity, while with the exception of China and evidence of some growth in real wages in the other economies, the evidence appears compelling to suggest that increased industrialization and integration into the capitalist economy has not succeeded in providing significant labour improvement. The evidence suggests that a proactive state, focusing on enhancing the material conditions of labour, is pertinent to ensuring sustainable long term industrialization and thus improving material conditions for workers.

This book was originally published as a special issue of the *Journal of the Asia Pacific Economy*.

Rajah Rasiah is Professor of Economics and Technology Management at University of Malaya, Kuala Lumpur, Malaysia. He is currently on sabbatical at Harvard University, Cambridge, MA, USA.

Bruce McFarlane was formerly Professor of Economics at Adelaide University, Australia, and Newcastle University, Australia.

Sarosh Kuruvilla is Professor of Industrial Relations, Asian Studies, and Public Affairs at the School of Industrial Relations, Cornell University, Ithaca, NY, USA.

Globalization, Industrialization and Labour Markets in East and South Asia

Edited by
Rajah Rasiah, Bruce McFarlane and Sarosh Kuruvilla

Routledge
Taylor & Francis Group

LONDON AND NEW YORK

First published 2016 by Routledge

2 Park Square, Milton Park, Abingdon, Oxon OX14 4RN
711 Third Avenue, New York, NY 10017, USA

Routledge is an imprint of the Taylor & Francis Group, an informa business

First issued in paperback 2017

British Library Cataloguing in Publication Data
A catalogue record for this book is available from the British Library

ISBN 13: 978-1-138-92493-2 (hbk)
ISBN 13: 978-1-138-08660-9 (pbk)

Typeset in Times New Roman
by RefineCatch Limited, Bungay, Suffolk

Publisher's Note
The publisher accepts responsibility for any inconsistencies that may have
arisen during the conversion of this book from journal articles to book chapters,
namely the possible inclusion of journal terminology.

Disclaimer
Every effort has been made to contact copyright holders for their permission to
reprint material in this book. The publishers would be grateful to hear from any
copyright holder who is not here acknowledged and will undertake to rectify
any errors or omissions in future editions of this book.

Contents

Citation Information

The chapters in this book were originally published in the *Journal of the Asia Pacific Economy*, volume 20, issue 1 (January 2015). When citing this material, please use the original page numbering for each article, as follows:

Chapter 1
Globalization, industrialization and labour markets
Rajah Rasiah, Bruce McFarlane and Sarosh Kuruvilla
Journal of the Asia Pacific Economy, volume 20, issue 1 (January 2015) pp. 2–13

Chapter 2
Globalization, industrialization and labour markets in China
Miao Zhang and Rajah Rasiah
Journal of the Asia Pacific Economy, volume 20, issue 1 (January 2015) pp. 14–41

Chapter 3
Growth, industrialisation and inequality in India
Jayati Ghosh
Journal of the Asia Pacific Economy, volume 20, issue 1 (January 2015) pp. 42–56

Chapter 4
Industrialization, globalization, and labor market regime in Indonesia
Dionisius Narjoko and Chandra Tri Putra
Journal of the Asia Pacific Economy, volume 20, issue 1 (January 2015) pp. 57–76

Chapter 5
Industrialization and labour in Malaysia
Rajah Rasiah, Vicki Crinis and Hwok-Aun Lee
Journal of the Asia Pacific Economy, volume 20, issue 1 (January 2015) pp. 77–99

Chapter 6
Globalization of industrialization and its impact on clothing workers in Myanmar
Myo Myo Myint, Rajah Rasiah and Kuppusamy Singaravelloo
Journal of the Asia Pacific Economy, volume 20, issue 1 (January 2015) pp. 100–110

Chapter 7
Growth and employment in de-industrializing Philippines
Rene E. Ofreneo
Journal of the Asia Pacific Economy, volume 20, issue 1 (January 2015) pp. 111–129

Chapter 8
Industrialization, globalization and labour force participation in Thailand
Voravidh Charoenloet
Journal of the Asia Pacific Economy, volume 20, issue 1 (January 2015) pp. 130–142

Chapter 9
Globalization, industrialization, and labor markets in Vietnam
Angie Ngoc Tran and Irene Nørlund
Journal of the Asia Pacific Economy, volume 20, issue 1 (January 2015) pp. 143–163

For any permission-related enquiries please visit:
http://www.tandfonline.com/page/help/permissions

Notes on Contributors

Voravidh Charoenloet graduated with a Ph.D. in Economics from the University of Paris X – Nanterre, France, and has worked for 20 years in the Faculty of Economics at Chulalongkorn University, Bangkok, Thailand. Now, he has been appointed to teach in the School of Economics at the University of Chiang Mai, Thailand. His fields of specialty are political economy, economic development and labour economics. His research focuses on industrialization and labour, with special emphasis on industrial relations, social protection, and welfare and occupational health and safety.

Vicki Crinis is a research associate with the Faculty of Law, Humanities and Creative Arts at the University of Wollongong, Australia. Her research focuses on the clothing industry in the Asia Pacific and migrant workers, trade unions and NGOs in Malaysia. She has published a number of book chapters and journal articles on these topics. Her current research is looking at Work and Care in Malaysia.

Jayati Ghosh is Professor and Chairperson at the Centre for Economic Studies and Planning, School of Social Sciences, Jawaharlal Nehru University, New Delhi, India. She is also the Executive Secretary of International Development Economics Associates.

Sarosh Kuruvilla is Professor of Industrial Relations, Asian Studies, and Public Affairs at the School of Industrial Relations, Cornell University, Ithaca, NY, USA.

Hwok-Aun Lee is Senior Lecturer in the Department of Development Studies, Faculty of Economics and Administration, University of Malaya, Kuala Lumpur, Malaysia. His research interests include affirmative action, inequality, labour, social policy, discrimination and education.

Bruce McFarlane was formerly Professor of Economics at Adelaide University, Australia, and Newcastle University, Australia.

Myo Myo Myint obtained her doctoral degree in economics from the University of Malaya, Kuala Lumpur, Malaysia in 2012. She is currently undertaking research on labour issues in Myanmar.

Dionisius Narjoko is a researcher at the Economic Research Institute for ASEAN and East Asia, Jakarta, Indonesia. He received his Ph.D. in Economics from the Australian National University, Canberra, Australia. His research focuses on topics related to industrial organization and international trade.

Irene Nørlund is Associate Professor in the Faculty of Health and Technology at the Metropolitan University College, Copenhagen, Denmark. Her books include: *The Politics of Vietnam's Poverty Reduction and Growth Strategy*; *The Emerging Civil*

Society in Vietnam CIVICUS; *Vietnam in a Changing World*; *The Bai Bang project – Swedish aid and paper production in Vietnam1969–96*; and *Textile Production in Vietnam 1880–1940*.

Angie Ngoc Tran is Professor of Political Economy at California State University, Monterey Bay, California, USA. Her books include: *Ties That Bind: Cultural Identity, Class, and Law in Vietnam's Labor Resistance*; *Corporate Social Responsibility (CSR) and Competitiveness for SMEs in Developing Countries*; and *Reaching for the Dream: Challenges of Sustainable Development in Vietnam* (with Melanie Beresford).

Rene E. Ofreneo holds a professorship at the University of the Philippines, Diliman, Quezon City, Philippines. He has done extensive research and field work on industrial relations and the labour market in the Philippines and Southeast Asia. His latest book, *Asia & the Pacific: Advancing Decent Work Amidst Deepening Inequalities*, was published in 2013.

Chandra Tri Putra is a Research Associate at the Economic Research Institute for ASEAN and East Asia, Jakarta, Indonesia. He received his Master Degree in Economics from the University of Indonesia, specializing in International Economics.

Rajah Rasiah is Professor of Economics and Technology Management at the University of Malaya, Kuala Lumpur, Malaysia. He is currently on sabbatical at Harvard University, Cambridge, MA, USA.

Kuppusamy Singaravelloo is a senior lecturer in the Faculty of Economics and Administration, University of Malaya, Kuala Lumpur, Malaysia.

Miao Zhang obtained her Ph.D. in Economics from University of Malaya, Kuala Lumpur, Malaysia, and is currently working as a post-doctoral researcher at the University of Malaya.

OBITUARY

Tribute to Melanie Beresford

I knew Melanie as a partner for 17 years including a long spell at Cambridge University (UK), where she completed — in brilliant fashion — three degrees — BA (honours), MA and PhD (doctorate).

Her many books and articles clearly show that we have lost a scholar of immeasurable value. As academics we have lost her penetrating framework for r understanding South-east Asia and, indeed for much else. And she had a readership outside universities. Her best book was her doctorate rewritten somewhat, *Unification and Economic Development in Vietnam* but she won the US Library of Congress prize for her book, *Vietnam - Economics, Politics and Society*. The pioneering question she asked and tried to answer was — What happens when two contradictory socio-economic systems inhabit the same geographical unit — the same boundaries? (Something we saw in North and South Vietnam, North and South Korea, West and East Germany, etc.) Her honest and incisive works made her one of the world's leading scholars on Vietnam.

Melanie was a quiet, gentle person, but passionate about her friends and her political causes, such as Australia—Vietnam friendship, aboriginal rights, environmental protection and social change.

She was also prepared to call a spade a spade when necessary — as when, after marking Economics 1 exam papers, she emailed the staff members 'Is anyone else as appalled as I am?'

On the whole she was treated fairly by Macquarie University except when someone asked why her articles did not contain the word 'economic'. While this was patently untrue, she was at that time heavily burdened with undergraduate lecture courses on The History of Economic Thought and the Economies of South-east Asia!

Melanie will be sorely missed by myself, Marcus (brother), Betsy (mother), Prue Kerr, Geoff Harcourt, and the many postgraduate students whom she supervised.

Bruce McFarlane
Formerly of Newcastle University, Australia

Globalization, industrialization and labour markets

Rajah Rasiah[a], Bruce McFarlane[b] and Sarosh Kuruvilla[c]

[a]Department of Development Studies, University of Malaya, Kuala Lumpur, Malaysia; [b]Economics Department, Newcastle University, Callaghan, NSW, Australia; [c]School of Labor and Industrial Relations, Cornell University, Ithaca, NY, USA

While mainstream accounts of globalization are telling us that liberalization is essential for engendering the conditions of prosperity across the world, we argue that selective interventions arc necessary to ensure that these processes open the path to the high road to industrialization. While recognizing the importance of relative surplus appropriation through technological deepening as the engine of capitalist accumulation, the extant evidence suggests that a proactive state focusing on enhancing labour is pertinent to ensure sustainable long-term industrialization and structural change so that the material conditions of workers improve over time. Hence, this article provides the introduction to globalization, industrialization and labour market experiences in selected East and South Asian economies.

1. Introduction

Two major processes have impacted extensively on the labour markets in Asia, namely globalization and industrialization. Whereas globalization refers to the integration of local and national economies globally with serious developmental consequences, industrialization refers primarily to the emergence and expansion of manufacturing activity, but also its appendages of construction and utilities (Kaldor, 1967). Advocates emphasizing the need to promote industrialization as a necessary condition to stimulate rapid economic growth have argued that its increasing returns characteristics is essential to evolve the productive forces of economies so that the material conditions of populations can be improved dramatically (Chang 2003; Reinert 2007).

However, Piore and Sabel (1984) and Pyke and Sengenberger (1992) argue that the road to industrialization does not necessarily guarantee that its fruits will trickle equally between capital and labour, distinguishing in the process the high and low roads to industrialization. While the increasing returns advocates of industrialization have focused wholly on its potential to drive rapid economic growth, the under-consumption theorists have targeted wage improvements for it to be sustainable (Hobson 1965; Brewer 1980). High wage regimes not only offer the demand for sustained growth with domestic consumption becoming a major driver of growth, it will also ensure that class contradictions could be kept from exploding. In addition, high-wage regimes are also an essential

---

This introduction has benefitted extensively from comments from participants at the Workshop on 'Globalization, Industrialization and Labour Markets in Asia', held on 9-10 January 2014 at Chiang Mai University.

component of flexible specialization practices that draw on workers knowledge capabilities. Flexible specialization regimes are the polar opposite of exploitative Taylorist regimes. Whereas the former are in sync with what Marx (1967) and Luxembourg (1951) referred to as focused on relative surplus value appropriation that is associated with industrial capitalism, the latter is predicated on absolute surplus value appropriation.

We examine here how the forces of globalization, especially the nature of capitalist integration into the global economy, have affected industrialization in selected Asian economies, including with varying degrees of national and local policy initiatives, and how these processes have influenced changes in domestic labour markets. We discuss the arguments and the evolution of globalization, industrialization and labour markets in this introduction. These were critical issues Beresford (1988, 1989, 2009) addressed in her works on Vietnam and Cambodia, including its effects on the labour force processes.

2. Globalization

Globalization can be traced to the seventeenth century when the historian Hopkins (2003) used the term proto-globalization to refer to the phase when trade links and cultural exchange began to rise rapidly as the age of discovery, colonization and sea links between Europe and other countries expanded (see also Hobsbawm 1998). Information flow and the physical movement of people took a new dimension following the advent of jets, transistors, computers and the Internet (Perez 1985; Best 2001). Humans have since evolved to engage in interactive brain circulation, such that knowledge development has not only received a quantum leap but it has also expanded the synergistic capacity of knowledge nodes through the installation of broadband technology. Concerns of an overexpansion of technology that could destroy planet earth are also increasingly allayed with efforts taken by several countries to check climatic change and global warming. Interestingly, Mathews (2014) argues that it is the most populous countries of China and India that are currently recording the fastest rate of industrialization-led GDP growth, and who are also poised to green capitalism by displacing fossil fuels with renewable fuels. While one cannot any longer question the power of science and technology in making the world both materially more comfortable, as well as, environmentally more inhabitable, serious questions still linger on whether globalization as a process will continue to exacerbate inequalities, thereby only allowing a handful of countries and the peoples to make the transition to developed and sustainable status.

In addition, the consequences of globalization continue to be interpreted differently by different scholars, and hence, the prescriptions for stimulating economic development have also varied widely. While the neo-Marxist argument that the process has given rise to the simultaneous occurrence of exploitation (the periphery) and accumulation (in the core) is now only a force in populist circles following rapid growth and structural change experienced by countries such as Korea, Taiwan, Singapore, China and India (Mathews 2014; Rasiah and Schmidt 2010), the lack of economic convergence involving most other countries means that the processes of global integration have been highly uneven with host-states becoming a major explanatory variable as to why some countries have managed it while others have failed.

3. Industrialization

The arguments on industrialization as the engine of growth and development arose largely from the advocates of increasing returns industries. Smith (1776) and Young (1928) had argued incisively on the capacity of industrialization to drive increasing returns activities.

Veblen (1915), Gerschenkron (1962) and Abramovitz (1956) provided evidence to argue that successful industrializers have used industrial policy to stimulate rapid economic growth and structural change.[1] As manufacturing matures, Rowthorn and Wells (1987) provided evidence to show that the shift towards services has been accompanied by continued improvements in productivity in a number of industries in the United States (positive deindustrialization) while it has declined in the United Kingdom (negative deindustrialization). Information and knowledge exchange synergies do support GDP growth, especially when countries achieve high income status.

Industrialization – both the growth in share of GDP and its diversification into higher value added activities – have been associated with the successful development of the Organization for Economic Cooperation and Development (OECD) countries in the initial years of rapid growth. East and Southeast Asia's successful developers – i.e. the first wedge of the flying geese stock of Japan, Hong Kong, Korea, Singapore and Taiwan – enjoyed rapid industrialization throughout their high growth years.[2]

Marx (1967) had argued over the superior productive forces that industrial capitalism generates over other modes of production, though his predicted route of class antagonism and revolution to communism did not happen. Kalecki (1976) acknowledged this dimension when formulating his model of economic development by focusing on the development of productive forces over simply the creation of jobs (see also McFarlane 1971, 1982). However, Lenin (1950) turned Marx on his head by claiming that capitalism had reached a monopoly stage, and hence, orchestrated the Bolshevik revolution in rural Russia. The inability of the vanguard to transform the productive forces comparable to the competitively driven capabilities evolved in industrial capitalism undermined the socialist experiment (Kontorovich and Ellman 1992), which eventually ended in 1991 with the fall of the Berlin wall. Also, the denial of individual freedom through centralized control acted as a powerful social glue to expand the reservoir of hatred against communism.

Economic transition from communism to industrial capitalism has helped countries such as Cambodia, Laos, Myanmar and Vietnam enjoy fairly strong economic growth, though the first three still had GDP per capita incomes less than US$1000 in 2012 (World Bank 2013). However, the fall of the Soviet Union did not herald the conditions of economic convergence for most countries. For example, the sub-Saharan countries have continued to languish in poverty with countries such as Angola, Benin, Burkina Faso, Cameroun, Chad, Congo, Ethiopia, Guinea Bissau, Kenya, Madagascar, Malawi, Niger, Senegal, Sierra Leone, Somalia, The Gambia, Togo, Uganda, Zambia and Zimbabwe failing to break away from least developed country (LDC) status. In Asia, the landlocked countries of Mongolia, Uzbekistan, Tajikistan, Afghanistan, Nepal and Bhutan, and the sea-linked countries of Bangladesh and Pakistan have also remained poor. The Pacific states of Cook Islands, Fiji, Marshall Islands, Papua New Guinea, Samoa, Solomon Islands, Tonga, Timor Leste and Vanuatu have also remained in the periphery with their external economics very much dominated by Australia and New Zealand.

Attempts to discuss the importance of industrialization will not be complete without a discussion of the trade and the structural orientation of industries that should be promoted. The 1950s advocates of industrial development recommended a focus on inward-oriented heavy and capital goods as an integral part of final consumption goods manufacturing. Advocates of this approach argue that the department two goods were critical complementary inputs for the development of other industries.[3] Britain, United States, Germany, Japan, South Korea and Taiwan very much enjoyed the development of both light manufacturing and complementary heavy industries, thereby making them versatile in entering a wide range of final goods industries. Yet, light manufacturing goods such as textiles and garments also grew rapidly in these countries. Because the expansion of these industries did not raise substantially the material living conditions of the masses, Adam (1975) referred to them as: 'banana republics' transforming into pyjama republics'.

The focus on heavy industries behind import-substitution – in both large and small domestic markets – failed in many countries because of a combination of a lack of scale and clientelist approaches that removed competitive pressures and the translation of subsidies and grants into productive rents to drive firm-level technological catch-up. For example, poorly coordinated and corrupt import-substitution policies failed in Indonesia (Rasiah 2010), the Philippines (Ofreneo 2008) and many Latin American countries (Jenkins 1987).

However, Korea managed to achieve international competitiveness in the heavy industries of steel, shipbuilding and cars, and machinery and steel by using import-substitution for export promotion (Amsden 1989), while Taiwan managed to achieve competitiveness in machinery and metals, and electronics (Fransman 1986; Amsden and Chu 2003) through deliberate promotional strategies and effective appraisal mechanisms. Governments in these countries enjoyed autonomy from clientelist groups to enforce stringent performance conditions on the manufacturers (Khan 1989). Hence, it can be argued that strategic industrial policy *a la* the Northeast Asian models have been successful. South Korea and Taiwan have also experienced a contraction in manufacturing's contribution to GDP with a trend expansion in services but manufacturing productivity has continued to rise.

Taking the argument of Poulantzas (1978) and later Jessop (1990) on state autonomy, Evans (1995) advanced the concept of the developmental state using the computer industry in Brazil, India and Korea as examples. This argument posits that state capacities distinguish development outcomes ranging from the developmental states of Korea and Taiwan to the predatory states of Zaire (Congo) and Kenya. The history of economic development has shown that natural endowments matter much less than governance capacity in transforming economies to developed status. South Korea and Taiwan are major examples of economies that became developed in one generation (see Amsden 1989; Wade 1990).

Although it was Smith (1776) who discussed industries' capacity to quicken differentiation and division of labour, heterodox economists identified manufacturing as the path to engender rapid growth and structural change because of the presence in the sector of increasing returns activities (Young 1928; Kaldor 1967).[4] Industrialization is viewed to drive its own growth, as well as that of the other sectors, including stimulating structural change from low value-added activities to high value-added activities and the consequent differentiation and division of labour to provide the opportunities for generating employment growth. Hence, the speed of industrialization among successful latecomer industrializers has always shortened (Gerschenkron 1962). Although industrial policy elements can be traced to Britain till 1485, the export taxes imposed on hides was targeted at raising income for Henry the VII rather through any explicit industrial policy to promote a viable textile industry (Reinert 2007). Following the introduction of industrial policy in the late sixteenth century, it took 150 years (1585–1735) for Britain to become the most industrialized country (Reinert 2007).

Finally, the attempt to examine the role of industrialization is justified on the grounds that it has been aggressively promoted in many countries either as an instrument to attract investment and generate jobs or as a channel for stimulating technological catch up. However, one may argue that industrialization may not be a meaningful route to engender rapid economic development in poor countries, such as the Pacific and the Caribbean

Islands, lacking the basic endowments. Nevertheless, industrialization is an important route for most other countries as it enjoys increasing returns characteristics. Also, even poor small island countries could stimulate industrialization at a later stage if the unique conditions of small size and scope economies become critical in the industries promoted or if systemic frameworks supporting industrialization enjoy scale through the integration of production factors and markets from the integration of several economies. The latter would of course require regional integration policy constructs. Asian economies, such as, Korea and Taiwan, achieved developed status in one generation through the promotion of rapid industrialization (Chang 2003). Despite its small size, Singapore's rapid economic progress was also driven strongly by industrialization, albeit primarily through inviting foreign capital.

4. Labour

Whereas globalization and industrialization have been major drivers of rapid growth in a number of countries, labour in a number of them not enjoyed significant improvement in their material conditions. The share of income enjoyed by capitalists and labour has varied between countries so much so that the low-income groups in the rich countries of the United States and United Kingdom have not been able to enjoy some of the basic needs, such as proper heating, compared to the lowest quintile of income groups in the Scandinavian countries of Denmark, Finland, Norway and Sweden. However, the poor in the developed countries are still exposed to far more opportunities than the poor in the poor economies of Bangladesh, Bhutan, Cambodia, Laos, Myanmar, Uzbekistan and Tajikistan. While more advanced electoral politics has reduced the potential for the expansion of the lumpen bourgeoisie[5] in the developed economies of the United States and United Kingdom, several neo-colonial states have been characterized by a dominant lumpen bourgeoisie that has done little to check the persistence of poverty and stagnation in real wages with significant sections of the masses living in squalor (see also Freire 1970). In addition, repressive political regimes have also undermined the emergence of responsible unions to address the plight of workers in many countries. In fact, the political leaderships in some countries have deliberately formulated policies to exclude trade unions from shaping development policies targeted at labour to stimulate foreign direct investment (see Jomo and Todd 1994).

Unfortunately, the dominant neo-classical arguments have focused on growth as one that will automatically push wages up as surplus labour evaporates in free market conditions so that it will bring about distribution. However, not only that perfect market conditions do not exist, they also discourage innovations (Schumpeter 1934), leaving the arguments of Heckscher and Ohlin (1991) that under conditions of perfect capital and labour mobility within borders and their immobility across borders, specialization on the basis of factor endowments will generate the best economic outcomes confined to a classroom academic exercise. While Keynes (1936) accepted the problems of information asymmetry and market imperfections to call for government intervention to generate full employment, Keynesian arguments do not broach effectively the specific strategies essential to stimulate improvements for labour. Instead, any effort to examine the implications of growth for labour would require a full understanding of institutions – both in the participation of labour in the process and in the instruments in place to ensure that there is effective distribution of value created between the owners and workers of the means of production. To this argument, we take a related argument that was taken up by political economists concerned with the impact of differentiation and division of labour on the quality of jobs created. Piore and Sabel (1984) and Pyke and Sengenberger (1992) and Zeitlin (1992) focused on the high road to industrialization. Examined through the same vantage point but with a focus on firm organization, Kochan and Osterman (1994) discussed the importance of mutual gains enterprises in which hierarchies are minimized with workers participating extensively in decision-making. In such enterprises, labour, management and government work together for mutual gains. Whereas the buzz word these days is on inclusive development, flexible specialization exponents discussed the active participation of all in the knowledge flows and interaction between skilled workers with a systemic structure that addresses collective action problems through a blend of competition and cooperation to form the basis of the high road to industrialization.

Unlike the traditional notions of trade unionism with the archetype Britain gripped by not only heavy antagonistic relations between labour and capital but also the latter's importance in championing workers' cause until Thatcher began dismantling the powers of trade unions since 1979, the evolution of electoral politics has driven a number of governments, including Germany, Sweden, Norway, Finland and Denmark, to assume a major responsibility to protect the welfare of workers (Edwards and Elger 1999). Using a similar framework, though some argue that it is overly dominated by the government, the National Trade Union Congress works with the ruling People's Action Party to protect the mutual interest of the different important stakeholders in Singapore (Wong 1998). Kuruvilla (1995, 1996) provided evidence from India, Malaysia, Philippines and Singapore to argue that import-substitution industrialization was associated with industrial relations and human resource strategies that were plural and stable, while countries that moved from low to higher value-added export-oriented industrialization strategy experienced a shift from low-cost to workforce flexibility and skills development. Countries that failed to upgrade, e.g. the Philippines, continued to experience the casualization of labour, and slow skills development (Ofreneo 2008).

The environment facing labour has varied between one country and another. Unlike the past when capital–labour relations have been so antagonistic that militancy and collective bargaining deadlocks have often culminated in strikes, layoffs and persistence of low wages, changes in the labour process necessitated by rapid advances in technology and modern capitalist relations has transformed to value labour in the labour process as a value creator. The Taylorist production organization had separated conception and execution from the labour process so that management performed the former and workers the latter (Braverman 1974). These processes gave rise to the creation of specialized high-wage skilled workers with mass production advanced by Ford (Best 2001) where large reserves of surplus labour or the industrial reserve army still existed, as in low value-added clothing and cement manufacturing activities in countries, such as, Bangladesh, India and Myanmar, Taylorist practices still dominate. Although both Taylorist and Fordist labour processes still exist, modern industrial capitalism – e.g. in the assembly of automotive and electronics products – have evolved to recognize that workers have the ability to create knowledge and with that add value to the labour process. This has led to the evolution of flexible rather than casual production systems, which is consistent with the arguments by Marx (1967) that relative surplus value appropriation is the central pillar of industrial capitalism.

In market economies such as Indonesia, Malaysia, Thailand and Philippines, trade unions have largely acted as an independent representative of workers in their relations with the state. On the one hand, states have tried to garner support from unions by enacting welfare instruments to govern employment relations and industrial relations. On the other hand, governments have offered generous incentives to woo investment that has included the prevention of the formation of trade unions, the banning of strikes and the enactment of a minimum wage act in certain industries. In some countries, trade unions are integral components of states, e.g. China, Laos and Vietnam.

5. Countries examined

We have included countries in South and East Asia where economic globalization has been important, and industrialization either enjoyed rapid growth in the past or has started to experience rapid expansion. Apart from Myanmar, which has faced trade sanctions since 2002 (Myint 2011), the remaining countries examined have strong integration into the global economy with the trade shares in GDP of Malaysia, Thailand and Vietnam exceeding GDP in 2011−2012 (see Table 1). China, India, Indonesia, Malaysia, Philippines, Thailand and Vietnam have continued to experience considerable manufacturing activity since 2000, though a number of them have begun to face deindustrialization. Although Myanmar had a small manufacturing sector in 2010, government policies have continued to target industrial expansion in these countries.

5.1. Trade in GDP

The dynamics of globalization cannot be captured holistically by any quantitative instruments as it is more a qualitative process. Nevertheless, we attempt to use some simple quantitative measures to show how much the countries selected here have integrated into the global economy. In doing so, we avoid capturing embodied knowledge flows (e.g. through movement of people, royalties, publications, licensing, manuals and media interactions) owing to problems of classification and a lack of a continuous series for a number of the countries examined. Instead, we use the usual variable of trade (imports plus exports) share in GDP. We have avoided using foreign direct investment and portfolio equity investment because of both the problems of data access and reliability of the information from some countries.

There are several ways of measuring economic globalization. Trade openness is one measure, and within that the share of trade (imports and exports) is often used to show how open an economy is to global economic relations.[6] Except for Myanmar, which has faced trade sanctions from the United States since 2003 (Myint 2011), there has been a trend rise in trade as a share of GDP in all the countries shown in Table 1. Myanmar's

Table 1. Share of import and export in GDP, selected countries, 1960−2012.

	1960	1970	1980	1990	2000	2012
China	NA	5.3	18.0	29.2	37.7	58.7
India	11.1	7.5	15.1	15.2	26.5	55.4
Indonesia	26.9	28.4	54.4	49.1	71.4	50.1
Malaysia	89.0	78.7	111.0	117.0	220.4	163.0
Myanmar	40.4	14.0	22.0	5.6	1.1	0.3*
Philippines	23.4	42.6	52.0	60.8	104.7	64.8
Thailand	32.7	34.4	54.5	75.8	124.9	118.8
Vietnam	NA	NA	23.2	81.3	112.5	180.0

Note: *For year 2010.
Source: From Myanmar Ministry of Planning; others from World Bank (2013).

share fell to 0.3% in 2010. The most dramatic expansion was experienced by Vietnam, which enjoyed a 180% share in 2012. Malaysia enjoyed its peak of 220% in 2000 before that share fell to 163% in 2012. Thailand enjoyed the next highest share, which rose from 33% in 1960 to 149% in 2012. The transition LDCs of Cambodia and Laos enjoyed reasonable shares of 114% and 82%, respectively, in 2011. The trade share in GDP of the large economies of China, India and Indonesia rose from 5%, 8% and 28%, respectively, in 1970 to 59%, 55% and 50%, respectively, in 2012.

5.2. Composition of manufacturing in GDP

We use the core component of the industry here, which is manufacturing. Meanwhile, utilities are included in services in a number of national account series. The attempt to confine the assessment to just manufacturing is also appropriate because its dynamics is considerably different from mining, construction (largely a non-tradable) and utilities. Hence, we present changes in the manufacturing share of GDP of the countries examined.

Except for Myanmar, the share of manufacturing value added in GDP in the remaining countries shown in Table 2 exceeded 10% in 2012. Myanmar's industrialization has been affected by trade sanctions imposed by the United States in 2003 (Myint 2011). The shares have fallen over the period from 1980 to 2010 in China, India and Philippines, and over the period from 2000 to 2012 in Indonesia and Malaysia. Industrial expansion in GDP resumed in Vietnam since 1990, while it has continued to grow in Thailand. Whether countries are facing an expansion or a relative fall, the importance of industrialization in national planning in all the countries examined cannot be understated. Hence, the choice of examining the implications of globalization on both industrialization and labour here is a useful exercise.

6. Outline

Following this introduction, the remaining articles analyse the impact of globalization and industrialization on labour markets in East and South Asia. Zhang and Rasiah (2014) examine in the next article the impact of global integration and industrialization on labour markets in China. Their evidence shows that rising trade and inflows of foreign direct investment has stimulated industrialization and structural change, which has consequently translated into a rapid rise in overall and manufacturing real wages, especially in eastern

Table 2. Manufacturing share in GDP, selected countries, 1960–2010.

	1960	1970	1980	1990	2000	2012
China	29.2*	33.7	40.2	32.7	32.1	29.5x
India	13.7	13.7	16.2	16.2	15.4	13.5
Indonesia	9.2	10.3	13.0	20.7	27.7	24.3@
Malaysia	8.1	12.4	21.6	24.2	30.9	24.3
Myanmar	9.5*	10.4	9.5	7.8	7.2	11.7x
Philippines	24.6	24.9	25.7	24.8	24.5	21.1@
Thailand	12.5	15.9	21.5	27.2	33.6	35.6@
Vietnam	NA	NA	20.5	12.3	18.6	18.9

Note: *For year 1965; x for year 2010; and @ for year 2011.
Source: The 2010 data for Myanmar from the Ministry of Planning, Myanmar; others from World Bank (2013).

China. Although marketization has widened regional inequalities with the Eastern coastal provinces enjoying higher growth and structural change than the Western and other inland provinces, rapid growth has also driven wages up.

Ghosh (2014) dissects in the third article the impact of rapid economic growth on India's labour markets in the subsequent article. She argues that capitalists in India have continued to benefit from socially segmented labour markets using such 'incentives' to appropriate absolute surplus value by suppressing wages of workers rather than focusing on relative surplus value extraction from productivity increases. Hence, the accumulation process in India has relied indirectly on persistent low wages that has not only discouraged structural change but also aggravated social inequality in the country.

Narjoko and Putra (2014) analyse in the fourth article, through exports, the impact of globalization and industrialization on labour markets in Indonesia using a case study manufacturing with three important findings. First, the responsiveness of output to employment and wages to employment declined substantially over the period 1996–2006 before recovering in 2009, which is assumed to be a consequence of the implementation of new labour laws since 2003. Second, though exporters' employment conduct is conditioned by demand, since the implementation of the new labour law, exporters have tended to retain employment more than non-exporters when wages rise. Third, exporters have responded to rising wages by substituting labour with machinery.

Rasiah, Crinis, and Lee (2014) discuss in the fifth article premature deindustrialization in Malaysia where the contribution of manufacturing to GDP has started to fall since the late 1990s before its component sectors have enjoyed structural transformation from low to high value-added activities. They argue that its consequences on the labour market include slow or negative change in real wages, which has been aggravated with the weakening role of trade unions and a massive influx of low-skilled foreign labour.

Myint, Rasiah, and Singaravelloo (2014) use the case of the clothing industry in the sixth article to show how foreign capital and export-orientation have increased employment and wages in Myanmar. While acknowledging that the clothing industry has integrated in the low-skill low-wage segment of the global value chain, their evidence shows gradual material improvements have been enjoyed by the workers despite economic sanctions from the United States that has lowered their export options. Indeed, national contract firms have also emerged with technological capabilities to compete in export markets.

Ofreneo (2014) argues in the seventh article that incoherent and poorly coordinated industrial policies that are driven by contradictory liberalization initiatives have prevented industrial structural change essential to stimulate the emergence of the high road to industrialization in the Philippines. The consequences of this development on the labour market include the continued casualization of labour and persistence of low wages.

Charoenloet (2014) analyses in the eighth article the impact of globalization and industrialization on Thailand's labour force. This article shows that over half of the labour force of Thailand has remained in non-wage employment. Also, the lack of technological upgrading in industry has left the bulk of the Thai labour force in low-wage activities. Outsourcing has also become rampant as employers seek to compete by cutting production costs. Hence, this article argues that it is important that workers from all forms of work are mobilized to strengthen the role of unions to ensure that workers' rights are protected.

Tran and Nørlund (2014) investigate in the ninth and final article the historical context and industrial policies to analyse the impact of capitalist integration of Vietnam with a focus on the labour-intensive, export-oriented industries of textile and garments and the electronics industry. Their evidence does not suggest the emergence of a 'high road' to industrialization path in Vietnam. Indeed, low-skilled assembly workers join the labour force with non-liveable wages and sub-standard working conditions.

Overall, the evidence amassed shows significant economic expansion in the countries examined as a consequence of globalization and industrialization. However, the story on labour markets has been mixed. While sustained expansion in productivity and wages has driven the high-road industrialization path in the Newly Industrialized Economies of East Asia, with the possible exception of China, the lack of similar policies have undermined the capacity of these economies to ensure sustained productivity growth and structural change towards higher value-added activities, thereby restricting improvements in the material conditions of labour. Even in China, rural migrant female labour is still disadvantaged because of vulnerabilities in informal labour markets.

Acknowledgements

We wish to thank the Economic Research Institute for ASEAN and East Asia (ERIA) for graciously funding the costs of the workshop in Chiang Mai on January 10–11, 2014 where the original papers were presented.

Notes

1. Countries such as the Netherlands, Switzerland and New Zealand developed without much industrialization.
2. See Hamilton (1983), Amsden (1989), Wade (1990) and Rodan (1989).
3. See Kalecki (1976) and McFarlane (1968, 1981).
4. The original argument on the differentiating capacity of industry can be traced to Smith (1776).
5. Fanon (1963) used the term lumpen bourgeoisie to refer to the pseudo-bourgeoisie who lived the luxurious lives of the bourgeoisie but drew their material wealth by living as parasites in society.
6. There is no exhaustive and precise measure of globalization and trade openness. Hence, we have used the easiest instrument used in the literature to do this (see Weiss 1988).

References

Abramovitz, M. 1956. "Resource and Output Trends in the United States since the 1870." *American Economic Review* 46(2): 5–23.
Adam, G. 1975. "Multinational Corporations and Worldwide Sourcing." In *International Firms and Modern Imperialism*, edited by Radice, H., 89–103. Harmondsworth: Penguin.
Amsden, A. 1989. *Asia's Next Giant: South Korea and Late industrialization.* New York: Oxford University Press.
Amsden, A., and W.W. Chu. 2003. *Beyond Late Industrialization: Taiwan's Upgrading Policies.* Cambridge: MIT Press.
Beresford, M. 1988. *Politics, Economics and Society.* London: Pinter.

Beresford, M. 1989. *National Unification and Economic Development in Vietnam*. London: Macmillan.

Beresford, M. 2009. "The Cambodian Clothing Industry in the Post-MFA Environment: A Review of Developments." *Journal of the Asia Pacific Economy* 14 (4): 366–388.

Best, M. 2001. *The New Competitive Advantage: The Renewal of American Industry*. Oxford: Oxford University Press.

Braverman, H. 1974. *Labour and Monopoly Capital*. New York: Monthly Review Press.

Brewer, A. 1980. *Marxist Theories of Imperialism: A Critical Survey*. London: Routledge.

Chang, H.J. 2003. *Kicking Away the Ladder*. London: Anthem Press.

Charoenloet, V. 2014. "Industrialization, Globalization and Labour Force Participation in Thailand." *Journal of the Asia Pacific Economy* 20 (1): 130–142.

Edwards, P.K., and T. Elger. 1999. *The Global Economy, National States, and the Regulation of Labour*. Hove: Phycology Press.

Evans, P.B. 1995. *Embedded Autonomy: States and Industrial Transformation*. Princeton: Princeton University Press.

Fanon, F. 1963. *The Wretched of the Earth*. New York: Grove Press.

Fransman, M. 1986. "International Competitiveness, Technical Change and the State: The Machine Tool Industries in Taiwan and Japan." *World Development* 14 (12): 1375–1396.

Freire, P. 1970. *The Pedagogy of the Oppressed*. New York: Heder and Heder.

Gerschenkron, A. 1962. *Economic Backwardness in Historical Perspective*. Cambridge: Belknap Press.

Ghosh, J. 2014. "Growth, Industrialisation and Inequality in India." *Journal of the Asia Pacific Economy* 20 (1): 42–56.

Hamilton, C. 1983. "Capitalist Industrialization in East Asia's Four Little Tigers." *Journal of Contemporary Asia* 13 (1): 35–73.

Heckscher, E.F., and B. Ohlin. 1991. *Heckscher-Ohlin Trade Theory*, translated, edited and introduced by H. Flam, and M.J. Flanders. Cambridge: MIT Press.

Hobsbawm, E. 1998. "The Nation and Globalisation." *Constellations* 5 (1): 1–9.

Hobson, J.A. 1965. *Imperialism: A Study*. Ann Arbor: University of Michigan Press.

Hopkins, A.G. ed. 2003. *Globalization in World History*. New York: Norton.

Jenkins, R. 1987. *Transnational Corporations and Uneven Development*. London: Methuen.

Jessop, B. 1990. *State Theory: Putting Capitalist States in Their Place*. Cambridge: Polity Press.

Jomo, K.S., and P. Todd. 1994. *Trade Unions and the State in Peninsular Malaysia*. Kuala Lumpur: Oxford University Press.

Kaldor, N. 1967. *Strategic Factors in Economic Growth*. Ithaca: Cornell University Press.

Kalecki, M. 1976. *Essays on Developing Economies*. Hassocks: Harvester.

Khan, M. 1989. "Clientelism, Corruption and the Capitalist State: A Study of Bangladesh and Korea." Doctoral thesis, Cambridge University.

Kochan, T.A., and P. Osterman. 1994. *The Mutual Gains Organization: Forging a Winning Partnership Among Labor, Management and Government*. Cambridge: Harvard Business School Press.

Keynes, J.M. 1936. *The General Theory of Employment, Interest and Money*. London: Macmillan.

Kontorovich, V., and M. Ellman. 1992. *The Disintegration of the Soviet Economic System*. London: Routledge & Kegan Paul.

Kuruvilla, S. 1995. "Economic Development Strategies, Industrial Relations Policies and Workplace IR/HR Practices in Southeast Asia." In *The Comparative Political Economy of Industrial Relations*, edited by K.S. Wever and L. Turner. Ithaca, NY: Cornell University Press.

Kuruvilla, S. 1996. "Linkages Between Industrialization Strategies and Industrial Relations/Human Resource Policies: Singapore, Malaysia, the Philippines, and India." *Industrial and Labor Relations Review* 49 (4): 635–657.

Lenin, V. 1950. *Imperialism: The Highest Stage of Capitalism*. Moscow. Progress Publishers.

Luxembourg, R. 1951. *The Accumulation of Capital*. London: Routledge.

Marx, K. 1967. *Capital: The Process of Circulation of Capital, Volume II*. Moscow: Progress Publishers.

Mathews, J.A. 2014. *Greening Capitalism: How Asia Is Driving the Next Great Transformation*. Stanford: Stanford University Press.

McFarlane, B.J. 1968. *Economic Policy in Australia: The Case of Reform*. Melbourne: F.W. Chesire.

McFarlane, B.J. 1971. "Michal Kalecki's Economics: An Appreciation." *Economic Record* 47 (117): 93–105.

McFarlane, B.J. 1981. *Australian Capitalism in Boom and Depression*. Kuala Lumpur: APCD Publishers.

McFarlane, B.J. 1982. *Radical Economics*. New York: St. Martin's Press.

Myint, M.M. 2011. "Export Performance, Labour Productivity and Institutional Environment of Myanmar Garment Manufacturing." PhD Thesis, submitted to University of Malaya, Kuala Lumpur.

Myint, M.M., R. Rasiah, and K. Singaravelloo. 2014. "Globalization of Industrialisation and Its Impact of Clothing Workers in Myanmar." *Journal of the Asia Pacific Economy* 20 (1): 100–110.

Narjoko, D., and C.T. Putra. 2014. "Industrialization, Globalization and the Labour Market Regime in Indonesia." *Journal of the Asia Pacific Economy* 20 (1): 57–76.

Ofreneo, R. 2008. "Arrested Development: Multinationals, TRIMs and the Philippines' Automotive Industry." *Asia Pacific Business Review* 14 (1): 65–84.

Ofreneo, R. 2014. "Growth and Employment in De-industrializing Philippines." *Journal of the Asia Pacific Economy* 20 (1): 111–129.

Perez, C. 1985. "Microelectronics, Long Waves and World Structural Change: New Perspectives for Developing Countries." *World Development* 13 (3): 441–463.

Piore, M., and Sabel, C. 1984. *The Second Industrial Divide*. Cambridge, MA: MIT Press.

Poulantzas, K. 1978. *Political Power and Social Classes*. London: Verso.

Pyke, F., and Sengenberger, W. (eds.). 1992. *Industrial Districts and Local Economic Regeneration*. Geneva: International Labour Organization.

Rasiah, R. 2010. "Industrialization in the Second-Tier NIEs." In *The New Political Economy of Southeast Asia*, edited by R. Rasiah and D.J. Schmidt, 44–102. Cheltenham: Edward Elgar.

Rasiah, R., and Schmitz, J.D. 2010. *The New Political Economy of Southeast Asia*. Cheltenham: Edward Elgar.

Rasiah, R., V. Crinis, and H.A. Lee. 2014. "Industrialization and Labour in Malaysia." *Journal of the Asia Pacific Economy* 20 (1): 77–99.

Reinert, E. 2007. *How the West Got Rich and . . . . Why the Poor Stay Poor?* London: Anthem Press.

Rodan, G. 1989. *The Political Economy of Singapore's Industrialization: National State and International Capital*. Basingstoke: Macmillan.

Rowthorn, R., and J. Wells. 1987. *Deindustrialization and Foreign Trade*. Cambridge: Cambridge University Press.

Schumpeter, J.A. 1934. *The Theory of Economic Development*. Cambridge: Harvard University Press.

Smith, A. 1776. *An Inquiry into the Nature and Causes of the Wealth of the Nations*. London: Strahan & Cadell.

Tran, A., and I. Nørlund. 2014. "Globalization, Industrialization and Labor Markets in Vietnam." *Journal of the Asia Pacific Economy* 20 (1): 143–163.

Veblen, T. 1915. *Imperial Germany and the Industrial Revolution*. New York: Macmillan.

Wade, R. 1990. *Governing the Market: Economic Theory and the Role of Government in East Asian Industrialization*. Princeton: Princeton University Press.

Weiss, J. 1988. *Industry in Developing Countries: Theory, Policy and Evidence*. London: Croom Helm.

Wong, E.S. 1998. "Social Tripartism and Employment in Singapore." In *Employment and Development,* edited by R. Rasiah and N.V. Hofmann. Singapore: Friedrich-Ebert Stiftung.

World Bank. 2013. *World Development Indicators*. Washington, DC: World Bank Institute.

Young, A. 1928. "Increasing Returns and Economic Progress." *Economic Journal* 38 (152): 527–542.

Zeitlin, J. 1992. "Industrial districts and local economic regeneration: overview and comment." In *Industrial districts and local economic regeneration,* edited by F. Pyke and W. Sengenberger, 279–294. Geneva: International Labour Organization.

Zhang, M. and R. Rasiah. 2014. "Globalization, Industrialization and Labour Markets in China." *Journal of the Asia Pacific Economy* 20 (1): 14–41.

Globalization, industrialization and labour markets in China

Miao Zhang and Rajah Rasiah

Department of Development Studies, University of Malaya, Kuala Lumpur, Malaysia

China's experience with globalization is still contested. This paper seeks to examine the impact of global integration and industrialization on labour markets in China. The evidence shows that rising trade and flows of foreign direct investment has not only quickened industrialization and structural change but it has also stimulated a rapid rise in overall and manufacturing real wages. The government's framework of absorbing marketization while maintaining planning control through decentralization has been critical in the development of technological capabilities in manufacturing. Although the nature of economic development after reforms has also widened regional inequalities with the Eastern coastal provinces enjoying higher growth and structural change than the Western and other inland provinces, rising wages suggest that the material conditions of the majority of workers in China have improved.

1. Introduction

When China announced its reform plans in 1978, few could have anticipated the miraculous growth that it will record, especially since 1992. Under the leadership of Mao, China had built the elements of nationalism for the central government to direct economic development, which helped a nationally united command economy to stimulate economic development through the unleashing of market forces, private dwellers and rapid integration into the global economy. Trade and investment flows brought China closer to the global economy. From specialization in light manufactured exports, China has undergone considerable structural change to participate in heavy and knowledge-intensive manufactured goods (Rasiah, Miao, and Xin, 2013). However, some economists have questioned China's rapid growth by either claiming that official statistics are not reliable or that it has largely been propelled by agriculture, land use and labour-intensive industries (Young 2003).[1] Even more so China's labour markets remain under-examined from the standpoint of whether rapid growth has been reflected in improvements to wages and working conditions. The latter is important to determine if China is following the high road to industrialization.

The historical precursor of industrialization in China can be traced to the Song Dynasty (960–1279) when steel was invented and produced and used extensively by the public. A series of pre-modern technological innovation and evolution of intellectual thought during the Song Dynasty made China one of the most prosperous and advanced economies in the medieval world.[2] However, the weak succeeding regimes that followed did not carry this forward. In fact, large parts of China were colonized by the Western countries and Japan. After the establishment of People's Republic of China (PRC), a real sense of industrialization did not happen until 1958 when the controversial campaign The Great Leap Forward was advanced by Mao Zedong. His aim to transform the newly born PRC from an agrarian economy to a modern communist society through state-led industrialization eventually failed. GDP per capita fell from 200 yuan in 1958 to 173 yuan in 1960. Thanks to reforms, industrialization resumed rapidly under the Deng Xiaoping Administration.

An assessment of globalization, industrialization and labour markets in China is important not only because of its rising importance as a major economic power but also because of its transformation from an agricultural economy to an industrial economy. The analysis will not only offer an opportunity to examine the contrasting passion scholars have on China. On the one hand, some accept the reality over the surge in industrialization and Chinese exports as an example of a successful development model in which the state has allowed market forces to operate within those social boundaries (e.g. Rasiah, Miao, and Xin, 2013). On the other hand, critics claim that Chinese data is fudged, and that the rapid growth is unsustainable owing to growing fuel deficits and environment disasters.

Hence, this paper seeks to examine the impact of globalization and industrialization on China's labour market since reforms began. Specifically, the paper seeks to capture the impact of industrial structural change on the domestic labour market. Unlike neoliberal expositions of globalization, we will provide evidence to show that the complex nature of government policy in China was structured to allow both the provincialization, as well as, the localization of planning (Zhang and Rasiah 2014). Also, industrialization was promoted by the government taking account of the specific characteristics of the industries, the targets set for them, and provincial and municipal endowments. The rest of the paper is organized as follows. Sections 2 and 3 examine globalization and industrialization in China with a focus on structural change. Section 4 analyses the demand–supply model of labour market and discusses the impact of globalization and industrialization on it. Section 5 concludes with policy implications.

2. Trade and investment flows

While the globalization concept has a wide meaning that includes qualitative exchange of information and the forces shaping the process, for measurement purposes we confine the assessment to quantitative flows of trade and investment. Hence, we discuss trade and inward and outward foreign direct investment flows in this section. Although integration into the global capitalist economy expanded since the launching of the Opening Door Policy in 1978, global flows of trade and investment into China was marked by two major waves, the first taking place in the mid-1980s followed by the early 1990s and subsequently since 2001.

2.1. Trade

Between 1978 and 2000, the Chinese economy grew gently but began to switch gears to rapidly expand since 2001 following its membership of the World Trade Organization. Except for a decline in 2009 due to the global financial crisis, exports, imports and total trade of goods grew from US\$266.1 billion, US\$243.5 billion and US\$509.6 billion, respectively in 2001 to US\$1898.4 billion, US\$1743.5 billion and US\$3641.9 billion, respectively in 2011 (Figure 1), which expanded the share of trade in GDP from 5% in 1979 to its peak of 70% in 2007 before falling to 59% in 2011 (Figure 2).

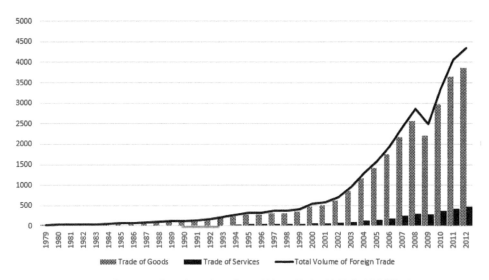

Figure 1.   Import and export of goods and services, China, 1979–2012 (US$ billion).
Source: Ministry of Commerce of China, various years.

China's share in world exports rose from 1.2% in 1983 to 11.4% in 2012 (Table 1). Figure 3 shows that growth in exports from China exceeded growth in world exports in the period 2001–2007. Although always less than exports the share of import in world merchandise also recorded significant expansion from 1.1% in 1983 to 10% in 2012. China ranked first in world exports of merchandise and second in trade (exports plus imports) totaling US$3867 billion in 2012 (Figure 4). The trade surplus of China reached US$230 billion in 2012 amounting to 2.8% of GDP.

Trade has played an important role in stimulating economic growth in China, but the biggest beneficiaries have been the sea-fronted Eastern provinces. Proximity to the sea has resulted in the proliferation of special economic zones (SEZs) in the coastal cities,

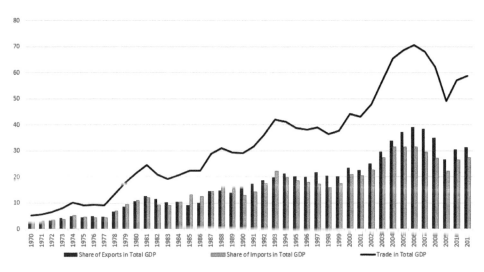

Figure 2.   Share of import and export in total GDP (Goods and Services), China, 1970–2011.
Source: World Bank Institute (2012).

Table 1.   Share of exports and imports in World Merchandise Trade, China, 1948–2012 (%).

	1948	1953	1963	1973	1983	1993	2003	2012
Export	0.9	1.2	1.3	1.0	1.2	2.5	5.9	11.4
Import	0.6	1.6	0.9	0.9	1.1	2.7	5.4	10.0

Source: World Trade Organization (2012).

such as Guangdong, which accounted for approximately one-third of China's trade, though it fell from 36% in 2000 to 26% in 2010 (Figure 5). Efforts by the central government to reduce provincial inequality saw the rise of inland provinces so that Jiangsu and Beijing recorded sizeable amount of trade in 2010. However, regional inequality has persisted as the outlying provinces of Tibet, Xinjiang and Guizhou have remained poor.

2.2.   Foreign direct investment

Aided by market reforms and accession to the WTO, China has become a major recipient of FDI in the world. China has also begun investing abroad, especially in the South countries. We examine China's integration in the global economy through FDI flows in this section.

2.2.1.   Inward foreign direct investment

China has also strongly integrated in the global economy through inward foreign direct investment (FDI), which rose from US$20.7 billion in 2000 to US$193.3 billion in 2005

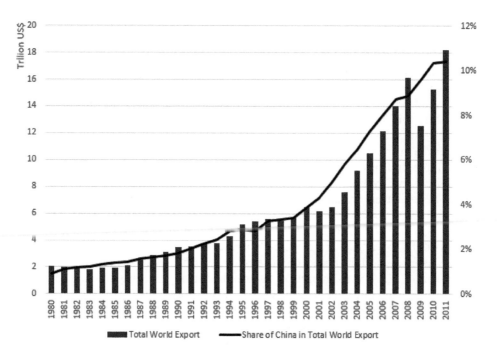

Figure 3.   China's share in world exports, 1980–2011.
Source: China Foreign Economic Statistical Yearbook (2012).

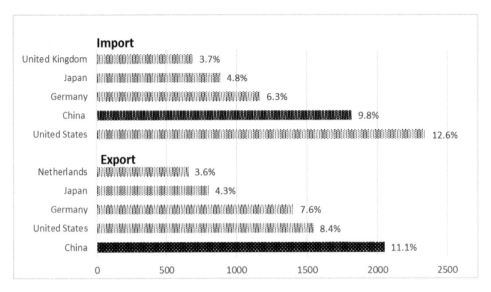

Figure 4.   Top five exporters and importers by trade value in the world, 2012 (US$ billion).
Source: World Trade Organization (2012).

and US$578.8 billion in 2010 (UNCTAD 2011, 193). Inward FDI as a share of GDP rose from 1% in 1991 to over 6% in 1993 before falling as a consequence of the Asian Financial Crisis. The jump in FDI in 1993 was a direct result of Deng Xiaoping's South Tour in the summer of 1992, which was accompanied by the opening of four SEZs in the country. The campaign to realize China's industrialization through joint ventures was launched to 'attract foreign technology in the industrial sector by leveraging on the domestic market.' FDI has not only helped modernize China's backward industrial sector by introducing cutting-edge technology, it has also quickened the shift in manufacturing operations from labour-intensive to technology-intensive operations. Except for the financial-crisis affected year of 2009, inward FDI registered over 3% of GDP over the period 2005−2013 (Figure 6).

The sectoral distribution shows that export-oriented labour-intensive manufacturing sector is the main destination of FDI, though its share fell from 71% in 2000 to 47% in 2010 (Table 2). However, despite falling shares, actual FDI into manufacturing experienced grew slightly from US$44 billion in 2000 to US$49 billion in 2010. However, except for equipment manufacturing − which enjoyed FDI shares rising from 4.3% in 2000 to 6.1% in 2010, the remaining sectors experienced falling FDI shares. Nevertheless, the growing real estate sector led by a price boom in 2003, began to attract strong inflows of FDI so that its share in overall FDI rose from 8.4% in 2000 to 22.7%.

Any assessment of the impact of globalization on China will not be complete without an account of FDI and its impact on International trade. Enjoying access to duty free imports when exporting, foreign firms share in exports rose from 0.2% in 1981 to its peak of 58.3% in 2005 before falling to 49.9% in 2012 (Table 3). Foreign firms' share in imports rose from 0.5% in 1981 to its peak of 59.7% in 2006 before falling to 47.9% in 2012. The export:import ratio improved in trend terms from 19.2 in 1981 to its peak of 124.3 in 2007. It has exceeded 100 over the period 1997−2012 demonstrating a positive trade balance over that period.

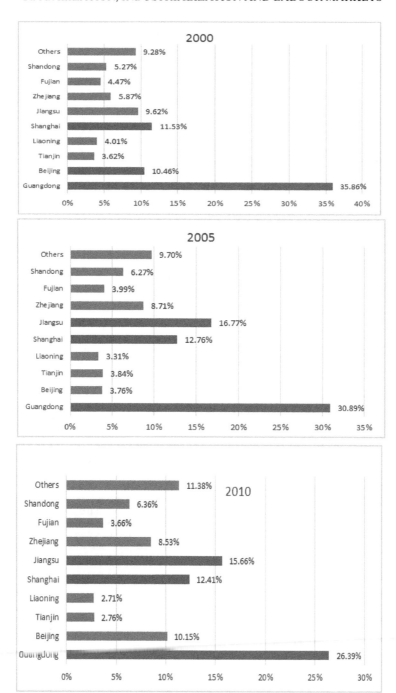

Figure 5.   Provincial trade, China, 2000–2010 (%).
Source: China Statistical Bureau (various years).

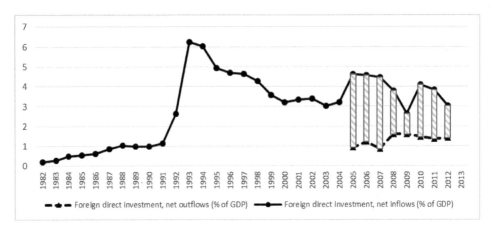

Figure 6. Share of foreign direct investment in GDP, Net Inflows and Outflows, China, 1982−2013.
Source: World Development Indicators (2012).

2.2.2. Outward FDI

Chinese FDI outflows have also become important especially after new century. Between 2005 and 2010, Europe, the United States and Australia attracted US$43.2 billion, US$30.4 billion and US$38.4 billion FDI, respectively from China (Figure 7). Regionally, China's outward FDI has also flowed considerably to South America (US$72.3 billion), Sub-Saharan Africa (US$56.4 billion), West Asia (US$51.7 billion), the Arab countries (US$43.7 billion) and East Asia (US$42.6 billion).

Sectorally, energy and power, especially in Sub-Saharan Africa, West Asia and the Arab countries, have been the leading destination of China's outward FDI, which

Table 2.   FDI in manufacturing and real estate, China, 2000−2010.

Year	2010		2008		2005		2000	
Item	Value[a]	%	Value	%	Value	%	Value[b]	%
Total	10,573,524		9,239,544		6,032,469		6,237,952	
Manufacturing	4,959,058	46.9	4,989,483	54.0	4,245,291	70.37	4,425,430	70.94
Textile and clothing	160,250	1.52	182,336	1.97	210,404	3.49	198,833	3.19
Chemistry raw material and chemical product	343,655	3.25	412,326	4.46	280,884	4.66	259,444	4.16
Medicine	102,847	0.97	65,753	0.71	55,549	0.92	91,153	1.46
General purpose equipment	345,762	3.27	350,809	3.80	203,213	3.37	163,003	2.61
Special purpose equipment	312,874	2.96	281,638	3.05	194,123	3.22	106,585	1.71
Computer and electronic	843,210	7.97	845,143	9.15	771,117	12.78	1,135,615	18.20
Real Estate	2,398,656	22.68	1,858,995	20.12	541,807	8.98	523,213	8.39

Note: [a]Value in 2005, 2008 and 2010 is actual use of FDI by US$10,000;
[b]Value in 2000 is contractual value by US$10,000.
Source: China Trade and External Economic Statistical Yearbook (various years).

Table 3.   Share of foreign-funded firms in imports and exports, China, 1981–2012.

Year	Imports and exports Value[a]	Imports and exports % in total	Exports Value	Exports % in total	Imports Value	Imports % in total	Export/import (%)
1981	1.43	0.33	0.33	0.15	1.1	0.5	19.20
1986	30.12	4.08	5.82	1.88	24.3	5.66	38.69
1991	289.55	21.33	120.47	16.75	169.08	26.5	65.82
1996	1371.1	47.3	615.06	40.71	756.04	54.46	96.37
2001	2590.98	50.82	1332.35	50.05	1258.63	51.66	105.86
2006	10,364.51	58.87	5638.35	58.18	4726.16	59.7	119.30
2007	12,549.28	57.73	6955.2	57.1	5594.08	58.53	124.33
2008	14,105.76	55.07	7906.2	55.34	6199.56	54.71	127.53
2009	12,174.37	55.16	6722.3	55.94	5452.07	54.22	123.30
2010	16,003.07	53.83	8623.06	54.65	7380.01	52.91	116.84
2011	18,601.56	51.07	9953.3	52.42	8648.26	49.6	115.09
2012	18,939.97	48.98	10,227.48	49.92	8712.49	47.93	117.39

Note: [a]In US$100 million.
Source: Ministry of Commerce (various years).

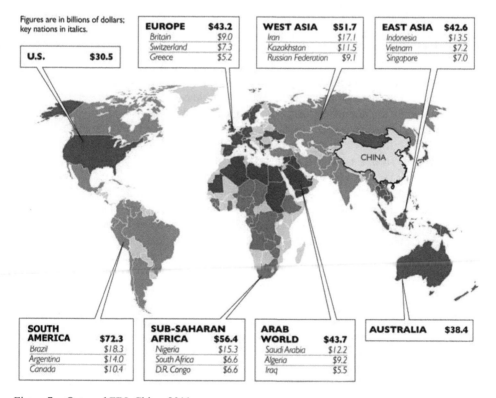

Figure 7.   Outward FDI, China, 2011.
Source: China Global Investment Tracker (2011).

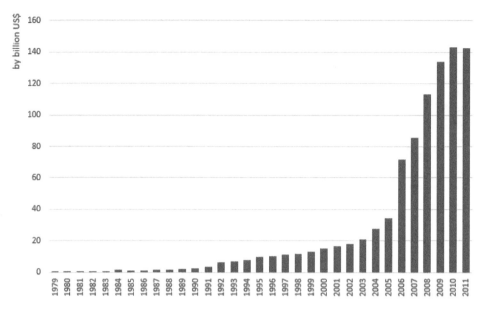

Figure 8. Outward FDI by contracted value, China, 1979–2011.
Source: China Statistical Bureau (2012a).

accounted for US$61.8 billion in 2011. In addition, large engineering and construction contracts, such as railway, roads, bridges and stadiums have also been important. The finance and real estate sectors attracted US$16.5 billion while agriculture received US$6.4 billion in 2011. Hence, despite the well-known fact that China's outward foreign capital has mostly been confined to portfolio investments in American government bonds, its non-bonds investment flows show strong sectoral and geographic diversification as a consequence of its increasing integration into the world economy.

Motivated by the national strategy of 'go-aboard' with a set of supportive policy diplomatically and financially since 1998, outward FDI (the contract value from China) rose from US$11.7 billion in 1998 to US$142 billion in 2011 (Figure 8). The huge current and capital account surpluses with foreign reserves reaching US$3.31 trillion in 2012 has made China a major capital exporter. Whereas traditionally, China invests extensively into energy and manufacturing in the developing economies, falling property prices following the global financial crisis has attracted massive Chinese investment into the developed economies of the US and Britain. Meanwhile, Chinese firms have also begun to acquire established foreign firms to quicken technological catch up. For example, *Lenovo* and *Geely* acquired International Business Machines (IBM) and Volvo in 2005 and 2010, respectively.

3. Industrialization

While global integration has been important, government focus on stimulating technological capability building was no less important in the rapid growth of manufacturing in China. Clearly, the focus on capital accumulation was directed at technological capability building.

Government promotion of manufacturing took on three different instruments. The first was a central government initiative that started in 1978 when four SEZs were created to attract export-oriented industries, 14 cities were declared as coastal open cities in 1984 and regional development plans involving the three Delta schemes of Yangze River, Min Jiang and Pearl River Valleys. Where the industries promoted were identified as strategic, import controls (duties, quotas and licenses were used by the central government to promote high technology industries, such as automobiles and electronics). Government policies emphasized technology transfer to national firms when the domestic market was important. This was the basis on which Volkswagen was approved to produce and supply cars in the Chinese market.[3] These controls were not used where production was largely for foreign markets. The Chinese government also offered special incentives by way of grants and tax breaks to promote high technology industries and technological upgrading.

At the same time, local governments were given the autonomy to implement central government initiatives (e.g. subsidized land lease rights and utilities, customs coordination), as well as, more importantly strategize to promote technological capability building in industries where the focus is on technological upgrading. Examples of successful local initiatives include efforts by the Shanghai government in the late 1980s to mandate that the Santana, a car produced by the Shanghai Volkswagen joint venture, be the only legitimate taxi to run in the city. Similarly, the Yongjia county and the Qiaotou municipality in Zhejiang province played a critical role in establishing cluster links between the firms and the designing and R&D centres with support from universities to stimulate technological upgrading in the button industry (Rasiah, Kong, and Vinanchiarachi 2011). Provincial governments also invested heavily into high-tech parks to stimulate technological upgrading in the high technology industries.

Led by government initiatives, FDI and international trade, the manufacturing sector in China has flourished since economic reforms began. As Zhang and Rasiah (2014) have shown market reforms helped raise efficiency and coordination, the state has remained in control of important decisions to stimulate technological upgrading and improvement of the material conditions of the people. China's share in world manufactured exports grew from 1.9% in 1990 to 4.7% in 2000 and to 16.8% in 2012. At the same time, manufacturing, which accounted for 94% of China's exports in 2012, saw a tremendous growth of its share in export in the world from 1.9% in 1990 to 4.7% in 2000 before it reached 16.8% in 2012.

The share of manufacturing in total imports expanded sharply to 58% in 1987 after bottoming to 26% in 1985 (Figure 9). However, manufacturing's share in exports and imports grew strongly in the 1990s to reach almost 80% each respectively in 1994. Whereas export shares have continued to rise to reach 94%, import shares fell to 56% in 2012. A combination of rising fuel imports and stronger domestic manufacturing production capabilities accounted for a fall in the share of manufactured imports in total imports (Rasiah, Miao, and Xin, 2013).

Manufacturing is the key component of the industrial sector with construction and utilities being the other components (Kaldor 1967). Although industrialization reached its highest share in GDP during the Great Leap Forward campaign in 1958, modern manufacturing did not seriously take off until the economic reforms. Its contribution to GDP has hovered around 30%–35% in the period 1984–2010 (Figure 10). In addition, the contribution of industrial output in GDP has remained strong to reach 47% in 2011. Although the contribution of manufacturing value added in GDP fell in 2008–2010 owing to a crash in exports caused by contracting imports from the developed economies, it grew in real prices from US$12 billion in 1965 to US$1243 billion in 2010 (Figure 11). Indeed, except for the steep growth recorded in 1967 (because of its small starting base), manufacturing value added grew strongest and in a sustained way in China since 1993.

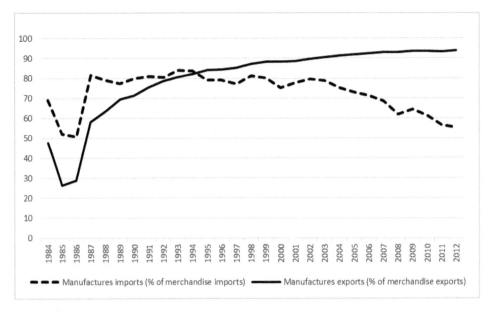

Figure 9.   Share of manufacturing in imports and exports, China, 1984–2012.
Source: World Bank (2012).

China has enjoyed significant manufacturing structural change as the capital goods industry of machinery and transport equipment recorded the highest share, which rose from 18% in 1992 to 24% in 2007 (Table 4). The contribution of textiles and clothing fell from 12.9% in 1992 to 10.0% in 2007. While growth in demand – both domestic and

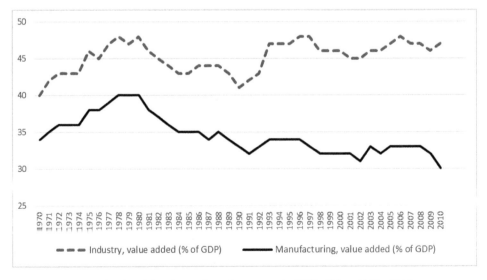

Figure 10.   Share of industrial and manufacturing sectors in GDP, China, 1970–2010.
Source: China Statistical Bureau (2010a).

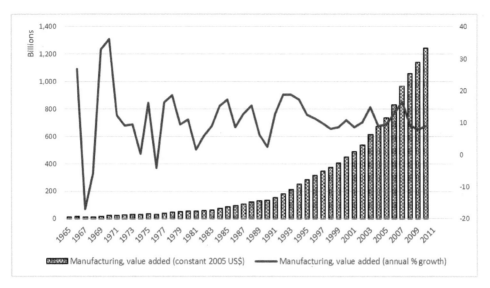

Figure 11.   Manufacturing value added, China, 1965–2011.
Source: World Bank Institute (2012).

foreign has been important, the role of the central, provincial and municipal governments have also been critical in stimulating innovation and technological upgrading in manufacturing.[4]

In short, it is clear that China has undergone significant globalization and structural change with manufacturing showing a shift towards the higher value added activities of machinery and transport equipment. It will be interesting to see if these developments have translated into a high road to industrialization in the next section.

4.   Labour markets

We discuss in this section the impact of internationalization and industrialization on China's labour market. In doing so, we analyse first the labour supply–demand patterns followed by an evaluation of the uneven rural–urban flows, and wages and labour unions in China. The analysis is to assess if globalization and industrialization has resulted in an improvement in the material conditions of workers in China.

4.1.   Supply–demand analysis

Labour supply and demand of China have increasingly been governed by a blend of policy directives and market forces after economic reforms. On the supply side, major changes in labour supply have taken place with the demographic restructuring, such as the one-child policy has lowered the dependency ratio. On the demand side, China's insertion into the global economy increased the demand for high-quality labour as government policies focused on transforming economic specialization in the country from low to high value added activities.

Table 4. Gross output, manufacturing industries, China, 2000–2011.

Year	2000		2002		2004		2006		2008		2010		2011	
	Actual amount	%	Actual amount	%	Actual amount	%	Actual amount	%	Actual amount	%	Actual amount	%	Actual amount	%
Manufacturing	83,990.55	100	10,8701.2	100	206,122.2	100	293,172.7	100	473,830.8	100	652,203.1	1100	789,971.8	100
Mining and washing of Coal	1276.81	1.52	1980.76	1.82	4735.20	2.30	7207.61	2.46	14,625.92	3.09	22,109.27	3.39	28,919.81	3.66
Extraction of petroleum and natural gas	3130.11	3.73	2756.59	2.54	4630.17	2.25	7718.8	2.63	10,615.96	2.24	9917.84	1.52	12,888.76	1.63
Mining and processing of ores	1048.25	1.25	1220.2	1.12	3056.34	1.48	4094.65	1.40	8368.33	1.77	12,923.59	1.98	16,803.38	2.13
Manufacture of food, beverages and tobacco	8368.88	9.96	10,778.02	9.92	18,166.37	8.81	24,801.03	8.46	42,373.24	8.94	61,273.84	9.39	76,813.58	9.72
Manufacture of textile	5149.3	6.13	6370.79	5.86	11,655.12	5.65	15,315.5	5.22	21,393.12	4.51	28,507.92	4.37	32,652.99	4.13
Manufacture of textile wearing apparel, footwear and caps	2291.16	2.73	2914.91	2.68	4668.52	2.26	6159.4	2.10	9435.76	1.99	12,331.24	1.89	13,538.12	1.71
Manufacture of leather, fur and feather	1345.17	1.60	1801.46	1.66	3133.23	1.52	4150.04	1.42	5871.43	1.24	7897.5	1.21	8927.54	1.13
Manufacture of wood and furniture	3636.33	4.33	4716.37	4.34	7801.75	3.79	10,309.44	3.52	15,307.19	3.23	20,228.74	3.10	22,465.66	2.84
Manufacture of paper product and publications	7272.66	8.66	9432.74	8.68	15,603.5	7.57	20,618.88	7.03	30,614.38	6.46	40,457.48	6.20	44,931.32	5.69
Processing of petroleum, coking, processing of nuclear fuel	4429.19	5.27	4784.98	4.40	9088.84	4.41	15,149.04	5.17	22,628.68	4.78	29,238.79	4.48	36,889.17	4.67
Manufacture of chemical products	5749.02	6.84	7220.05	6.64	14,027.74	6.81	20,448.69	6.97	33,955.07	7.17	47,920.02	7.35	60,825.06	7.70

(continued)

Table 4. (Continued)

Year	2000		2002		2004		2006		2008		2010		2011	
	Actual amount	%	Actual amount	%	Actual amount	%	Actual amount	%	Actual amount	%	Actual amount	%	Actual amount	%
Manufacture of medicines	1781.37	2.12	2378.44	2.19	3365.85	1.63	5018.94	1.71	7874.98	1.66	11,741.31	1.80	14,941.99	1.89
Manufacture of chemical fibber	1243.07	1.48	1121.82	1.03	1994.19	0.97	3205.63	1.09	3970.16	0.84	4953.99	0.76	6673.67	0.84
Manufacture of rubber	112.7	0.97	1064.6	0.98	2047.60	0.99	2731.85	0.93	4228.61	0.89	5906.67	0.91	7330.66	0.93
Manufacture of plastics	1199.7	2.26	2487.92	2.29	5253.29	2.55	6381.01	2.18	9897.17	2.09	13,872.22	2.13	15,579.54	1.97
Manufacture of non-metallic mineral products	3692.85	4.40	4557.04	4.19	9951.20	4.83	11,721.52	4.00	20,943.45	4.42	32,057.26	4.92	40,180.26	5.09
Smelting and manufacture of metal products	9452.89	11.25	12,386.72	11.40	29,913.55	14.51	46,869.74	15.99	80,706.31	17.03	10,0087.2	15.35	12,3324.6	15.61
Manufacture of machinery and transport equipment	23,856.73	28.40	33,946.39	31.23	67,673.54	32.83	96,853.36	33.04	151,920.3	32.06	216,861.4	33.25	253,248.1	32.06%
Manufacture of artwork and others	4611.39	5.49	5889.05	5.42	2119.76	1.03	2533.22	0.86	4088.63	0.86	5662.66	0.87	7189.51	0.91

Source: China Statistical Bureau (various years).
Note: Actual amount is by 100 million yuan.

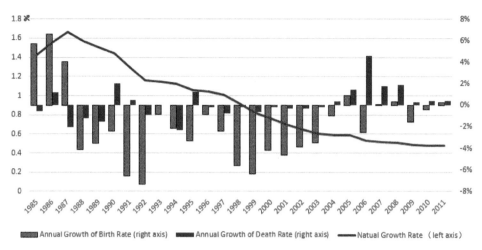

Figure 12.   Birth, death and population growth rates, China, 1978–2011.
Source: China Statistical Bureau (2012a).

4.1.1.   Labour supply

Ostensibly, labour supply did not seem to be a problem for a large country like China with a population of over 1.3 billion in 2010. Industrialization drove large numbers of workers from agriculture to industry and services so that in the initial stages the massive supply of labour contributed to a low wage elasticity of economic growth[5] in manufacturing in the 1990s. Rapid urbanization and industrialization helped raise the wage elasticity of growth as the industrial reserve disappeared. These changes were influenced by both export growth as well as demographic changes in China.

Demographic changes have contributed to a strong long-term shift in labour supply as the one-child policy sharply reduced population growth, which over the long run has eliminated the advantages of cheap labour. Labour-intensive industries have come under pressure as population growth slowed down sharply following a steep fall in birth rates from 1987 (Figure 12). Falling birth rates alongside a relatively stable death rate led to decline in population growth, which fell dramatically from 1.6% in 1982 to 0.5% in 2011.

The impact of demographic changes has not only affected the quantity but also in the age structure of labour supply. The disaggregation of population composition shows that although the population aged between 15 and 64 increased from 0.7 billion in 1978 to 1.0 billion in 2011, the population aged 0–14 dropped from 0.3 billion in 1978 to 0.2 billion in 2011, which shows that China will be facing a problem of a small young population in the long run. Hence, while the rapid expansion in human capital has improved job opportunities (demand), the one-child family policy has been a major cause of sharply contracting labour supply market in China.

4.1.2.   Labour demand

Whereas labour supply in China is determined by endogenous demographic factors, labour demand is sensitive to exogenous forces, such as globalization and industrialization. The transition of China from an agrarian to an industrial society has been driven by reforms since 1978, which has been the primary engine of global integration and economic structural change in the country. Since the focus here is on manufacturing, we

Table 5. Annual industrial employment elasticity, China, 1998–2010.

Year	Nominal gross industrial output[a]	Constant 2000 price[b]	Output growth	Employment[c]	Employment growth	Industrial employment elasticity[d]
1998	67,737.14	68,266.55	N/A	6195.81	N/A	N/A
1999	72,707.04	74,206.42	8.70%	5805.05	−6.31%	(0.72)
2000	85,673.66	85,673.66	15.45%	5559.36	−4.23%	(0.27)
2001	95,448.98	93,528.94	9.17%	5441.43	−2.12%	(0.23)
2002	110,776.48	107,917.66	15.38%	5520.66	1.46%	0.09
2003	142,271.22	135,072.14	25.16%	5748.57	4.13%	0.16
2004	201,722.19	179,131.78	32.62%	6622.09	15.20%	0.47
2005	251,619.50	214,992.53	20.02%	6895.96	4.14%	0.21
2006	316,588.96	260,638.13	21.23%	7358.43	6.71%	0.32
2007	405,177.13	310,003.71	18.94%	7875.20	7.02%	0.37
2008	507,284.89	360,050.81	16.14%	8837.63	12.22%	0.76
2009	548,311.42	391,492.71	8.73%	8831.22	−0.07%	(0.01)
2010	698,590.54	467,902.81	19.52%	9544.71	8.08%	0.41

Notes: [a]Nominal Gross Industrial Output figures converted to constant 2000 prices using the GDP deflator of China from World Bank Institute (2011).
[b]In 10,000 yuan.
[c]In 10,000.
[d]Industrial Employment Elasticity is calculated by dividing growth rate of employment over growth rate of real gross output.
Source: Calculated by authors based on China Statistical Bureau (2012a) & World Bank (2011).

estimate employment elasticity figures over the period where data is available, i.e. 1998–2010[6]. Employment elasticity refers to the growth in employment for every unit output generated.

Annual industrial employment elasticities over the period 1998–2012, which is estimated by dividing industrial employment growth by industrial output growth, is shown in Table 5. Real output grew every year over the period 1998–2012, while employment fell over the years 1999–2001 and 2009. Large scale retrenchments by state owned enterprises (SOEs) saw employment facing negative growth rates in 1999–2001, which resulted in negative employment elasticities. The massive layoffs that followed painful reforms targeted at SOEs in the late 1990s were absorbed by the emerging non-state sector.[7] Except for 2009 (affected by the global financial crisis), positive industrial employment elasticities were recorded over the period 1999-2012.

The employment rate, the equilibrium point between labour supply and demand, jumped three times from 207 million to 761 million over the period 1952–2010 (Figure 13). Gripped by low wages and disguised unemployment during the communist rule, the social-market experiment following reforms boosted employment growth, which grew 553 million in 1989 to 647 million in 1990, recording its highest annual average growth rate of 17% in that period (Figure 14). The steady increase in labour force participation rate is a reflection of the nature of social market reforms China introduced to integrate with the global economy.

As a consequence of rapid labour absorption, the unemployment rate[8] fell from 4.9% in 1980 to its trough of 1.8% in 1985 before a two-decade-long rise to 4.3% in 2003

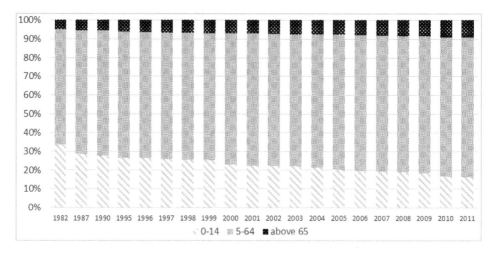

Figure 13. Population composition by age, China, 1982–2011.
Source: China Statistical Bureau (2012a).

(Figure 15). Reforms instituted on SOEs led to a rise in unemployment to 3.1% in 1989. Despite labour absorption, unemployment rose steadily until 2003 owing to structural unemployment caused partly by reforms faced by the SOEs. It has since either fallen or kept steady in trend terms, reaching 4.1% in 2011.

Rapid industrialization transformed the sectoral labour force participation rates as the share of employment in agricultural sector fell from 83.5% in 1952 to 34.8% in 2011, while the commensurate shares in the industrial sector rose from 7.4% in 1952 to 29.5% in 2011 (Figure 16). Employment by services grew from a share of 9.1% in 1952 to 35.7% in 2011. Economic reforms and the integration into the global economy transformed China from an agricultural to an industrial economy. Labour migration into the

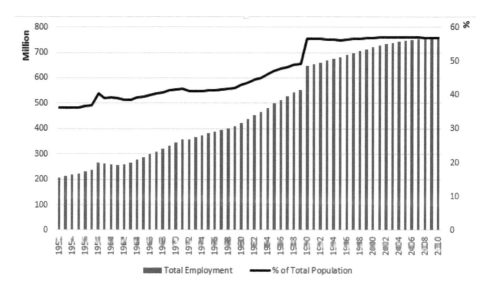

Figure 14. Employment, China, 1952–2010.
Source: China Statistical Bureau (various years).

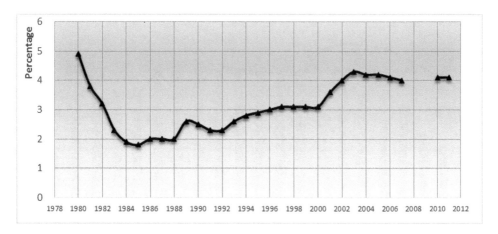

Figure 15. Unemployment rate, China, 1980–2011.
Source: World Bank Institute (2013).
Note: Data for 2008 and 2009 not available.

booming industrial and service sectors was the major reason, the introduction of large-scale agricultural production using high technology was also important.

Manufacturing employment grew rapidly over the first reform period of 1978–1988 (Figure 17). A declining share of manufacturing in total employment from 15.9% in 1988 to 13.3% in 1990 is due to the fact that other sectors grew faster than manufacturing. Both employment, and the employment share of manufacturing in total employment grew in 1990–1996 as China enjoyed rapid growth similar to East Asia. Manufacturing employment fell again in 1997–2001 as a consequence of the Asian financial crisis of 1997–1998, and the relocation of labour-intensive manufacturing to Vietnam, Laos and Cambodia.

4.2. Uneven distribution of labour

Globalization and industrialization have also reproduced uneven regional distribution of labour in China. The huge size of China, and its diverse geographical and socio-economic

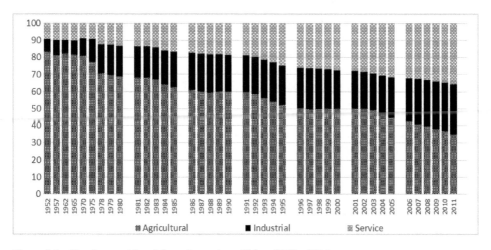

Figure 16. Employment breakdown by sectors, China, 1952–2011.
Source: China Statistical Bureau (2012b).

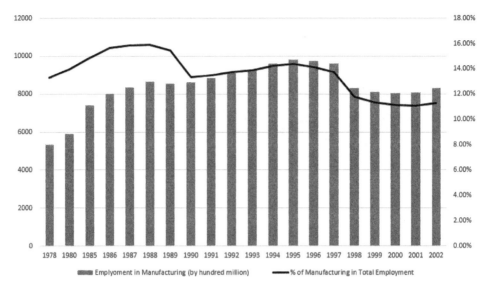

Figure 17. Employment in manufacturing, China, 1978–2008.
Source: China Statistical Bureau (various years).

background has given the labour market multifarious development patterns. Global integration benefited the coastal provinces more than the inland provinces owing to both a greater focus on the former than the latter in the initial reform period, as well as, the proximity offered by the seafront. Hence, the Eastern coastal provinces have enjoyed structural change towards medium and high technology industries and higher wages than the inland provinces. In the meanwhile, household registration system (*hukou*), as a population control scheme, separated labour supply and demand geographically, so that labour supply from rural and Western inland regions is institutionally constrained to fill up strong labour demand generated by the urban and East coastal regions.

Until around 2000, government policy to promote trade and FDI favoured the East coastal areas. After 2000, the significant improvement of trade conditions offered by accession to the WTO resulted in the government extending trade and investment focus to the whole of China. However, the importance of access to trade routes prevented the movement of labour-intensive industries to the Western inland provinces. Hence, the growth of export-driven industries drove massive movement of labor from the Western inland provinces to the coastal Eastern provinces, aggravating regional inequality in employment and wages. Compared to the middle and western provinces, the Eastern coastal provinces account for around half of national employment in the period 2003–2011 (Figure 18). In 2010, 50.3% of national employment was created by 11 out of 33 provinces/municipals in the Eastern China. The concentration in manufacturing was even higher at around 60% of national employment.

4.3. Wages

From a country that seemed like a base for unlimited cheap labour supply, China has transformed to experience rising real wages following a sustained rise in demand for labour and skills. Industrial exports aided strongly by important contributions from foreign capital, and foreign technology in particular has generated the demand for labour

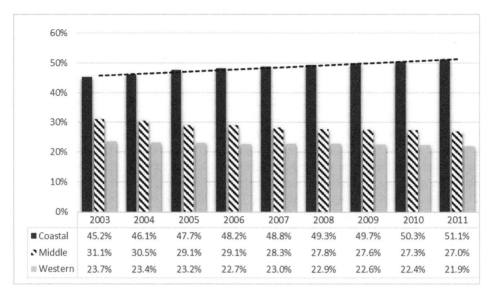

	2003	2004	2005	2006	2007	2008	2009	2010	2011
■ Coastal	45.2%	46.1%	47.7%	48.2%	48.8%	49.3%	49.7%	50.3%	51.1%
↘ Middle	31.1%	30.5%	29.1%	29.1%	28.3%	27.8%	27.6%	27.3%	27.0%
▥ Western	23.7%	23.4%	23.2%	22.7%	23.0%	22.9%	22.6%	22.4%	21.9%

Figure 18.   Share of employment by regions, China, 2003–2011.
Source: National Statistical Bureau (various years).

to record significant improvements in wages. The jump in real wage growth started in around 1998 when it was clear that the Multi-Fibre Arrangement – which gave preferential market access in the developed countries to particular developing economies – will be terminated by 2004 (Rasiah 2012). Although real wage growth fell below 7% in 2004, both overall and manufacturing enjoyed a massive annual growth in real wages between 7% and 20% over the remaining 1998–2012 period (Table 6). Growth in manufacturing wages exceeded growth in overall wages in 1995, 1998–2000 and 2003. The higher growth in non-manufacturing real wages since 2005 is largely a case of catching up with manufacturing.

Clearly, the rapid growth in real wages in the world's most populous country demonstrates that the infusion of market forces in a protracted manner with the state retaining control to ensure that the interests of the poor are shielded is arguably a great example for

Table 6.   Wages, overall and manufacturing, China, 1994–2009.

	Overall			Manufacturing		
Year	Nominal	Constant 2000 prices	Growth rate	Nominal	Constant 2000 prices	Growth rate
1995	5348	5773.44	4.51%	5199	5612.59	6.60%
1997	6444	6438.60	6.15%	5979	5973.99	3.82%
1999	8319	8490.55	13.14%	7874	8036.37	12.03%
2001	10,834	10,616.06	13.75%	9891	9692.03	9.69%
2003	13,969	13,262.15	10.03%	12,671	12,029.83	10.73%
2005	18,200	15,550.71	10.00%	15,934	13,614.56	7.58%
2007	24,721	18,914.20	10.16%	21,144	16,177.41	7.82%
2009	32,244	23,022.11	12.24%	26,810	19,142.25	10.51%

Source: China Statistical Bureau (2010b).

other economies to study. The high increase in real wages obviously also suggests that China has managed to experience the high road to industrialization as defined by Piore and Sabel (1984), and Pyke and Sengenberger (1992). Rapid economic growth led by manufacturing has been accompanied by tangible improvements in the material conditions of labour as wages have grown significantly over the years.

As shown in Table 7, all manufacturing industries recorded rapid average annual real wage growth over the period 2001–2011. Overall (8.5%) wages grew faster than manufacturing (8.1%) wages for the reasons explained earlier. Tobacco and special purpose machinery recorded the highest wage growth in the manufacturing sector at 10.2% per annum. Between these two industries, tobacco by far enjoyed a massive real wage growth as mean wages 2000 prices in the industry reached 57,749 yuan compared to only 25,740 yuan in special purpose machinery. In addition, the manufacturing industries of textile, timber, bamboo and straw, furniture, paper and paper products, chemicals, nonmetallic mineral products, and general purpose machinery also enjoyed higher real wage growth than overall wage growth in China over the period 2001–2011.

In addition to rising wages caused by a greater rise in labour demand over labour supply and the rising premium for skilled and knowledge-based labour, the Chinese government has also reviewed its minimum wages every two years to ensure that the formal labour market is properly regulated. Minimum wages in China vary according to the regional and provincial differences in socio-economic conditions, as well as the concentration of labour across China. Although the national regulations, *Regulations on Minimum Wage*, was enforced in 2004 as a guideline to protect employees being fairly remunerated, the provincialization and decentralization processes following reforms allow local governments the regulatory space to initiate their own regulations based on specific socio-economic conditions. Moreover, the changing external economic environment caused by factors, such as, inflation,[9] have often required the authorities to calibrate minimum wages to reflect market conditions so as to protect the welfare of employees. Following the law to encourage provincial authority to adjust the minimum wage once every two years until it is lifted up to 40% of average wage of urban employees in 2015, the national average annual growth rate of minimum wage was increased by 22% in 2011 and 20.5% in 2010. Among the provinces, Shanghai enjoyed the highest monthly and hourly minimum wages of 1620 yuan and 14 yuan, respectively, while the landlocked provinces/regions such as Guizhou and Chongqing recorded lower monthly and hourly minimum wages (Table 8). The dynamic economic provinces of Guangdong, Shenzhen, Jiangsu and Zhejiang also enjoyed relatively high minimum wages.

4.4. Female labour

We examine the gender issue in China's labour market here because female labour is attracting strong attention as they emerge from a background of subordination to males. Because China's early history has been dominated by men, the gender inequality that persisted since the *Han Dynasty* had remained until the establishment of People's Republic in 1949 when the Communist Party announced that the liberalization of women as a sign of modernization. Encouraged by Mao Zedong's motto of 'woman can also hold up half sky,' women were given equal rights to participate in the social relations of production.

Women's participation in the formal labour market became more pronounced since market reforms were introduced in 1978. Attracted by the better urban incomes, young migrant women left their homes from rural areas to seek employment in industrial areas

Table 7. Manufacturing wages, China, 2001–2011.

Year / Item	2001 Nominal	2001 2000 Prices	2003 Nominal	2003 2000 Prices	2005 Nominal	2005 2000 Prices	2007 Nominal	2007 2000 Price	2009 Nominal	2009 2000 Prices	2011 Nominal	2011 2000 Prices	2001–2011 Average annual growth
National average	10,834	10,616	13,969	13,262	18,200	15,550	24,721	18,914	32,244	23,022	41,799	25,978	8.5
Manufacturing	9,391	9,692	12,671	12,030	15,934	13,614	21,144	16,177	26,810	19,142	36,665	22,787	8.1
Processing of food from agricultural products	7,172	7,028	8,727	8,285	11,214	9,581	14,869	11,376	19,740	14,094	27,901	17,340	8.6
Foods	9,125	8,942	11,157	10,592	13,408	11,456	17,533	13,414	22,713	16,217	34,483	21,431	8.3
Beverage	8,919	8,740	10,746	10,202	13,506	11,540	18,135	13,875	24,986	17,840	34,105	21,196	8.4
Tobacco	20,269	19,862	27,143	25,770	42,355	36,188	52,418	40,105	67,156	47,949	92,919	57,749	10.2
Textile	6,681	6,547	8,079	7,670	10,531	8,998	13,968	10,687	18,241	13,024	26,973	16,764	8.9
Clothing, footwear, caps and wearing apparel	8,367	8,199	10,090	9,579	12,512	10,690	16,924	12,949	20,579	14,693	29,026	18,040	7.4
Furniture	7,721	7,566	9,501	9,020	12,639	10,799	16,871	12,908	20,543	14,668	30,700	19,080	8.8
Printing and publishing	9,616	9,423	11,707	11,115	14,984	12,802	19,350	14,805	25,029	17,871	34,095	21,190	7.6
Chemical products	9,288	9,101	12,129	11,515	15,770	13,474	21,835	16,706	27,583	19,694	38,113	23,687	9.1
Medicine	11,626	11,392	14,556	13,819	17,170	14,670	21,595	16,522	28,857	20,604	38,612	23,997	7.0
Rubber	9,089	8,906	11,024	10,466	14,233	12,161	18,994	14,532	23,841	17,022	32,289	20,068	7.7
Plastic	8,990	8,809	11,317	10,744	13,661	11,672	18,078	13,831	22,272	15,902	31,668	19,682	7.6
Smelting & processing of ferrous metals	13,266	12,999	17,989	17,079	24,030	20,531	30,786	23,554	36,686	26,194	44,238	27,494	7.0
Transport equipment	12,141	11,897	16,313	15,488	20,204	17,262	26,922	20,598	34,730	24,797	45,635	28,362	8.2
Communication equipment	16,350	16,021	18,922	17,965	21,213	18,124	26,934	20,607	32,236	23,017	41,009	25,487	4.3
Measuring instrument and office equipment	11,091	10,868	15,044	14,283	17,644	15,075	23,669	18,109	28,836	20,589	40,185	24,975	7.9

Source: China Statistical Bureau (various years).

Table 8.   Minimum wages by province, China, 2013.

	January		May		June		July	
	Monthly	Hourly	Monthly	Hourly	Monthly	Hourly	Monthly	Hourly
Shenzhen	1500	13.3	1600	14.5	1600	14.5	1600	14.5
Zhejiang	1470	12	1470	12	1470	12	1470	12
Shanghai	1450	12.5	1620	14	1620	14	1620	14
Beijing	1400	15.2	1400	15.2	1400	15.2	1400	15.2
Xinjiang	1340	13.4	1340	13.4	1520	15.2	1520	15.2
Jiangsu	1320	11.5	1320	11.5	1320	11.5	1480	13
Hebei	1320	13	1320	13	1320	13	1320	13
Tianjin	1310	13.1	1500	15	1500	15	1500	15
Guangdong	1300	12.5	1550	15	1550	15	1550	15
Shandong	1240	13	1380	14.5	1380	14.5	1380	14.5
Fujian	1200	12.7	1200	12.7	1200	12.7	1200	12.7
Inner Mongolia	1200	10.2	1200	10.2	1200	10.2	1200	10.2
Hunan	1160	11.5	1160	11.5	1160	11.5	1160	11.5
Heilongjiang	1160	11	1160	11	1160	11	1160	11
Shaanxi	1150	11.5	1150	11.5	1150	11.5	1150	11.5
Tibet	1150	10.5	1150	10.5	1150	10.5	1150	10.5
Jilin	1150	10	1150	10	1150	10	1150	10
Shanxi	1125	12.3	1290	14	1290	14	1290	14
Hubei	1100	10	1100	10	1100	10	1100	10
Liaoning	1100	11	1100	11	1100	11	1300	12.5
Ningxia	1100	11	1300	12.5	1300	12.5	1300	12.5
Yunnan	1100	10	1265	11	1265	11	1265	11
Henan	1240	11.7	1240	11.7	1240	11.7	1240	11.7
Qinghai	1070	10.8	1070	10.8	1070	10.8	1070	10.8
Sichuan	1050	11	1050	11	1050	11	1200	12.7
Chongqing	1050	10.5	1050	10.5	1050	10.5	1050	10.5
Hainan	1050	9.2	1050	9.2	1050	9.2	1050	9.2
Anhui	1010	10.6	1010	10.6	1010	10.6	1010	10.6
Guangxi	1000	8.5	1200	10.5	1200	10.5	1200	10.5
Gansu	980	10.3	1200	12.7	1200	12.7	1200	12.7
Guizhou	1030	11	1030	11	1030	11	1030	11
Jiangxi	870	8.7	1230	12.3	1230	12.3	1230	12.3

Source: Bureau of Human Resource and Social Security, various provinces, (2013).

to supplement household incomes or to support their male siblings to attend college. Statistics from Shenzhen General Labour Union (2003) show that 70% of the 5.5 million migrant workers were females in the Shenzhen Special Economic Zone in 2003. In one of its sub-districts, i.e. *Nanshan*, female labour accounted for 80% of the entire workforce with an average age of 23. However, lacking the skills and knowledge of urban educated woman, most rural female migrants are employed in segmented labour markets in the informal and low-wage employment sectors. Young migrant workers, with minimal education and awareness of labour-related rights found are largely exposed to low-wage employment with weak labour protection and physical and psychological problems.

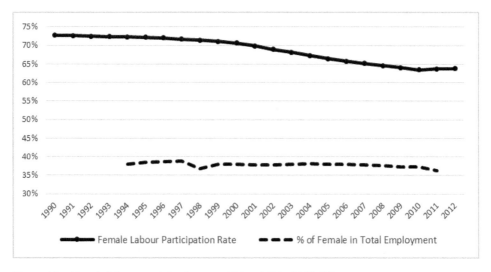

Figure 19.   Female labour participation rate, China, 1990–2012 (%).
Source: World Bank (2012).

The development of female employment since the Communist Party took over is asso-ciated with the following: first, the modernization of household relations as women began to enter education stream in large numbers, (including in technical fields), and second, market reforms since 1978 provided massive demand for female labour. However, while these two developments unleashed strong motivation for women to work, the gradual withdrawal of the state from economic activities triggered a gradual fall in female labour force participation rates, which dropped from 72.7% in 1990 to 63.8% in 2012 (Figure 19). The steep decline happened since 1998 until middle 2000s, which is believed to be a consequence of large-scale SOE reforms as a massive number of employees were retrenched. Rising incomes also led a number of females to stay home and take care of household chores. Hence, females in the labour force stabilized at 36%–38% in the period 1994–2011.

Overall and female employment in manufacturing has started to decline since 1994 before both of them experienced a rise after bottoming in 2003. The female composition declined from its highest of 45% in 1995 to its lowest of 39% in 2011(Figure 20). The declining trend in the female share of employment in manufacturing is a consequence of industrial upgrading from low technology labour-intensive industries, such as, clothing and tools manufacturing, to middle technology industries, such as, machinery manufacturing. While the former is dominated by female workers, the latter is dominated by male workers. Nevertheless, manufacturing alone accounted for 30.9%–42.4% of overall female employment over the period 1994–2011 (Figure 21).

Although China has enjoyed a relatively high female labour participation rate compared to most developing economic and the smallest rural-urban and gender wage gaps among developing countries (World Bank Institute 2012), female labour in manufacturing shows longer working hours than workers (including female) in the overall economy over the period 2001–2011. This gap has narrowed since over the period 2007–2011. In general, both male and female working hours in manufacturing is much longer compared to other sectors (Table 9). However, there is no discernible difference in male–female working hours over the period 2001–2011 to suggest that women work longer than men in

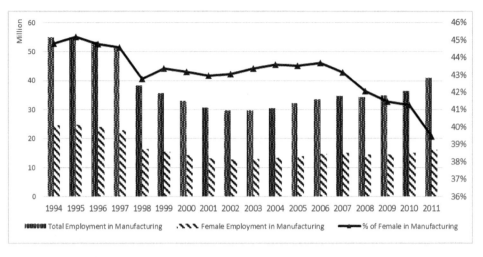

Figure 20.   Manufacturing employment, China, 1994–2011.
Source: China Statistical Bureau (various years).

manufacturing. The narrowing gap in working hours between manufacturing and other sec-tors also shows a shift in economic activity away from manufacturing to the other sectors, such as, services.

However, severe challenges still face China's female workers. Although industrializa-tion and globalization have improved wages, female workers earned less than 31% on average the wages of man in 2011 for doing the same job. Also, gender discrimination also affected female job seekers in the employment market with many employers prefer-ring male employees owing to legal protection for maternity leave and other preferential treatment given to women. In addition, urban migrant female workers often face serious social problems. Given the special characteristic of unions in China, which are a subordi-nate organ of government, female labour often lacks empowerment to seek their labour-related rights. The government's sanctioning of other forms of unionization denied the All-China Federation of Trade Unions the legitimacy to fight for worker's rights. As a

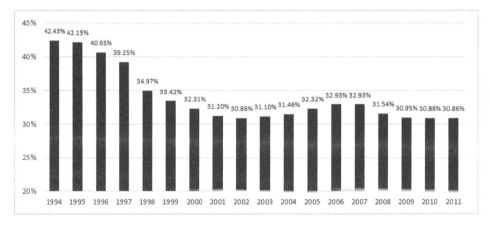

Figure 21.   Female manufacturing employment in total employment, China, 1994–2011.
Source: China Statistical Bureau (various years).

Table 9. Urban female average weekly working hours, China, 2001–2011.

Year	National	Male National	Female National	Manufacturing	Male in manufacturing	Female in manufacturing
2001	44.9	45.2	44.5	44.7	44.8	44.7
2002	45.2	45.6	44.7	46.0	45.6	46.5
2003	45.4	45.8	44.9	46.4	46.2	46.6
2004	45.5	46.0	44.9	46.9	46.5	47.5
2005	47.8	48.7	46.1	51.1	51.0	51.3
2006	47.3	48.3	45.9	50.4	50.3	50.5
2007	45.5	46.8	44	49.4	49.6	49.2
2008	44.6	45.7	43.1	47.9	48.0	47.7
2009	44.7	45.9	43.2	48.5	48.6	48.4
2010	47.0	47.7	46.1	49.0	49.0	49.0
2011	46.2	47	45.2	48.1	48.2	47.9

Source: China Statistical Bureau (various years).

consequence, the collective bargaining power of migrant women workers is largely absent to assist them to seek their rights from employers. Hence, unrests involving worker abuse have continued to explode in China, such as, the notorious Foxconn suicide scandal.

5. Conclusions

Although we have not examined the state of freedom and happiness the people of China may have enjoyed when the gates to global integration were opened in 1978, the evidence shows that massive trade and investment flows have followed since reforms began, which has not only stimulated rapid economic growth and structural change but it has also generated significant improvement in real wages, especially from the 1990s. The advantages offered by the seafront and an earlier focus by the government made the Eastern coastal provinces the largest beneficiaries of globalization in China. Manufacturing value added and structural change and wages have grown the fastest in these states. Nevertheless, the middle inland provinces and federal territories of Jiangsu and Beijing have also benefited considerably from the transformation. Although regional inequalities have widened as a consequence of the faster development of the Eastern provinces compared to the Western provinces the evidence shows that material progress has been felt by most provinces.

The evidence shows that global integration through the infusion of capitalist organization under a socialist structure where the central government has increasingly decentralized planning to absorb provincial and municipal participation in decision-making has been successful in ensuring long run growth, structural change and improvements in wages. The government's focus on targeting technological capability has been important in the structural transformation of manufacturing from lower to higher value added activities. Elsewhere Mathews (2014) has offered convincing evidence to show how China is driving Asia's new great transformation through a focus on renewable energy to power economic growth.

However, China's massive industrial labour market has also been gripped by social problems. Manufacturing workers on average still work longer than other workers in the economy. While female labour force participation rates are high compared to other developing countries, rising wages has also capped further increases since the 2000s as women have chosen to handle household chores more. However, not everything has been rosy as vulnerable industrial rural migrant workers have also been exposed to abuse by factories from time to time. Also, women on average still earn around one-third of men for similar work done in China.

Acknowledgements

We are grateful to comments from two referees. The usual disclaimer applies.

Notes

1. In general, the collection and reporting of statistics raise a number of problems. Nevertheless, statistics from a large and rapidly growing economy like China will be superior to those backward countries.
2. Moroccan geographer Muhammad al-Idrisi had recorded the appearance of Chinese merchant ships in the Indian Ocean in 1154, and their voyages extended as far as Yemen.
3. Interviews with a senior German engineer of Shanghai Volkswagen on 29 September 2000 in Shanghai.
4. For an account of the role of the central, provincial and municipal governments in the growth of button manufacturing in Qiaotou.
5. The low price elasticity may also be explained by the absence of a well-established market mechanism.
6. The observation period extends from 1998 to 2010 in order to capture the industry development after reforms and insertion of global economy, especially the entrance of WTO in 2000. The period before 1998 was not taken into discussion, as the changes in elasticity was not significant enough to examine the impact of globalization and industrialization on labour market.
7. The aggregate number of laid-off workers was 27 million from 1998 to 2004. The number of layoffs reached its peak of 6.6 million in 2000.
8. It indicates the share of unemployment on total labour force.
9. According to the Law, the minimum wage is a function of a set of socio-economic factors, which is expressed as follows:

$$M = f (C, S, A, U, E, a)$$

where M: Level of Minimum Wage; C: Urban Average of Life Expenses; S: Social Security Fund and Housing Provident Fund by Employees; A: Average Wage of Employees; U: Unemployment Rate; E: Level of Economic Development; and a: adjustment factor.

References

China Global Investment Tracker. 2011. *American Enterprise Institute & The Heritage Foundation.* Accessed October 21, 2014. http://www.heritage.org/research/projects/china-global-investment-tracker-interactive map

China Statistical Bureau. 2010a. *China Statistics Yearbook,* edited by J.T. Ma. Beijing: State Statistical Bureau.

China Statistical Bureau. 2010b. *China Labour Statistical Yearbook,* edited by Z.B. Zhang. Beijing: Department of Population and Employment Statistics of the State Statistics Bureau & Department of Planning and Finance of the Ministry of Human Resources and Social Security.

China Statistical Bureau. 2012a. *China Statistics Yearbook*, edited by J.T. Ma. Beijing: State Statistical Bureau.

China Statistical Bureau. 2012b. *China Labour Statistical Yearbook,* edited by Z.B. Zhang. Beijing: Department of Population and Employment Statistics of the State Statistics Bureau & Department of Planning and Finance of the Ministry of Human Resources and Social Security.

Kaldor, N. 1967. *Strategic Factors in Economic Development.* New York, NY: New York State School of Industrial and Labor Relations, Cornell University.

Mathew, J.A. 2014. *Greening Capitalism: How Asia is Driving the New Great Transformation.* Stanford: Stanford University Press.

Piore, M.J., and C.F. Sabel. 1984. *The Second Industrial Divide: Possibilities for Prosperity.* New York, NY: Basic Books.

Pyke, F., and W. Sengenberger. 1992. *Industrial Districts and Local Economic Regeneration.* Geneva: International Labour Organization (ILO).

Rasiah, R. 2012. "Beyond the Multi-Fibre Agreement: How are Workers in East Asia Faring?." *Institutions and Economies* 4 (3): 1–20.

Rasiah, R., X.-X. Kong, and J. Vinanchiarachi. 2011. "Moving Up in the Global Value Chain in Button Manufacturing in China." *Asia Pacific Business Review* 17 (2): 161–174. doi:10.1080/13602381.2011.533508

Rasiah, R., Z. Miao, and K.X. Xin. 2013. "Can China's Miraculous Economic Growth Continue?" *Journal of Contemporary Asia* 43 (2): 295–313. doi:10.1080/00472336.2012.740940

Shenzhen General Labour Union. 2003. "The Cooperative of Female Migrant in Shenzhen. 2014." http://gd.news.sina.com.cn/local/2003-03-10/18107.html.

UNCTAD. 2011. *World Investment Report.* Geneva. http://unctad.org/en/PublicationsLibrary/wir2012_embargoed_en.pdf

World Bank. 2011. *World Development Indicators.* http://data.worldbank.org/country/china#cp_wdi

World Bank. 2012. *World Development Indicators.* http://data.worldbank.org/country/china#cp_wdi

World Bank Institute. 2011. *World Development Indicators.* Washington, DC: World Bank Institute.

World Bank Institute. 2012. *World Development Indicators.* Washington, DC: World Bank Institute.

World Bank Institute. 2013. *World Development Indicators.* Washington, DC: World Bank Institute.

World Development Indicators. 2012. *The World Bank.* http://data.worldbank.org/country/china#cp_wdi

World Trade Organization. 2012. *International Trade Statistics.* Geneva: World Trade Organization.

Young, A. 2003. "Gold into Base Metals: Productivity Growth in the People's Republic of China During the Reform Period." *Journal of Political Economy* 111: 1220–1261.

Zhang, M., and R. Rasiah. 2014. "Institutional Change and State Owned Enterprises in China's Urban Housing Market." *Habitat International* 41 (Jan.): 58–68.

Growth, industrialisation and inequality in India

Jayati Ghosh

Centre for Economic Studies and Planning, School of Social Sciences, Jawaharlal Nehru University, New Delhi, India

The Indian growth process has been marked by the relative absence of structural change and the inability of faster output expansion to shift people out of low-productivity activities into higher value ones. Recent rapid growth has also been based on and resulted in growing inequalities. Private accumulation has relied upon existing social inequalities that create segmented labour markets that keep wages of certain social categories low, and on types of exclusion that allow large-scale displacement and dispossession without adequate compensation. The associated boom has required debt-driven bubbles to provide domestic demand since incomes of the masses have not risen in tandem, but such a strategy is inherently unsustainable. This growth process is now reaching the limits of its viability and is facing constraints posed by economic, social, political and environmental challenges.

1. Introduction

Until recently, India was regarded (along with China) as one of the 'success stories' of globalisation, likely to emerge into a giant economy and global economic power in the twenty-first century. The perception of a vibrant democracy on the move, especially in economic terms, was reinforced by an economic boom that has been relatively prolonged, with a confident capitalist class increasingly taking on the world not only in exports but also through investment abroad, euphoria in the financial markets and growing self-confidence among the elite, professional and middle classes.

Of course that happy picture has since been blurred, and global investors have suddenly come to recognise the features that were evident even during the boom phase to those with the willingness to look: the fragility of the Indian balance of payments, the internal imbalances and lack of employment generation and infrastructure development. However, there is still a somewhat perverse and misleading rendering of the economic trajectory of the past two decades, one in which it is assumed that growth in the period until the end of the first decade of the current century was driven by the inherent strengths of the Indian economy that were unleashed by forces of globalisation and liberalisation, while the recent slowdown has been ascribed to 'policy paralysis' and lack of continuing market-oriented and privatising reforms.

This is a substantial misinterpretation of both the past boom and the current slowdown. Recent high economic growth in India was related to financial deregulation that sparked a retail credit boom and combined with fiscal concessions to spur consumption among the richest sections of the population. This led to rapid increases in the aggregate gross domestic product (GDP) growth, even as deflationary fiscal policies, poor employment generation and persistent agrarian crisis reduced wage shares in national income and kept mass consumption demand low. There was a substantial rise in profit shares in the economy and the proliferation of financial activities. As a result, finance and real estate accounted for more than 15% of GDP in 2009–2010. This combined with the rising asset values to enable a credit-financed consumption splurge among the rich and the middle classes especially in urban areas. And this in turn generated higher rates of investment and output over the upswing. The earlier emphasis on public spending as the principal stimulus for growth in the Indian economy was thus substituted in the past two decades with debt-financed housing investment and private consumption of the elite and burgeoning middle classes (Ghosh and Chandrasekhar 2009).

The recent Indian growth story in its essentials was, therefore, not unlike the story of speculative bubble-led expansion that marked the experience of several other developed and developing countries, and was, therefore, subject to similar problems of lack of sustainability. It is well known now that debt-driven bubbles usually end in tears, whether in rich developed countries or in 'emerging markets' or even in resource-rich least developed countries. In the Indian case, the lack of sustainability is accentuated by the social and political problems that are increasingly emerging, driven by the unequal pattern of growth. Extremist movements are powerful and dominate in 150 backward and relatively undeveloped districts that are the location of extractive industries; lack of productive employment generation has given rise to powerful demands for regional autonomy and exclusion of 'non-natives' within the different states; other forms of criminality are increasing; and there is widespread public anger not only at the evident corruption that has been characteristic of this phase but also at the explicit ways in which state policy has favoured the rich. These create potent sources of instability that may rebound on the growth process in unpredictable ways.

Further, to paraphrase Charles Dickens, while these were the best of times for some, particularly the elite and some sections of professional middle classes, they were also the worst of times for others. And the 'others' in this case may well include the majority of Indians, given the growing divisions in conditions of living. Despite more than six decades of independence, the development project is nowhere near completion in India. It is also clear that over time, some elements of that project seem even less likely to be achieved than in the past, despite relatively rapid economic growth.

Taking a long view, there are some clear achievements of the Indian economy since Independence – most crucially the emergence of a reasonably diversified economy with an industrial base. The past 25 years have also witnessed rates of aggregate GDP growth that are high compared to the past and also compared with several other parts of the developing world. Significantly, this higher aggregate growth has thus far been accompanied by macroeconomic stability, with the absence of extreme volatility in the form of financial crises such as have been evident in several other emerging markets. There has also been some reduction (although not very rapid) in income poverty.

However, there are also some clear failures of this growth process even from a long-run perspective. An important failure is the worrying absence of structural change, in terms of the ability to shift the labour force out of low productivity activities, especially in agriculture, to higher productivity and better remunerated activities. Agriculture continues to account for more than half the work force even though its share of GDP is now less than 15%. In the past decade, agrarian crisis across many parts of the country has impacted adversely on the livelihood of both cultivators and rural workers, yet the generation of more productive employment outside this sector remains woefully inadequate. Other major failures, which are directly reflective of the still poor status of human development in most parts of the country, are in many ways related to this fundamental failure. These include: the persistence of widespread poverty; the sluggishness of employment, especially in the formal sector; the absence of basic food security (and growing food insecurity) for a significant proportion of the population; the inability to ensure basic needs of housing, sanitation, adequate health care to the population as a whole; the continuing inability to ensure universal education and the poor quality of much school education; and the sluggish enlargement of access to education and employment across different social groups and for women in particular. In addition, there are problems caused by the very pattern of economic growth: aggravated regional imbalances; greater inequalities in the control over assets and in access to incomes; and dispossession and displacement of people from land and livelihood without adequate compensation and rehabilitation.

Seen in this light, it becomes apparent that a basic feature of the process of economic development thus far has been exclusion: exclusion from control over assets; exclusion from the benefits of economic growth; exclusion from the impact of physical and social infrastructure expansion; and exclusion from education and from income-generating opportunities. This exclusion has been along class or income lines, by geographical location, by caste and community, and by gender. However, exclusion from these benefits has not meant exclusion from the system as such − rather, those who are supposedly marginalised or excluded have been affected precisely because they have been incorporated into market systems. We, therefore, have a process of exclusion through incorporation, a process that has actually been typical of capitalist accumulation across the world, especially in its more dynamic phases. Thus, peasants facing a crisis of viability of cultivation have been integrated into a market system that has made them more reliant on purchased inputs in deregulated markets while becoming more dependent upon volatile output markets in which state protection is completely inadequate. The growing army of 'self-employed' workers, who now account for more than half of our work force, has been excluded from paid employment because of the sheer difficulty of finding jobs, but is nevertheless heavily involved in commercial activity and exposed to market uncertainties in the search for livelihood. Those who have been displaced by developmental projects or other processes, and subsequently have not found adequate livelihood in other activities, are victims of the process of economic integration, though excluded from the benefits.

2. Inadequate structural change

The issue of lack of structural change specifically in terms of employment may prove to be the most critical failure of all. Indeed, the recent experience of the Indian economy is startling in the extent of its deviation from almost all of the expected features of the classic pattern that was outlined by Lewis, Kuznets and Kaldor. Some of the central paradoxes of the recent pattern of growth and employment in India can be briefly stated as follows: growth has not been associated with much employment generation, and in fact the employment elasticities of output growth have actually declined as the economy has become more exposed to global competition that was supposed to have favoured more labour-intensive activities. The share of manufacturing in both output and employment has been stubbornly constant at relatively low levels. Low productivity work continues to dominate in total employment, so in the aggregate there is little evidence of labour moving to higher productivity activities. Interestingly, this is true across sectors, such that low productivity employment coexists with some high value-added activities in all of the major sectors, and there are extremely wide variations in productivity across enterprises even within the same sub-sector. The expected formalisation of work and the concentration of workers into large-scale production units have not occurred – rather, there has been widespread persistence of informal employment and increase in self-employment in non-agricultural activities. Most striking of all is that the period of rapid GDP growth has been marked by low and declining work force participation rates of women, in a pattern that is unlike almost any other rapidly growing economy in any phase of history over the past two centuries.

Remarkably, these features have persisted through different growth models and policy regimes in the post-independence period, whether Nehruvian mixed economy or open economy market-based strategies, and through varying periods of slow growth, stagnation and rapid growth. The specific concern for our purposes is with the more recent period, when the significantly accelerated expansion of economic activity over the past two decades could have been expected to generate more significant structural changes as well.

First, aggregate rates of growth of employment in India have been disappointingly low, even with the rather loose and flexible definition of work that is adopted by our National Sample Surveys (Figure 1). Indeed, it is evident that total employment (in terms of usual status of work, principal and subsidiary activities) actually grew faster when the economy was growing more slowly and has tapered off significantly in the period since 2004–2005, with rural employment actually showing a decline in absolute numbers and urban employment growing by only 2.5% annual compound rate between 2004–2005 and 2011–2012.

Second, the persistence of low productivity employment has been evident in the continuing significance of primary activities in total employment and the domination of low productivity service activities accounting for the bulk of non-agricultural jobs. While the share of agriculture and allied activities in GDP fell from around 55% in 1960–1961 to less than 18% in 2011–2012, the share of employment it accounted for declined much more slowly over the entire period, from 72% in 1960–1961 to 48% in 2011–2012 (Figure 2).

Meanwhile, the share of manufacturing has stagnated at low levels of both output and employment – in 2011–2012 it accounted for only 14.4% of GDP and 12.6% of the work force. This has led some to argue that India can successfully become a post-industrial 'service-driven' economy on the basis of modern services that are associated with rapid productivity increases. However, it would be foolhardy to presume that the difficult but necessary stage of industrialisation can simply be bypassed in this manner, especially as the newer services also generate very little additional employment.

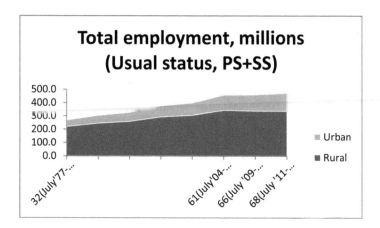

Figure 1.   Total employment, India, 1977–2011 (millions).
Source: NSSO, Reports on Employment and Unemployment, various issues.

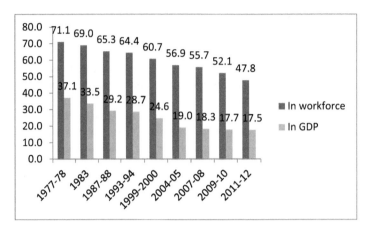

Figure 2. Share of agriculture in economy, India, 1977–2012.
Source: NSSO various rounds and CSO, National Income Accounts.

The period since the early 1990s has been marked by stagnation of formal employ-ment growth despite accelerated output growth, and lower intensity of employment in the most dynamic manufacturing and services sub-sectors (Kannan and Raveendran 2009; Arora 2010). Even within sectors that are perceived as more dynamic, the majority of workers persist in low productivity activities, with only a small minority in each sector involved in highly remunerated and high-productivity work. The most rapidly expanding activities in terms of GDP share, such as finance, insurance and real estate (FIRE), IT-related services and telecommunications which together now account for nearly 20% of the GDP, still employ less than 2% of the work force. The persistence of the vast majority of workers in extremely low-productivity activities is, therefore, evident. Figure 3 shows different sectors in terms of their labour productivity (as percentage of the average labour

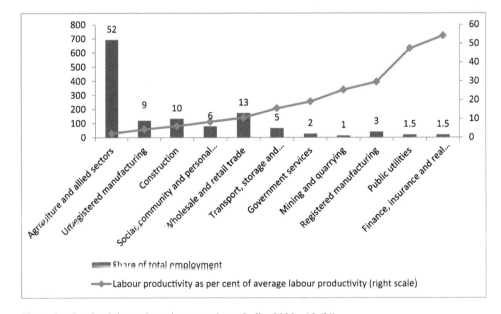

Figure 3.   Productivity and employment share, India, 2009–10 (%).
Source: Government of India, Economic Survey 2012–13, page 32.

productivity in the economy as a whole) and share of employment, in the year 2009−2010.[1] It is clear that the sectors that are very low productivity relative to the average (agriculture and allied activities along with unregistered manufacturing) together account for the bulk of the workforce, more than 60%.

Further, there are extremely large variations in productivity within the manufacturing sector, with the registered (organised) manufacturing industry showing nearly seven times the labour productivity levels of unregistered (unorganised) manufacturing in 2009−2010 − and also employing less than one-third the numbers of workers. This is in marked contrast to the experience of China, for example, where the period of rapid growth has been associated not only with industrialisation but particularly the emergence and preponderance of medium- and large-scale units that provide formal employment to workers. The persistence and continued domination of low productivity work in all the major sectors despite several decades of rapid aggregate income growth suggests a particularly unusual growth pattern in India.

3. Low-productivity informal work

Third, associated with this, informal work overwhelmingly dominates total employment. In 2004−2005, informal workers were estimated to account for 96% of all workers, and there is little to suggest that the share of formal work would have increased greatly since then. It is important to bear in mind that many informal workers are actually employed in the formal sector, in registered manufacturing and service companies, as contractual workers or even daily wage workers. As Figure 4 indicates, in 2004−2005, the number of

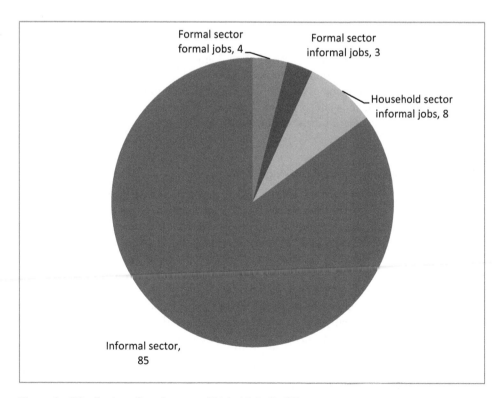

Figure 4.   Distribution of employment, 2004−05, India (%).
Source: NSSO, quoted in Government of India, Economic Survey 2012−2013.

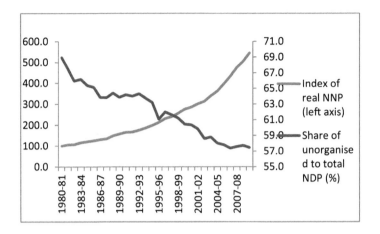

Figure 5.   Share of unorganised sector in NDP, India, 1980−2008 (%).
Source: CSO, Factor incomes in India, 2009−2010.

informal jobs in the formal sector (at 3% of the total estimated work force) was nearly as large as the number of formal jobs in the formal sector!

The incidence of self-employment (most of it highly fragile and vulnerable) has actually increased as a proportion of non-agricultural work, and the only reason for its overall stagnation is the decline in agricultural employment, particularly in the number of women workers self-employed in agriculture. Meanwhile, the share of the informal sector in GDP has fallen quite sharply during this period of high growth. Indeed, the recent period of most rapid acceleration of national income (NNP) was also the period of sharpest fall in the share of unorganised incomes (Figure 5). Thus, while the formal organised sector has substantially increased its share of national income, it has done so without drawing in more workers in the standard Lewisian trajectory.

4.   Low and declining women's work participation

Finally, unlike most other cases of rapid economic growth that have been observed historically, recognised work participation rates (WPRs) of women have not only not increased, but actually declined. This is significant for several reasons. It is now generally accepted that most women work, even when they are not recorded as 'workers' by official and other data gatherers. The tasks associated with social reproduction and the care economy are largely (though not solely) borne by women, but in many societies these are not counted among economic or productive activities. Similarly, many women are engaged in what is recognised otherwise as productive work, but as unpaid household helpers who are, therefore, only marginally seen as workers in their own right. The general invisibility of women's work is itself a mostly accurate reflection of their status in society: where women's official work participation is low, this is typically a sign of less freedom and mobility of women, lower status and lower empowerment. Indeed, where more women are active in the labour market and are employed (especially in formal activities), the share of unpaid work tends to come down and even the unpaid labour performed by women is more likely to be recognised and valued. This is why looking at the extent,

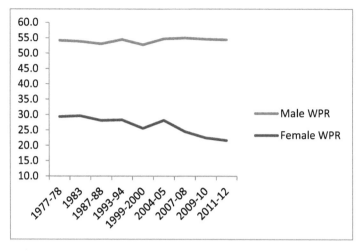

Figure 6. Labour force participation rates, India, 1977−2012 (%).
Source: NSSO Surveys of Employment and Unemployment.

coverage, conditions and remuneration of women's work is often a useful way of judging the extent to which their broader status in society has improved.

Female WPRs in India have historically been significantly lower than male rates, and are among the lower rates to be observed even in the developing world (Figure 6) (Ghosh 2009). What is more surprising is that despite three decades of relatively rapid GDP growth, these rates have not increased, but have actually fallen in recent times. The gap between male and female WPRs (for the 15+ age group) has grown, as male rates have remained stable and female rates have declined below their already very low levels. The decline is particularly sharp for rural women (Figure 7). The sharp decline in 2009−2010 was dismissed as a statistical aberration when it first emerged in the NSS large survey, but the subsequent large survey in 2011−2012 has revealed a further decline, implying that there is a real tendency at work that has to be understood and explained. In urban

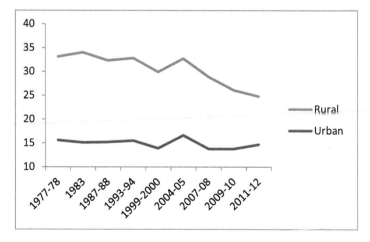

Figure 7. Female work participation rates, India, 1977−2012 (%).
Source: NSSO Surveys of Employment and Unemployment.

areas, women WPRs have been very volatile (possibly reflecting the vagaries of the sample survey) but nonetheless over a mildly declining trend.

It is widely believed that the decline in WPRs is chiefly because of increasing participation in education, which is to be welcomed. It is certainly true that female participation in education has increased in both rural and urban areas, and especially so since 2007. However, this still does not explain fully the total decline in female labour force participation, which has been significantly greater (relative to the increase in those engaged in education) in rural India and somewhat greater in urban India. Also, the decline is clearly evident even for the age group 25−59 years, where there is little indication of increasing involvement in education. It is worth noting that labour force participation rates (which include workers and those openly unemployed, that is searching but not finding jobs) closely track the WPRs, to the point that open unemployment rates of women have been falling because of declining labour force participation. It may be that the 'discouraged worker' effect is particularly strong for women, or it may reflect other social causes that inhibit engagement in recognised work.

Of course, India is a country of vast dimensions and enormous variation. There are significant differences across states, with female WPRs varying from a low of 5.3% in rural Bihar to a high of 52.4% in rural Himachal Pradesh. However, what is striking is how widespread has been the decline in women's work force participation. The north-eastern states of Tripura and Sikkim are the *only* ones that shows a substantial improvement in women's work participation in both rural and urban areas from 2004−2005 to 2011−2012. There were minor increases in West Bengal and rural Himachal Pradesh. Everywhere else, the same depressing tendency that marks the all India pattern is evident, even in states that earlier showed much higher proportions of female workers.

What explains this extraordinary deterioration in one of the more obvious indicators of the economic empowerment of women in India? Much of the decline in work participation has been among self-employed workers, including (but not only) those involved in agriculture. The growing mechanisation of agriculture has played a role in reducing demand for women's work. In addition, changes in ecological conditions have led to declines in many rural activities earlier performed mainly by women, such as the collection of minor forest produce. It should further be noted that women's displacement from agricultural activities and increased informalisation are likely to be associated with not only a real decline in women's participation rates but also a greater degree of undercounting of their participation rates. The undercounting of women's work in rural India may be particularly marked because of growing phenomenon of seeking brides from other areas in regions with very low female sex ratios, as these women are then used as unpaid drudges performing work in homes and fields.

Other changes, such as the growing difficulties of collecting fuel wood and water, have increased the time that has to be devoted to unpaid labour. Indeed, the time that has to be allocated to unpaid labour − in the form of not just various economic but unrecognised activities like provisioning essential items for household consumption but also the care economy generally − is likely to be an important reason for the withdrawal of women from the labour force (Mukherjee 2012). This is confirmed by the strong inverse relationship between work participation and involvement in what the NSS surveys classify as domestic work (Code 92: looking after children, taking care of the sick and the elderly, preparing food and other tasks associated with home management) and expenditure-saving activities (Code 93: expenditure-saving activities geared mainly towards household consumption, such as maintenance of kitchen gardens, and orchards, taking care of household poultry and cattle, free collection of firewood, fish etc., husking of paddy, grinding of food grains, preparation of cow dung cakes, fetching water, making baskets and mats for household use, sewing, tailoring, weaving, and tutoring children and so on).

Most women, even and especially those classified as 'non-workers', are engaged in these activities, which are clearly economic activities even when they are not socially recognised as such. It is also clear from the NSS surveys that the greater proportion of women who engage in these tasks do so because 'there is no one else to do this for the household', which suggests that the requirement to engage in such unpaid domestic labour can constrain the possibility of women engaging in outside work for remuneration. It is clear that in addition to broader socio-economic processes, state action has a critical role to play in affecting the extent to which such unpaid work is required. The lack of basic infrastructure and amenities, such as piped water or cooking fuel, obviously adds to the time required to procure or collect fuel wood or water for household use. The lack of social provision of care services including medical care increases the burden of care work that falls on household members. And so on.

Social perceptions about women and their capacities are also important factors. It is ironic but true that mechanisation has tended to displace women workers, particularly in agriculture and construction. Just as some activities become *less* arduous and physically taxing, women who were previously engaged in such work are replaced by male workers. However, there is really no physical reason why women should be less able than men to drive tractors and harvester-threshers or to operate construction machines. Rather, it reflects the persistence of what should be archaic attitudes towards women and the work that they are fit to perform.

However, it is also likely that women themselves may wish to quit the labour force when there is no pressing need simply because the paid work that is available for most of them is so arduous, taxing and poorly paid. Indeed, this is why it has been noted that much of women's work participation in India is of the 'distress' variety, engaged in when the household is very poor or when there is a natural calamity, economic shock or other decline in household income (Srivastava and Srivastava 2010; Himanshu 2011). Since paid work is not so readily available, and what is tends to be both difficult and low remuneration, as well as associated with the double burden of paid and unpaid work, it is not implausible that some improvement in household income levels could result in reduced pressure for women to seek outside employment.

5. Social relations and the accumulation process

These, then, are some of the more unusual features of structural change and labour market behaviour in the recent phase of rapid growth in the Indian economy. The question is why – what are the underlying reasons for such relatively unexpected patterns to emerge? I would like to argue that these outcomes are not accidental or inadvertent results of an otherwise successful growth trajectory, but emerge from the very strategy of accumulation and its location in certain social structures.

One reason for this is the reliance on growth strategies that did not seek to develop the home market for mass consumption goods through asset redistribution and dismantling of traditional monopolies. Indeed, the absence in post-Independence India of comprehensive land reforms (which were so instrumental in dismantling traditional structures of economic control in Japan, South Korea and Taiwan China) has been a major underlying feature of the continuing structural inequality that has prevented broad-based economic growth. This was related to the (possibly resulting) persistent hold of gender, caste and other forms of social discrimination, which in turn allowed segmented labour markets to persist and even intensify.

So workers in the informal economy have not simply been excluded from formal employment – they are deeply integrated into it both directly and indirectly. The perception that the informal economy exists because low wages allow it to compete with the formal sector in a host of non-agricultural activities is essentially misplaced in much of the Indian economy. Rather, in many instances, the informal economy is not in competition with the formal sector, but actually services its requirements, and low wages in the informal economy help sustain profits in the formal sector. Consider, for example, the software industry, which is generally seen as a shining example of hyper-modernity, an outlier of high productivity that is somehow separate from the vast sea of low productivity work that surrounds it. In actual fact, the ability of this industry to be competitive globally relies crucially on the very cheap supporting services in the form of logistics, security, transportation, cleaning and catering that are provided by companies or individuals that use workers on informal contracts that are well beyond the pale of labour protection. Similarly, the ability to hire highly skilled professionals in this industry at what are clearly salaries below global averages is dependent upon such workers' ability to access goods and services provided cheaply by India's informal workers.

This is equally true of other formal sectors. There is strong evidence of substantial increases in sub-contracting by the formal manufacturing industry to more informal production arrangements since 2001 (Bairagya 2010). The value chains evident in a number of important exporting industries in sectors as varied as readymade garments, gems and jewellery, automotive components, leather and leather products and sports goods, which are often co-ordinated by large and possibly multinational corporate entities, provide evidence of the significant and increased contribution of informal activities to what are seen as formal sector production (Damodaran 2010). These are only some examples of a wide and pervasive process of extremely close intertwining of formal and informal sectors, and the effective subsidisation of the formal sector by low-paid informal activities.

These tendencies have been reinforced by the nature of the growth strategy adopted in India over the past two decades. The focus of the Indian state (and of most state forces at the regional level) has been on generating growth through various incentives designed to encourage the expansion of private capital. It is now obvious that this can very quickly become prey to corruption, crony capitalism and the like. However, it is possibly less obvious that this strategy in itself generates incentives for such private players that effectively militate against a more broad-based and egalitarian economic expansion. So, new forms of capital certainly do emerge and proliferate as a result of this strategy, but they do so in a wider context in which capitalist accumulation is based essentially on extraction: of land and other natural resources, of the labour of differentiated workers, of the products of peasant cultivators and small producers of goods and services. This has reduced the incentives to focus on productivity growth and innovation as routes to more rapid growth, since state-aided primitive accumulation and socially determined extra-economic relationships provide easier and more reliable means of generating private surpluses. All this has actually been reinforced under globalisation, rather than being diminished by external competition.

The point is that these transactions in land, labour and product markets are not simply voluntary exchanges between equivalent parties. Instead, the game is played with dice that are heavily loaded in favour of capital, especially large capital, through various means: social institutions that allow for discriminatory labour market practices; legal and regulatory institutions that can be and are mobilised to enhance the bargaining power of capital; and political forces that actively engage in supporting all of these. The process of capitalist accumulation in India has utilised the agency of the state to further the project of primitive accumulation through diverse means (including land use change as well as substantial fiscal transfers) and has also exploited specific sociocultural features, such as caste, community and gender differences, to enable greater labour exploitation and therefore higher surplus generation. These are in turn associated with various other more 'purely economic' patterns that pile on the imbalances: financial institutions, input and product markets that do not provide reasonable credit access and so on.

It can be argued (Harriss-White 2005) that the greater part of the modern Indian economy is implicitly regulated or determined by social institutions derived from 'primordial identity' such as gender, caste and community. These interact with political forces, generating forms of patronage, control and clientelism that vary across regions. This makes the outcomes of government strategies, including those connected with liberalisation, privatisation and deregulation, different from those generally expected. Take the large bourgeoisie, for example, which is dominated by diversified joint family enterprises extending across different economic sectors. Even in the phase of globalisation, caste, region and linguistic community have been crucial in shaping these groups, determining their behaviour and influencing their interaction with each other as well as with global capital (Damodaran 2008). The very emergence of such capital has often reflected social forces: for example, there are no major business groups in the North and East that are not from 'traditional' business communities, and nationally no Dalit business group of significance. Existing practices, such as gender discrimination in property ownership and control, have often been reinforced by corporate behaviour, such as the ability to utilise the existence of legal forms (such as the Hindu Undivided Family form of ownership) that deny any role to women (Das Gupta 2012). These obviously added to the weight of socially discriminatory practices – and they affected how business houses at large and medium levels dealt with more purely economic forces, and their attitudes to investment, employment and output.

However, it could also be argued that these features of the Indian economic landscape are precisely what have been crucial in generating the recent phase of rapid growth, even as they have allowed the persistence of backwardness and accentuated inequalities in the course of that expansion. The complex nexus between politics and different levels of local, regional and national businesses has allowed for the appropriation of land and other natural resources that has been an integral part of the accumulation story and fed into the way that central and state governments have aided the process of private surplus extraction. More overt economic policies such as patterns of public spending and taxation are only one part of this – a substantial part relates to laws, regulations and their implementation (or lack of it) that provide the contours for the expansion of private capital.

These processes of direct and indirect underwriting of the costs of the corporate sector have been greatly assisted by the ability of employers in India to utilise social characteristics to ensure lower wages to certain categories of workers. Caste and other forms of social discrimination have a long tradition in India, and they have interacted with capitalist accumulation to generate peculiar forms of labour market segmentation that are unique to Indian society. Studies (such as of Thorat 2010) have found that social categories are strongly correlated with the incidence of poverty and that both occupation and wages differ dramatically across social categories. The National Sample Surveys reveal that the probability of being in a low wage occupation is significantly higher for STs, SCs, Muslims and OBCs (in that order) compared to the general 'caste Hindu' population. This is only partly because of the differences in education and level of skill, which are also important and which in turn reflect the differential provision of education across social categories (Table 1).

Table 1. Predicted urban/rural differences in caste inequalities.

	Metro cities	Other urban	Developed villages	Less developed villages
Consumption expenditure adjusted for household size				
Forward castes	31,191	27,122	18,280	15,185
Brahmin	31,987	26,524	17,929	16,936**
OBCs	28,930***	24,224**	16,381**	14,259*
Dalit	28,979	22,668**	15,281**	12,986
Adivasi	31,025	22,390**	14,568**	12,011**
Annual income from wage, cultivation and business for males 25−49				
Forward castes	52,102	37,532	16,558	12,964
Brahmin	62,302**	36,757	18,346*	12,440
OBCs	49,502	36,757**	15,476*	11,900
Dalit	51,093	31,276**	14,142**	12,234
Adivasi	NA	28,559**	14,053**	9933**
Ability to read children ages 8−11+				
Forward castes	0.52	0.70	0.59	0.62
Brahmin	0.76X	0.73	0.71X	0.66
OBCs	0.58	0.64	0.60	0.55
Dalit	0.55	0.56**	0.45**	0.48**
Adivasi	NA	0.52X	0.51	0.50**

Notes: Predicted value from the regression holding all control variables at their mean value.
X = p.10 in comparison with forward castes (excluding brahmin).
**p 0.01 in comparison with forward castes (excluding brahmin).
*p 0.05 in comparison with forward castes (excluding brahmin).
+Sample sizes for children get very small when broken down by residence and castes; result should be treated with caution.
NA = sample size: 50.
Source: Desai and Dubey 2011, page 45, Table 4.

While in many cases class and caste do overlap, the latter always supersedes the former at least in socio-economic factors. Caste is an extra-economic factor that acts in two forms, inequality of opportunity and inequality of outcome. Economic well-being cannot always overturn the inequalities of caste distinction, and that is reflected in the education levels, job opportunities, wage levels, access to social benefits and basic facilities, etc. Caste clearly affects family income, consumption and other parameters like education, health, etc.

Such caste-based discrimination has operated in both urban and rural labour markets. One study of Delhi (e.g. Banerjee and Knight 1985) found that significant discrimination against Dalit workers operating dominantly through the mechanisms of recruitment and assignment to jobs led to Dalits largely entering poorly paid 'dead-end' jobs that are essential but significantly lower paid. Similarly, empirical studies of caste behaviour in rural India (Shah et al. 2006; Thorat et al. 2009) have found that there are many ways in which caste practices operate to reduce the access of the lower castes to local resources as well as to income earning opportunities, thereby forcing them to provide their labour at the cheapest possible rates to employers. In addition to the well-known lack of assets, a large number of social practices effectively restrict the economic activity of lower caste and Dalit groups and force them to supply very low wage labour in harsh and usually precarious conditions. These practices in turn can be used to keep wages of Dalit workers (who are extremely constrained in their choice of occupation) low, even in period of otherwise rising wages. The persistence of such practices and their economic impact even during the period of the Indian economy's much-vaunted dynamic growth has been noted (Human Rights Watch 2007).

Gender-based differences in labour markets and the social attitudes to women's paid and unpaid work are also reflections of this broader tendency. The widespread perception that women's work forms an 'addition' to household income, and therefore commands a much lower reservation wage, is common to both private and public employers. Therefore, for private employers, women workers within Dalit or other discriminated groups typically receive even lower wages for similar work. In public employment, the use of underpaid women workers receiving well below minimum wages as anganwadi workers or ASHAs has become institutionalised in running several major flagship programmes that are designed to deliver essential public services of health, nutrition, support for early child development and even education. Further, the role played by the unpaid labour of women in contributing not only to social reproduction but also to what would be recognised as productive economic activities in most other societies has been absolutely crucial in enabling this particular accumulation process.

6. Implications for growth and inequality

Therefore, it may not be surprising that private agents find little value in accumulation strategies that are designed to enable structural transformation. Indeed, such transformation may even be to the detriment of their short-term interests, if it reduces their bargaining power. The low tolerance levels of capitalists in India to anything that can even slightly improve the bargaining power of workers is evident in the growing impossibility of even forming workers unions in most activities controlled by the private sector. It is clearly indicated by the ferocious and orchestrated backlash against something as limited as the MNREGA, only because it has provided some relief to rural workers who could at last begin to demand wages closer to the legal minimum from employers.

The point to note here is not simply that such practices continue to exist, but that they have become the base on which the economic accumulation process rests. In other words, capitalism in India, especially in its most recent globally integrated variant, has used past and current modes of social discrimination and exclusion to its own benefit, to facilitate the extraction of surplus and ensure greater flexibility and bargaining to employers when dealing with workers. So social categories are not 'independent' of the accumulation process – rather, they allow for more surplus extraction, because they reinforce low employment generating (and therefore persistently low wage) tendencies of growth. The ability to benefit from socially segmented labour markets in turn has created incentives for absolute surplus value extraction on the basis of suppressing wages of some workers, rather than requiring a focus on relative surplus value extraction resulting from productivity increases. High productivity enclaves have not generated sufficient demand for additional workers to force an extension of productivity improvement to other activities; instead the accumulation process has relied indirectly on persistent low wages in supporting activities or on unpaid labour to underwrite the expansion of value added. So, the particular (possibly unique) pattern of Indian inequality has led to a long-run growth process that generates further and continued inequality and does not deliver the expected structural change.

Acknowledgements

I wish to thank Rajah Rasiah for enabling all of us to pay tribute to Melanie Beresford as a scholar and a rare human being, and to an anonymous reviewer for helpful comments that led to improvements in the text.

Note

1. It should be noted that estimates of 'productivity' for several service activities that are provided in Chart 3, and particularly those for finance, insurance and real estate (the FIRE sector) are dubious at best, since they simply reflect unsustainable asset price bubbles and associated remuneration, rather than increases in real output.

References

Arora, A. 2010. "Economic Dualism, Openness and Employment in Manufacturing Industry in India." M. Phil. Thesis, Jawaharlal Nehru University.

Bairagya, I. 2010. "Liberalization, Informal Sector and Formal–Informal Sectors' Relationship: A Study of India." Paper presented at 31st General Conference of the International Association for Research in Income and Wealth, St. Gallen, August 24, 2010.

Banerjee, B., and J.B. Knight. 1985. "Caste Discrimination in the Indian Urban Labour Market." *Journal of Development Economics* 17 (1): 277–307

Damodaran, H. 2008. *India's New Capitalists: Caste, Business and Industry in a Modern Nation.* London: Palgrave Macmillan.

Damodaran, S. 2010. "Global Production, Employment Conditions and Decent Work: Evidence from India's Informal sector." ILO Working Paper. New Delhi: International Labour Office.

Das Gupta, C. 2012. "Gender, Property and the Institutional Basis of Tax Policy Concessions: Investigating the Hindu Undivided Family." http://www.macroscan.net/index.php?view=search&kwds=Chirashree%20Das%20Gupta

Desai, S., and A. Dubey. 2011. "Caste in the 21st Century India: Competing Narratives." *Economic & Political Weekly*, March. Vol. XLVI (11).

Ghosh, J. 2009. *Never Done and Poorly Paid: Women's Work in Globalising India.* New Delhi: Women Unlimited.

Ghosh, J., and C.P. Chandrasekhar. 2009. *After Crisis: Adjustment, Recovery and Fragility in Asia.* New Delhi: Tulika Publishers.

Harriss-White, B. 2005. *India's Market Economy.* New Delhi: Three Essays Collective.

Himanshu. 2011. "Employment Trends in India: A Re-examination." *Economic & Political Weekly*, September 10. Vol. XLVI (37).

Human Rights Watch. 2007. India: Hidden Apartheid: Caste Discrimination Against India's "Untouchables." Shadow Report to the UN Committee on the Elimination of Racial Discrimination. http://www.chrgj.org/docs/IndiaCERDShadowReport.pdf

Kannan, K.P., and G. Raveendran. 2009. "Growth Sans Employment: A Quarter Century of Jobless Growth in Indian Organised Manufacturing." *Economic & Political Weekly*, March 7.

Mukherjee, A. 2012. "Exploring Inter-state Variations of Rural Women's Paid and Unpaid Work in India." *Indian Journal of Labour Economics* 55 (3): 371–392.

Shah, G., H. Mander S. Thorat, S. Deshpande, and A. Baviskar. 2006. *Untouchability in Rural India.* New Delhi: Sage.

Srivastava, N., and R. Srivastava. 2010 "Women, Work and Employment Outcomes in Rural India." *Economic & Political Weekly*, July 10.

Thorat, A. 2010. "Ethnicity, Caste and Religion: Implications for Poverty Outcomes. *Economic and Political Weekly*. December 18.

Thorat, S., P. Negi, M. Mahamallik, and C. Senapati. 2009. *Dalits in India: Search for a Common Destiny.* New Delhi: Sage.

Industrialization, globalization, and labor market regime in Indonesia

Dionisius Narjoko and Chandra Tri Putra

Economic Research Institute for ASEAN and East Asia, Indonesia

This paper examines globalization, industrialization, and labor markets in Indonesia using a case study of manufacturing. It attempts to answer the question of how changes in the labor market after the 1997–1998 Asian Financial Crisis affected industrialization and labor market performance. The paper generates three main findings. First, the responsiveness of output to employment and wages to employment declined substantially over the period 1996–2006 but recovered in 2009. The decline could be a consequence of the implementation of rigid labor laws since 2003. The recovery in 2009 may reflect firms' adjustment period to the new environment or simply that firms found different opportunities. Second, exporters generally show higher employment elasticity than non-exporters. However, since the implementation of the labor law, exporters tend to retain employment more than non-exporters when wages rise. Third, exporters began substituting labor with machinery as wages started rising.

1. Introduction

Globalization plays an important role in the industrialization of many countries in East and Southeast Asia. An open trade and investment regime as well as outward/export orientation are the main characteristics of industrialization in these countries. More recently, since early 1990, character of industrial development in these regions has gone more to advance it with establishment of networks of production involving firms across countries within the regions. This exhibits a model of industrial development, commonly known as regional/ international production networks (Kimura and Ando 2005; Kimura 2008), based on the framework of product fragmentation (e.g., Arndt and Kierzkowski 2001; Cheng and Kierzkowski 2001; and Deardorff 2001) and it is probably unique only to these regions.

Indonesia subscribed to this model for its industrialization. While it is debatable whether or not Indonesia is deep into the networks of production in the regions, what seems to be clear is that its industrialization – at least at the beginning during the late 1980s and the 1990s before the 1997/1998 Asian Financial Crisis (ACF) – has strong outward orientation. Important to note however that it happened only after the country had done a series of market reforms to respond to the 1980s oil crisis which altogether marked the end of import substitution industrialization strategy the country adopted before the oil crisis. The path of industrialization in Indonesia since then continued to resemble those of its neighbors and the East Asia model, and as often cited by many, this has put the country's industrial sector in a high-growth path until it was disrupted by the AFC in 1997/1998.

As in the general model of East Asia industrialization, the high manufacturing growth in Indonesia at least in the 1990s was facilitated by an open trade and investment regime. But not only these, it was also facilitated by initial condition of labor market, which is abundant in the stock of low-skilled workers in traditional sectors, and flexible labor market regime. The latter was also found in other countries in the regions, and in fact it is considered as one important factor in the success of the regions' export-oriented industrialization (Manning 1998).

While the relationship between globalization and industrialization is often discussed, the interrelationship between the two and labor market regime is much less often touched in the literature. This paper attempts to enrich our understanding about this interrelationship, using Indonesia as a case study. Indonesia fits for study mainly because it offers a natural experiment to test the importance of labor market regime in its interrelationship with globalization and industrialization. As described in the next section, the regime in the country swung from very flexible before AFC to be very rigid after it. This paper is not intended to test some specific hypotheses; instead, it is intended to collect some basic facts in regard to how industrial performance or labor market outcome changed over the period of two distinct labor market regimes.

Tighter labor market regime post AFC echoed the more state intervention in the labor market. Examining how it affects industrial performance provides insights to the idea of Melanie Beresford of a more state-guided industrialization approach. Beresford (2008), for example, argues that state-led development remains an alternative for a robust growth and development to the market-led development as in many East Asian countries, provided an existence of a clear and more authoritative industrial policy.

Section 2 describes the evolution policies affecting industrialization in Indonesia since early 1990s, including one that governs the labor market. Section 3 briefly describes manufacturing development, focusing on output growth and export performance. Section 4 presents our empirical analysis on the employment response to the changes in output and wage, and Section 5 concludes the study.

2. Policies affecting the industrialization

2.1. Pre AFC

The early Indonesian manufacturing adopted import substitution policy strategy. A wide range of protective measures was put in place during the implementation period of this strategy, i.e., since early 1970s and to mid-1980s. Among the measures, the most important ones have been tariff and non-tariff barriers (NTBs), as well as restriction on foreign direct investment (FDI) and import. The tariffs were implemented to support the earlier stage of import substitution which focuses on downstream industries, such as final consumers good, and the NTBs were used to support the second stage of import substitution that focuses on upstream industries (i.e., intermediate and capital goods) (Thee 1994). These measures create what the so-called 'cascading effect,' whereby the effective tariff rates for consumer goods were set higher than the rates for intermediate and capital goods (Ariff and Hill 1985).

As for restrictive foreign investment and import, the government, through its Investment Coordinating Board (*Badan Koordinasi Penanaman Modal*, BKPM) was given discretionary authority to approve both foreign and domestic investment. BKPM published an annual Priority Investment List that detailed the economic sectors in which investment was allowed, for both domestic and foreign investors. The number of industries that were closed to foreign investors continuously increased during this import-substitution period.

Despite the inward orientation of the industrial strategy, some reforms were introduced in the early 1980s in response to falling oil and commodity prices. Exchange rate devaluation and banking sector deregulation were undertaken. The latter included removal of the interest rate ceiling, the credit ceiling and a reduction in liquidity credits. Apart from the macroeconomic and financial sector reforms, the government also introduced tax and trade reforms during this period.

The continuing threat of falling oil prices between 1982 and 1986 forced the government to initiate an export promotion policy objective. The government reacted quickly by devaluating the Rupiah by a massive 45% in 1983, while at the same time controlling inflation using monetary and fiscal policies. Furthermore, the government introduced a major financial sector reform in 1988, which principally removed entry restrictions for new banks. Foreign banks could enter Indonesia as joint ventures, with equity up to 85% and without any product or geographical restrictions. As a result of this reform, the banking sector boomed and funds available to firms were greatly increased.

A series of deregulation packages aiming to liberalize trade and investment regimes, and the financial sector, were also introduced. Bold measures were taken to reduce the export bias. Included in these were measures to reduce the costs of exports and to increase the flow of investment. In May 1986, a new and improved duty drawback scheme was introduced. Unlike the old system, this scheme allowed exporters to source imported input at international prices and exempted them from all duties and regulation on imported inputs. Moreover, the scheme also allowed exporters to import directly without having to deal with import licensing.

The measures to reduce protection included the reduction of the general level of tariffs and the removal of many NTBs. These were undertaken in a series of deregulation packages from 1987 to 1997 before the 1997/1998 crisis. The NTB removal was done by transforming them to equivalent tariffs and export taxes. One example was the removal of the import monopoly on plastics. Before the reform, the right to import plastic raw materials had been awarded to a single government trading company, which then appointed a sole agent from a well-connected group. All of the imports had to be undertaken by the agent, who charged a fee and took a longer time to deliver the goods than would have happened if they had been imported directly.

As for the liberalization in investment regime, equity restriction and divestment rules were gradually removed in a series of deregulations between 1986 and 1995. Several policy changes were important during this period. First, the obligation for foreign firms to establish joint ventures with Indonesian partners was relaxed. In particular, joint venture with a maximum of 95% of foreign ownership was allowed, which had not been the case earlier. In addition, and more importantly, the government also allowed 100% of foreign ownership albeit this is only applied to only nine public sectors which are now opened for foreign investment. Second, the minimum capital for foreign investment was reduced from about $1 million to $250,000 in 1992 and finally removed in 1994. Third, the government finally opened up nine sectors which had previously been closed for foreign investment, which are ports, electricity generation, telecommunications, shipping, air transport, drinking water, railway, automatic generation plants, and mass media.

Fourth, the obligation to divest the majority of capital over a certain period of time was substantially relaxed. The divestment rule for a joint-venture with at least 5% domestic ownership is no longer mandatory, and the divestment decision is left to shareholders. Meanwhile, for companies with 100% of foreign ownership, there is still phasing-out provision, but it is relaxed significantly, and that is, the amount of the divested investment is not officially ruled and left to the investors' decision. Lastly, the provision governing the foreign investment license was made greatly less restrictive. The 30-year license is now automatically be renewed as long as the Investment Board acknowledges that the investment brings positive benefit for the economic development in general. Earlier, under the 1967 Investment Law, the 30-year license is non-renewable, and at the end of 30-year limit, foreign ownership must all be transferred to domestic investors, or else the company will be mandatory liquidated.

Although economic reforms supporting export orientation were the dominant feature of policy changes between 1985 and 1995, there were remaining regulations that preserved the protectionist industrial policy. Some sectors remained closed to foreign investors and untouched by the reforms. In terms of NTBs, some industries continued to be assisted by restrictive licensing, administratively determined local-content requirements, restrictive marketing arrangements and export taxes (World Trade Organization [WTO] 1998).

2.2. During AFC

Further trade liberalizations were implemented over the 1998–1999 period, which is the peak of the crisis, and as a part of the agreements between Indonesian government with International Monetary Fund (IMF) for the IMF's crisis support program. Significant trade reforms were undertaken as a result of the first two agreements with the IMF. These reforms aimed at reducing tariffs, promoting exports, and particularly NTBs. The latter largely captured The World Bank's proposal to continue the stalled trade reform in the early 1990s (Soesastro and Basri 2005). These reforms are briefly summarized as follows.

2.2.1. Tariffs

In the IMF agreement, Indonesia committed to gradually reduce tariffs on items subject to 15%–25% tariff rates prior to the crisis by 5 percentage points. The items included iron, steel and chemical products. Tariffs on these products were mostly reduced in 1999.

The reforms also substantially reduced trade protection in the automotive industry. Import tariffs on completely knocked down (CKD) and completely built up (CBU) vehicles were substantially reduced by the June 1999 automotive deregulation package. The tariff reductions, and the deregulation package in particular, were significant in regard to the protectionist policy aimed at supporting the National Car Program.

As a result of trade reforms in the mid-1990s, and the acceleration of the reform by the IMF agreements, the simple average tariff rates were reduced from 20% in 1994 to 9.5 in 1998 and 7.5 in 2002 (WTO 1998, 2003).

2.2.2. Non-tariff barriers

The government removed many trade restrictions affecting import licenses, the local content schemes, trade monopolies and marketing arrangements. In 1998, it discontinued the tax, customs and credit privileges granted to the National Car program and local content scheme for dairy products. Through the automotive deregulation package in 1999, the government ended the local content scheme in the automotive industry and permitted general importers to import CBU vehicles. It also removed a number of restrictive formal and informal marketing arrangements, including those for cement, paper and plywood.

Other reforms related to NTBs included in the IMF agreements were aimed at reducing restrictions on exports. In the second IMF agreement, the government committed to gradually remove export taxes and eliminate all other types of export restrictions, such as quotas and provincial taxes levied on inter-provincial and inter-district trade. In addition, the government in 1998 reformed the export licensing system by removing many products from the regulated export lists and allowed cement producers to export with a general export license.

To promote exports, the government granted export-oriented companies duty exemption and drawbacks. Eligible exporters operating in export processing zones or export-oriented manufacturing were eligible for tariff exemptions for all capital equipment, machinery and raw materials needed for initial investment and production. Exporters were also allowed to bypass import monopolies as long as the imported goods were used in export production.

2.3. Post AFC

There are at least two elements or aspects of business environment that seem to have limited the growth of the manufacturing sector after the crisis. First, FDI flows to Indonesia have lagged significantly behind practically all major East Asian economies since 1997. Indonesia was the only crisis-affected economy to register negative FDI flows for several years after the onset of the crisis. The comparison with Thailand, where 'fire-sale' FDI was significant in the wake of the crisis, is particularly pronounced. Moreover, the foreign investment approvals data, which are not comparable to the balance of payments estimates of realized flows, shed light on the changing nature of FDI after the crisis. In addition to much reduced investor interest, the proportion of FDI taking the form of greenfield investment has declined, with both expansions and mergers and acquisitions (M&As) rising. This is consistent with the theory of post-crisis, 'fire-sale' FDI behavior more generally (Lipsey 2001): there is excess capacity, and asset prices fall sharply owing to the effects of the exchange rate depreciation and the crisis.

Second, Indonesia's business regulatory regime continues to be complex, opaque and costly. The World Bank's 2008 Doing Business Survey, for example, ranks Indonesia 123rd out of 178 economies for ease of doing business, with particularly poor rankings in categories dealing with licenses, employing workers, enforcing contracts, and closing a business. While corruption has always been a serious problem, under the Soeharto regime the process and outcomes were largely predictable, whereas in the new environment, the links between bribes and 'outcomes' are much weaker and more uncertain. The financial sector has also experienced major changes. Financial health has been restored as the major financial institutions were rescued, merged or shut down after the crisis. However, financial institutions are now considerably more prudent and cautious, particularly towards SME borrowers with limited or ill-defined collateral.

2.4. Labor market policies

In general, before the AFC, during the Soeharto era, labor market outcomes more or less accorded with 'East Asian norms.' Rapid economic growth generated rising real wages, with a lag. Trade unions existed, but were heavily managed. Minimum wages were prescribed but they were generally below market levels in the formal sector, and were not enforced systematically.

Provisions under the new Manpower Law introduced in 2003 (Law No. 13/2003) were the ones that contribute to the changes in labor market outcomes after AFC. These are especially the following (Manning and Roesad 2007, p. 65): hiring and firing of workers (in particular, severance pay), sub-contracting and fixed-term contracts, and the setting of minimum wage.

Provisions for the setting of minimum wage are the most controversial area governed by the law. The key point is that they (the provisions) significantly increase the level of minimum wage. This is relative to the level of the wage set under the older law and regulations. Sources of the increase coming from the new law are the following, which work in combination to create the much higher level of minimum wage: first, authority to set minimum wage is moved from central government to regional governments (province and district level). This is to make the mechanism consistent with decentralization law introduced in 2001. Second, the anchor by which the level of minimum wage is based. Under the older regulations, the anchor is 'minimal' living standard; under the new law, this is changed to be 'decent' standard. The last factor that contributes to the higher level of minimum wage is the frequency to reset the wage; under the older regulations, review of minimum wage is done every three years; under the new law, it must be done every year. All in all, not only all of these could significantly increase the level of minimum wage — because the 'decent' living standard could be much higher than the 'minimal' living standard, but they also could make minimum wages to vary considerably in their level between regions. Moreover, there is now much higher degree of uncertainty in the rate of increase over the time because they are set at very short time duration (i.e., one year only).

The issue with provisions on severance pay has made it to be the most expensive regime among developing countries. As Table 1 shows, the increase in the cost for severance pay is as high as 30% even for employees that have worked only for three years. Inclusive in this increase is not only the basic severance pay, but also 15% gratuity and long-service pay. In addition to making the expected severance pay high, provisions on severance pay are controversial in that they apply the rate for dismissal due to non-economic causes (e.g., retirement, illness) to be the same with dismissal due to economic causes (e.g., bankruptcy).

In terms of its impact to employment, the minimum wage set under the provisions of the new law will likely be at the level above productivity for most/average low-skilled

Table 1. Severance costs and rates, and minimum wage rates, 2000–2003 (%).

Years of service	% of increase in severance costs due to rise in[a]			Increase in real severance costs 2000–2003[c]
	Severance pay rate	Real minimum wage[b]	Total	
3	30	70	100	84
5	23	77	100	72
10	49	51	100	170
20	47	53	100	158

[a] For employee dismissed for economic reasons
[b] Unweighted mean for all Indonesian provinces, using Bandung and Surabaya as proxy for West and East Java, respectively.
[c] Nominal rates/costs deflated by the CPI.
Source: Ministry of Manpower, unpublished data on minimum wage rates; Ministerial Decrees 3/1996 and 150/2000 and Law 13/2003, taken from Manning and Roesad (2007).

workers. In fact, even before the AFC, observers have noticed that the increase in minimum wage over the time, especially after around 1992, has already exceeded labor productivity in some sectors (in particular, labor-intensive sectors such as manufacturers of garment or footwear) (Manning 1998).

Although the new law likely increases the cost for severance pay and minimum wage, previous works indicate that the real application of the law might not be as influential as previously predicted. Del Carpio et al. (2012), for example, observed that the employment effect of minimum wages is only significant and negative among smaller firms and less-educated workers; it is not significant for larger firms with semi-skilled and skilled workers. Brusentsev et al. (2012) concluded that the compliance rate for the payment of severance pay is low; that is, only a third of entitled workers report receiving the severance pay and workers collect only about 40% of the payment. While there are indications that impact of the new labor is limited, one cannot neglect that some impacts do exist.

Changes in labor market policy were perhaps the only major policy change that substantially affected the post-crisis performance of the Indonesian manufacturing. In short, not only that they increased the cost for hiring and firing, but also introduced rigidities into hiring processes that discourage firms from taking on additional labor, with the result that Indonesia's labor policies have become among the most restrictive in Asia (Manning and Roesad 2006). These are illustrated by Table 2 that provides figures that show relative position of Indonesia among other developing countries in terms of flexibility of labor market regime, including the extent of cost for hiring and firing. All these means that distortion prevailed in labor market outcomes has gone way beyond market clearing level. As noted, the distortion – albeit probably only small extent – has actually been noticed since around 1992 when minimum wage is expected to have exceeded productivity.

3.   Brief description of the industrial performance[1]

Growth of industrial output in the 1990s, i.e., over the period 1994–1996 (Table 3), has been very high, averaging to about 10% per annum over the period. This represents the high-growth industrialization in Indonesia. Economic reforms over the period contributed the high growth.

There has been considerable inter-industry variation in growth rates both before and especially after AFC (Table 3). Food processing and related products (ISIC 31) are the only manufacturing sector not to record negative growth during the crisis. This reflects both the inelastic demand for food staples and the fact that some of the export-oriented food processing activities benefited from the exchange rate decline. Textiles' clothing and footwear (TCF, ISIC 32) grew more slowly than the industry average, but declined less sharply during the crisis. The slower export growth of these labor-intensive activities in the wake of the exchange rate declines. The resource-based sectors, wood products (ISIC 33) and paper products (ISIC 34) have grown slowly after the crisis, again in spite of the boost to competitiveness. In both cases, notwithstanding higher international prices, the problems are on the supply-side, as access to reliable natural resource supplies has become a serious constraint.

Among the mineral-resource-based activities, chemicals and related products (ISIC 35) experienced only a mild decline during the crisis. This was partly due to the close connection with the resilient agriculture sector for major sub-sectors such as the fertilizer industry. By contrast, non-metallic mineral products (ISIC 36) contracted sharply, reflecting the collapse of the construction industry in 1997–1999. Basic metals (ISIC 37) and machinery and equipment products (ISIC 38) also contracted sharply. The former is

Table 2. Employment flexibility, hiring and firing costs, selected countries, 2005[a].

	Hiring		Firing				Average index[b] (0–100)
	Difficulty of hiring index (0–100)	Cost of hiring (% of salary)	Difficulty of firing index (0–100)	Cost of firing (weeks of wages)	Rigidity of hours index (0–100)		
More restrictive (rigidity of employment index >50)							
India	56	12	90	79	40		62
Cambodia	67	0	30	39	80		59
Indonesia	61	10	70	145	40		57
Brazil	67	27	20	165	80		56
Vietnam	44	17	70	98	40		51
Less restrictive (rigidity of employment index <50)							
Korea	44	17	30	90	60		45
Philippines	56	9	40	90	40		45
China	11	30	40	90	40		30
Chile	33	3	20	51	20		24
Thailand	33	5	0	47	20		18
Malaysia	0	13	10	65	20		10
Singapore	0	13	0	4	0		0
Mean for all countries	39	40	35	38	13		80

[a] A higher index denotes greater difficulty.
[b] Termed the 'rigidity of employment index,' this is average of the three other indices.
Source: Adapted from World Bank/International Finance Corporation 2006, <http://www.doingbusiness.org>, taken from Manning and Roesad (2006).

Table 3. Industrial growth by sector (real value added, % per annum), 1994–2006.

ISIC	Sector	1994–1996	1997–1999	2000–2002	2003–2006
31	Food, beverages and tobacco	17.5	5.6	1.6	3.5
32	Textile, clothes and leather industry	8.7	−3.4	4.9	3.2
33	Wood and wood products	4.0	−14.0	2.7	−0.6
34	Paper and paper products	11.4	2.2	1.0	5.1
35	Chemicals and chemical products	10.7	−0.8	4.1	8.2
36	Non-metallic mineral products	16.9	−7.0	10.4	5.2
37	Basic metal industries	11.1	−9.2	3.6	−2.4
38	Fabricated metal, machineries, and eq.	7.3	−21.2	26.3	11.6
39	Other manufacturing industries	10.3	−10.2	4.8	9.2
–	Non-Oil and Gas Manufacturing	10.5	−6.3	7.4	6.2

Source: CEIC database, taken from Aswicahyono et al. (2000).

dominated by inefficient state enterprises selling most of their output to firms in the latter sector. ISIC 38 is dominated by two industries, automotive products and electronics. The auto industry has a history of high levels of protection and was thus dependent on the domestic market up to the AFC. As demand collapsed in 1997–1998, the industry came to a standstill. Electronics weathered the crisis more effectively, primarily owing to its export-oriented components assembly activities. However, these exports remain small in aggregate (see below), with thin domestic value added. Output then recovered strongly after 2000. Protection for the auto industry was reduced quickly as part of the government's agreement with the IMF (see the previous section), and the resulting rationalization, combined with some technological learning during the period of high protection, forced firms towards more economic production runs and an increased focus on exports (Aswicahyono 2000).

Since early 1990s when industrialization is directed to export, its share of global non-oil exports almost doubled, from 0.5% to 0.9%, at about the rate for Southeast Asia as a whole (3%–6.9%). Immediately after AFC, exports responded significantly to the exchange rate depreciation with a lag. However, in spite of buoyant commodity prices in the early years of the twenty-first century, export growth since 1998 has been sluggish. These data refer to growth and shares in nominal dollar exports. For manufactures, they therefore obviously understate the growth in domestic currency terms, and also in volumes. For total exports, by contrast, the nominal price data overstate the volume growth from 2001, since the growth rates are inflated by increased international prices for commodities (Athukorala 2006). Thus, the overall picture for manufactured exports is a clear 'bounce' in the wake of the sharp exchange rate depreciation in 1997–1998, followed by a trend growth rate that is substantially lower than the decade of in the 1990s.

Table 4 classifies manufactured exports into five main categories, broadly corresponding to factor intensity groupings. These are unskilled labor-intensive, resource-based (labor and capital intensive), footloose capital intensive, and electronics. The latter is a separate category owing to its size and the ambiguity of its factor proportions. In each case, the four largest exports at a disaggregated SITC level are identified. There are significant differences in performance across these major product groups, and these reflect the interplay of external and domestic policy factors. The two labor-intensive product groups have performed very poorly. The resource-based group, mainly wood products, shrank for most of the period, reflecting mainly supply mismanagement. For the footloose group, export

Table 4. Export growth by sector (% per annum, based on nominal USD), 1990–2006.

		1990–1993	1994–1996	1997–1999	2000–2002	2003–2006
1-ULI	Unskilled labor intensive	37.7	6.0	-0.8	0.5	7.9
821	Furniture and parts thereof	44.7	12.1	10.1	7.6	5.6
651	Textile yarn	41.7	35.3	9.7	1.8	10.1
851	Footwear	74.2	9.5	-9.3	-9.5	8.0
843	Women, girls, infants outwear, textile, not knitted or crocheted	35.4	-0.8	3.0	4.2	6.8
845	Outwear knitted or crocheted, not elastic nor rubberized	21.8	-1.6	2.4	3.9	16.8
2-RB-LI	Resource-based labor intensive	19.9	-1.7	-9.7	-4.6	0.9
634	Veneers, plywood, "improved" wood and other wood, worked, nes	17.9	-4.4	-12.3	-6.9	-0.9
635	Wood manufactures, nes	53.6	16.8	-2.5	0.7	4.8
663	Mineral manufactures, nes	53.4	18.5	35.5	8.2	5.8
662	Clay and refreactory construction materials	74.6	5.6	117.8	10.8	7.8
667	Pearl, precious and semi-precious stones, unworked or worked	27.0	-5.5	19.3	-8.4	32.0
3-RB-CI	Resource-based capital intensive	8.4	19.0	18.8	4.6	15.6
641	Paper and paperboard	34.1	22.3	38.2	-2.9	18.9
625	Rubber tires, tire cases, inner and flaps, for wheels of all kinds	10.5	45.7	0.9	12.1	23.0
674	Universals, plates, and sheets, of iron or steel	-2.8	38.1	1.6	0.4	61.3
511	Hydrocarbons, nes and derivatives	205.8	39.8	55.2	31.8	36.6
522	Inorganic chemical elements, oxides and halogen salts	3.0	44.2	-9.3	37.2	34.2
4-ELE	Electronics	93.5	36.9	0.6	37.9	4.7
752	Automatic data processing machines and units thereof	1875.6	78.0	-10.2	182.9	16.6
778	Electrical machinery and apparatus, nes	46.6	27.6	3.1	8.7	18.8
764	Telecommunication equipment, nes; parts and accessories, nes	81.0	46.2	2.4	29.8	2.5
763	Gramophones, dictating machines and other sound recorders	441.6	36.1	-15.6	49.8	-4.1
772	Electrical apparatus for making and breaking electrical circuits	702.3	27.6	0.1	107.4	14.6

(continued)

Table 4. (*Continued*)

5-FLCI		1990–1993	1994–1996	1997–1999	2000–2002	2003–2006
	Footloose capital intensive	42.7	22.1	10.7	8.7	20.0
784	Motor vehicle parts and accessories, nes	50.5	35.9	46.0	27.4	32.6
582	Condensation, polcondensation and polyaddition products	23.7	115.8	18.6	13.2	14.2
583	Polymerization and copolymerization products	29.2	44.1	23.0	1.9	16.9
513	Carboxylica acids, and their derivatives	16.6	64.8	37.8	10.7	13.1
512	Alcohols, phenols, etc., and their derivatives	48.3	56.4	9.9	6.2	19.7
	Manufacturing exports	29.5	9.6	0.8	9.9	7.9

Source: UN Comtrade database, taken from Aswicahyono et al. (2000).

growth was also slowing before the crisis, but there was no recovery in response to the large exchange rate depreciation. The declining growth rates were evident in both quota-constrained products (for example, most garments) and products for which quotas do not apply (such as footwear). All these points to a general export competitiveness issue.

4. Output and wage elasticities

This section presents our main empirical analysis, which makes use elasticity to gauge the responsiveness of employment to the change in output and wage.

As for the method, first, for the industry classification, labor-intensive industries include 'two digit' ISIC (International Standard Industrial Classification) codes 32, 33 and 39; resource-based industries comprise ISIC codes 31, 34 and 35; and capital-intensive industries cover ISIC codes 36−38. The labor-intensive industries are textiles, garments and footwear; wood products and furniture; and miscellaneous manufactures. The resource-based are food and related products; paper products; and chemical, rubber and plastic products. The capital-intensive group includes non-metallic minerals; steel products; and metal and machine goods, electronics and autos.

Elasticity of employment with respect to output and wage change is estimated by the following regression equation:

$$ln(L)_{i,t} = \alpha_0 + \alpha_1 ln(w)_{i,t} + \alpha_2 ln(Q)_{i,t} + \alpha_3 DFor_{i,t} + \alpha_4 DExp_{i,t}$$

$$+ \sum_{\alpha_5}^{\alpha_k} DIndustry_{i,j,t} + \varepsilon_{i,t}, \tag{1}$$

where i is firm/plant, j is industry, defined at three-digit ISIC, L is employment, defined as total (head-count) labor force, w is wage per labor, defined as labor expenditure per employee, Q is output, defined as real value added, $DFor$ is dummy variable for foreign ownership ($DFor$ equal to one if firm i has any foreign ownership share, or $DFor$ equal to zero otherwise), $DExp$ is dummy variable if engaged in exporting ($DExp$ equal to one if firm i exports any of its output, or $DExp$ equal to zero otherwise) and $DIndustry$ is dummy variable for industries, defined at three-digit ISIC.

Estimation used the annual manufacturing surveys/censuses of medium- and large-scale establishments (*Statistik Industri*, or SI). This study performed a cross-section regression using the data for the following years: 1990, 1996, 2006, and 2009, which cover the period before and after AFC. The establishments are defined as those with 20 or more employees. SI data are considered one of the best by the standard of developing countries. The data are known to have reliable and robust information, except perhaps for the data quality for the capital stock, and cover a wide range of information on the establishments, many of which are needed to conduct the estimation.

In general, we perform the regression equation to each annual sample and collect the elasticity parameters of wage and output. Tables 5 and 9 are elasticity parameters from the regression using different samples. Besides using the whole year sample, we also use samples of two-digit ISIC revision 2 (ISIC 31-39) and samples based on factor intensity (labor, capital and resource) constructed based on the combination of 3 two-digit ISIC revision 2. Table 4 comprises output to employment elasticities from each year, each factor intensity and each two-digit ISIC as described above. Table 6 comprises wage to employment elasticities in the same structure as Table 5. In Table 7, we focus on the difference of wage and output elasticities using the sample of exporting and non-exporting

Table 5. Output elasticities, large and medium manufacturing plants, 1990–2009

ISIC code and industry		1990	1996	2006	2009
Output elasticity	All large and medium-sized manufacturing firms	0.60^{***}	0.59^{***}	0.49^{***}	0.56^{***}
	Labor-intensive	0.66^{***}	0.65^{***}	0.57^{***}	0.66^{***}
	32 Textiles and garments	0.66^{***}	0.68^{***}	0.59^{***}	0.68^{***}
	33 Wood products	0.66^{***}	0.61^{***}	0.55^{***}	0.61^{***}
	39 Other manufacturing	0.65^{***}	0.57^{***}	0.45^{***}	0.66^{***}
	Resource-intensive	0.56^{***}	0.55^{***}	0.43^{***}	0.51^{***}
	31 Food and beverages	0.55^{***}	0.54^{***}	0.42^{***}	0.51^{***}
	34 Paper products	0.56^{***}	0.57^{***}	0.43^{***}	0.52^{***}
	35 Chemical, rubber and plastic products	0.59^{***}	0.55^{***}	0.44^{***}	0.50^{***}
	Capital-intensive	0.55^{***}	0.54^{***}	0.50^{***}	0.52^{***}
	36 Non-metallic mineral products	0.53^{***}	0.52^{***}	0.46^{***}	0.56^{***}
	37 Basic metal industries	0.50^{***}	0.45^{***}	0.55^{***}	0.43^{***}
	38 Machinery and transport equipment	0.56^{***}	0.55^{***}	0.51^{***}	0.53^{***}

Note: $^{***}\,p < 0.01$, $^{**}\,p < 0.05$, $^{*}\,p < 0.1$.
See the text for the basis of industry grouping by factor intensity.
Source: SI data, BPS; various years.

firms. Table 8 provides output and wage elasticities using only exporting-firms sample in the same structure of Tables 5 and 6. Finally, Table 9 gives the same structure as Table 8, but using the sample of non-exporting firms. The following are key observations or basic facts derived from the figures in the table.

Table 5 presents the elasticities, which are the estimates of α_2 in Equation (1), for the whole manufacturing and by two-digit ISIC industries, which are further grouped by the industries' factor intensity. The following are key observations or basic facts derived from the figures in the table.

Overtime pattern. For the whole manufacturing, there is a pattern of relatively flat output elasticities for the period 1990–1996, after which is followed by a substantial decline in the next period up to 2006. The elasticity, rather surprisingly, seem to have recovered in 2009 toward its level in 1996. In other words, there is a U-shape pattern over the time from 1996 – just one year before the AFC – to 2009. Casual observation of overtime pattern in unemployment and average wage rate for the national level indicates that the bottom could have happen either in or just before 2006.

Recall the description of labor market policies in Section 2, we expect that a more rigid labor regime should be responded by some decline in the output elasticity. Indeed, this seems to have happened, i.e., a sharp declining output elasticity between 1996 and 2006. This may reflect adjustment period for firms which experience a change in labor market regime from flexible to a very rigid after the AFC.

The magnitude. Output elasticity for the whole manufacturing is considered high. For pre-AFC period, in 1996, for example, 10% increase in output would have been translated to 6% increase in employment. The figure was relatively the same in 2009 when it has more or less recovered – this is about 10 years or so after the AFC.

Cross-section pattern, i.e., across industry groups (defined by factor intensity) and across two-digit ISIC industries. Consider the pattern across industry groups, employment

Table 6. Wage elasticities for large and medium-sized manufacturing plants, 1990–2009.

ISIC Code and Industry		1990	1996	2006	2009
Wage Elasticity	All large and medium-sized manufacturing firms	−0.44***	−0.41***	−0.30***	−0.44***
	Labor-intensive	−0.50***	−0.43***	−0.33***	−0.50***
	32 Textiles and garments	−0.50***	−0.51***	−0.39***	−0.56***
	33 Wood products	−0.48***	−0.34***	−0.27***	−0.37***
	39 Other manufacturing	−0.64***	−0.28***	−0.22***	−0.56***
	Resource-intensive	−0.37***	−0.37***	−0.22***	−0.41***
	31 Food and beverages	−0.31***	−0.34***	−0.18***	−0.41***
	34 Paper products	−0.34***	−0.40***	−0.26***	−0.36***
	35 Chemical, rubber and plastic products	−0.50***	−0.41***	−0.36***	−0.42***
	Capital-intensive	−0.42***	−0.35***	−0.39***	−0.38***
	36 Non-metallic mineral products	−0.39***	−0.30***	−0.30***	−0.40***
	37 Basic metal industries	−0.31***	−0.19***	−0.46***	−0.24***
	38 Machinery and transport equipment	−0.45***	−0.41***	−0.45***	−0.41***

Note: *** $p < 0.01$, ** $p < 0.05$, * $p < 0.1$.
See the text for the basis of industry grouping by factor intensity.
Source: SI data, BPS; various years.

responsiveness to a change in output is the highest in labor-intensive group, with the responsiveness in capital- and resource-intensive industry groups is relatively the same. The cross-section pattern between two-digit ISIC industries in general follows the one showed by the pattern between industry groups; there is no industry that exhibits extreme elasticity value/estimate.

Three points are worth mentioning based on the cross-section pattern. First, the pattern is consistent with the standard Lewis-type of model in which assume abundant stock of low-skilled workers that still can be drawn from traditional sector (by the modern – i.e., manufacturing – sector). Second, to some extent this also tells us that Indonesia still relies on labor-intensive industries for in its comparative advantage, and, finally, the pattern may also suggest that firms/plants in labor-intensive industries 'expend' much of their profit, or value added, to create jobs, more than what the other industries (i.e., resource- and capital-intensive industries).

Another important point, or perhaps question, to highlight is concerning the recovery of output elasticity in 2009. One needs to explain why output elasticity recovered despite a very different labor market regime after the crisis, which was a very rigid one. While a deep and perhaps extensive investigation is warranted by another study, it is worth at this

Table 7. Output and wage elasticities, exporters and non-exporters, 1990–2009.

All large and medium-sized manufacturing firms		1990	1996	2006	2009
Output elasticity	Exporter	0.65***	0.64***	0.55***	0.60***
	Non-exporter	0.59***	0.56***	0.47***	0.55***
Wage elasticity	Exporter	−0.55***	−0.45***	−0.32***	−0.36***
	Non-exporter	−0.42***	−0.38***	−0.28***	−0.45***

Note: *** $p < 0.01$, ** $p < 0.05$, * $p < 0.1$.
Source: SI data, BPS; various years.

Table 8.   Output and wage elasticities, exporters, 1990–2009.

ISIC code and industry, exporter		1990	1996	2006	2009
Output elasticity	All large and medium-sized manufacturing firms	0.65***	0.64***	0.55***	0.60***
	Labor-intensive	0.68***	0.68***	0.62***	0.68***
	32 Textiles and garments	0.64***	0.72***	0.66***	0.74***
	33 Wood products	0.72***	0.67***	0.62***	0.64***
	39 Other manufacturing	0.85***	0.54***	0.52***	0.71***
	Resource-intensive	0.61***	0.57***	0.44***	0.49***
	31 Food and beverages	0.61***	0.58***	0.46***	0.52***
	34 Paper products	0.83***	0.55***	0.50***	0.59***
	35 Chemical, rubber and plastic products	0.60***	0.55***	0.40***	0.43***
	Capital-intensive	0.55***	0.57***	0.52***	0.58***
	36 Non-metallic mineral products	0.56***	0.61***	0.55***	0.61***
	37 Basic metal industries	0.61***	0.45***	0.46***	0.49***
	38 Machinery and transport equipment	0.53***	0.57***	0.51***	0.57***
Wage elasticity	All large and medium-sized manufacturing firms	−0.55***	−0.45***	−0.32***	−0.36***
	Labor-intensive	−0.52***	−0.39***	−0.34***	−0.33***
	32 Textiles and garments	−0.47***	−0.42***	−0.40***	−0.32***
	33 Wood products	−0.54***	−0.42***	−0.35***	−0.31***
	39 Other manufacturing	−0.95***	−0.06	−0.09	−0.56***
	Resource-intensive	−0.58***	−0.45***	−0.26***	−0.33***
	31 Food and beverages	−0.63***	−0.51***	−0.32***	−0.39***
	34 Paper products	−0.23	−0.25**	−0.26**	−0.39***
	35 Chemical, rubber and plastic products	−0.54***	−0.36***	−0.18***	−0.27***
	Capital-intensive	−0.49***	−0.42***	−0.37***	−0.34***
	36 Non-metallic mineral products	−0.57**	−0.06	−0.27***	−0.20**
	37 Basic metal industries	0.10	−0.27	−0.06	−0.12
	38 Machinery and transport equipment	−0.50***	−0.56***	−0.46***	−0.42***

Note: *** $p < 0.01$, ** $p < 0.05$, * $p < 0.1$.
Source: SI data, BPS; various years.

point to speculate on few possible answers. The first possible explanation is that firms may have used the time between shortly after the introduction of the new manpower law to 2006 and 2006 to learn how to adjust to new/more rigid labor market regime. The second possible explanation is related to the first, that is, in learning to adjust, firms may have found some ways to get around the very restrictive law and hence, at the end, the restrictiveness nature of the law is — in practice — is not, or much less, restrictive. In the literature, there are casual observations that reflect this 'getting around the law' phenomenon. The third potential explanation is simply existence of economic opportunities/prospects (high demand growth) that allow firms to start hiring again.

Brusentsev et al. (2012) observed a downward trend in compliance from 2007 to 2008. This observation can be viewed as the one indicating how firms get around the law,

GLOBALIZATION, INDUSTRIALIZATION AND LABOUR MARKETS

Table 9. Output and wage elasticities, non-exporters, 1990–2009.

ISIC code and industry, Non-exporter		1990	1996	2006	2009
Output elasticity	All large and medium-sized manufacturing firms	0.59***	0.56***	0.47***	0.55***
	Labor-intensive	0.65***	0.62***	0.53***	0.65***
	32 Textiles and garments	0.66***	0.66***	0.56***	0.67***
	33 Wood products	0.63***	0.52***	0.49***	0.58***
	39 Other manufacturing	0.63***	0.60***	0.41***	0.62***
	Resource-intensive	0.56***	0.54***	0.43***	0.51***
	31 Food and beverages	0.54***	0.53***	0.42***	0.51***
	34 Paper products	0.55***	0.57***	0.42***	0.50***
	35 Chemical, rubber and plastic products	0.58***	0.55***	0.46***	0.52***
	Capital-intensive	0.55***	0.53***	0.49***	0.51***
	36 Non-metallic mineral products	0.53***	0.51***	0.43***	0.54***
	37 Basic metal industries	0.46***	0.45***	0.59***	0.41***
	38 Machinery and transport equipment	0.56***	0.55***	0.51***	0.52***
Wage elasticity	All large and medium-sized manufacturing firms	−0.42***	−0.38***	−0.28***	−0.45***
	Labor-intensive	−0.49***	−0.42***	−0.32***	−0.52***
	32 Textiles and garments	−0.50***	−0.50***	−0.37***	−0.57***
	33 Wood products	−0.45***	−0.27***	−0.22***	−0.38***
	39 Other manufacturing	−0.61***	−0.47***	−0.24***	−0.54***
	Resource-intensive	−0.35***	−0.35***	−0.22***	−0.42***
	31 Food and beverages	−0.29***	−0.31***	−0.17***	−0.41***
	34 Paper products	0.34***	−0.42***	−0.26***	−0.35***
	35 Chemical, rubber and plastic products	−0.48***	−0.42***	−0.41***	−0.47***
	Capital-intensive	−0.42***	−0.34***	−0.39***	−0.38***
	36 Non-metallic mineral products	−0.38***	−0.31***	−0.29***	−0.40***
	37 Basic metal industries	−0.32***	−0.18	−0.60***	−0.27***
	38 Machinery and transport equipment	−0.45***	−0.36***	−0.44***	−0.40***

Note: *** $p < 0.01$, ** $p < 0.05$, * $p < 0.1$.
Source: SI data, BPS; various years.

albeit longer time frame is certainly needed to convince us with a robust indication. It can also explain how the recovery in labor market rigidity was made after the introduction of the new labor law.

Table 4 presents the elasticities that reflect the responsiveness of employment to a change in wage. The elasticities are the more direct measures for the effects of any changes in the labor market environment. The wage data refer to the total labor costs divided by the total workforce for each plant. In principle, therefore they should include all costs of employing workers, extending to any separation costs incurred by firms. As with the approach above, the results are derived from the coefficients in our equation (i.e., the estimates of α_1).

Consider, first, the overtime pattern. For the whole manufacturing, it is similar to the one observed for the output elasticities, i.e., a relatively stable responsiveness from 1990 to 1996, which was followed by a decline in 2006, and a recovery observed in 2009. Employment was less sensitive to the change in wage over the 1996–2006 period which may have reflected the period for firms to adjust to the new/more rigid labor market regime introduced by the new manpower law in 2003. Here, more specific to what may have happened during the adjustment period is an indication of a behavior by firms that considers labor more as quasi-fixed fixed rather than variable cost; this is because, as discussed, the new law has created a very expensive hiring and firing costs.

As for the pattern across industry groups and two-digit ISIC industries, as in the case of output elasticities, labor-intensive sector in general is more sensitive compared to the wage-employment responsiveness of resource- and capital-intensive groups, suggesting that labor costs are relatively unimportant for resource- and capital-intensive groups. It is also important to note the relatively very low wage elasticities of basic machinery (ISIC 37) as recorded in 2009; this indicates that this industry has become even less relied on labor even compare to the other capital-intensive industries.

Tables 7, 8, and 9 present the elasticties (output and wage) by group of exporters and non-exporters. These are calculated as an attempt to draw observations/patterns with a more direct relationship between globalization and labor market regime. We consider exporting as a key variable representing globalization.

Consider the elasticities presented by Table 7, exporters tend to hire more workers than non-exporters in respond to a change in output. It is completely a different picture in the case of wage elasticity (wage to employment responsiveness). That is, as the last two rows of Table 7 show, in the beginning – during period 1990–1996, before the AFC, exporters were more responsive in lowering employment than non-exporters for a given increase in wage. After the AFC, however, exporters were less responsive than non-exporters. In other words, after the AFC, exporters tend to retain employment more than non-exporters should there be an increase in wage level. This is interesting to note, and one possible explanation is that exporters, which usually employ skilled workers more than non-exporters (e.g., Bernard, Jensen, and Lawrence 1995; Bernard and Jensen 1999), do not want to easily lose the economic return from their investment to train their workers.

Turning to Tables 8 and 9, observing first cross-section pattern of output elasticities, for exporters, it is found that employment responsiveness to a change in output was the highest for labor-intensive industry group (see Table 8). This is also observed for non-exporters (see Table 9). Output elasticity of capital-intensive industry group is also found to have been relatively high for exporter, which was not the case for non-exporters (i.e., around 0.6 for exporters in comparison with 0.5 for non-exporters for the elasticity estimated for 2009).

Consider now wage elasticities presented by Tables 8 and 9. Important observation is that, for exporters, the estimates of wage elasticity are about the same across all industry groups (labor-, resource-, and capital-intensive groups) (see Table 8). This is not observed for non-exporters (see Table 9). Therefore, dependency of exporters on labor input tends to be the same across the three industry groups, while this is not the case for non-exporters.

Combining this with earlier observation on the pattern of wage elasticity over the time suggests a general inference exporters operated in Indonesian manufacturing were less relied on labor input after the AFC or after the implementation of new – but more rigid – labor law; the reliance of the exporters before the crisis, or before the implementation of

Table 10. Average plant-level capital intensity, 1990–2009.

	Non-wage VA (thousand IDR)		Energy expenditure (thousand IDR)	
	Non-exporter	Exporter	Non-exporter	Exporter
1990	3290	7383	648	1077
1996	7457	13,312	1242	2092
2006	45,523	95,338	15,048	16,409
2009	75,411	205,007	21,672	24,116

Note: Capital intensity is proxied by non-wage value added and energy expenditure.
Source: SI data, BPS; various years.

the new law, seems to have been higher. The new labor law therefore may have forced exporters to change their production technology by substituting labor by machineries. This is supported by the increase in the ratio of capital intensity between exporters and non-exporters over the period before and after the AFC (see Table 10).

5. Conclusion

This study examines the interrelationship between globalization, industrialization and labor market regime using the case study of Indonesian manufacturing for the period 1990–2009. It attempts to collect some basic facts concerning the question of how the change in labor market regime, from flexible to rigid, may have affected industrial and/or labor market performance.

A number of basic facts are observed. Among other, the study finds that the responsiveness of output to employment (output elasticity) and of wage to employment (wage elasticity) decline substantially over the period 1996–2006, which may have been contributed as an effect of the implementation of the new but rigid labor law since 2003.

Equally important observation in this context is the one that show a recovery in the responsiveness of output and of wage to employment after 2006, which is recorded by the estimate of the elasticities in 2009. A number of possible explanations can be put forward, first, there is time spent by firms to adjust or to learn how to survive under the setting of new labor law. Second, firms may have found some ways to get around the very restrictive law, which makes operating under the new law less costly that it should have been. Third, there are simply economic opportunities/prospects (high demand growth) that allow firms to start hiring again despite a more expensive hiring and firing environment.

Estimating for and comparing the elasticities between groups of exporters and non-exporters yield some more direct inferences concerning the importance of globalization in moderating the effect of labor market regime on industrial performance and labor market outcome. First, exporters tend to hire more workers than non-exporters in respond to a change in output. Second, in the period after the implementation of the new labor law, exporters tend to retain employment more than non-exporters should there be an increase in wage level. One possible explanation for this observation is that exporters, which usually employ skilled workers more than non-exporters do not want to easily lose the economic return from their investment to train their workers. The less reliance of exporters on labor input suggests that the new labor may have forced exporters to change their production technology by substituting labor by machineries.

Acknowledgements

We are grateful to Economic Research Institute for ASEAN and East Asia for financial assistance.

Note

1. Considerable description in this section was drawn from Aswicahyono et al. (2010).

References

Ariff, M., and H. Hill. 1985. *Export-Oriented Industrialisation: The ASEAN Experience.* Sydney: Allen and Unwin.

Arndt, S.W., and H. Kierzkowski. 2001. *Fragmentation: New Production Patterns in World Economy.* Oxford: Oxford University Press.

Athukorala, P-C. 2006. "Post-crisis Export Performance: The Indonesian experience in regional perspective." *Bulletin of Indonesian Economic Studies* 42 (2): 177–211.

Aswicahyono, H. 2000. "How Not to Industrialise? Indonesia's Automotive Industry." *Bulletin of Indonesian Economic Studies* 36 (1): 209–241.

Aswicahyono, H., H. Hill, and D. Narjoko. 2010. "Industrialisation after a Deep Economic Crisis: Indonesia." *Journal of Development Studies* 46 (6): 1084–1108.

Beresford, M. 2008. "Doi Moi in Review: The Challenges of Building Market Socialism in Vietnam." *Journal of Contemporary Asia* 38 (2): 221–243.

Bernard, A.B., and J.B. Jensen. 1999. "Exceptional Exporter Performance: Cause, Effect, or both?" *Journal of International Economics* 47 (1): 1–25.

Bernard, A.B., J.B. Jensen, and R.Z. Lawrence. 1995. "Exporters, Jobs, and Wages in U.S. Manufacturing: 1976-1987." *Brookings Papers on Economic Activity, Microeconomics*, 67–119. Digital document available at http://www.jstor.org/discover/10.2307/2534772?uid=3738224&uid=2&uid=4&sid=21105093859613

Brusentsev, V., D. Newhouse, and W. Vroman. 2012. "Severance Pay Compliance in Indonesia." *World Bank Policy Research Working Paper 5933.*

Cheng, L.K., and H. Kierzkowski. 2001. *Global Production and Trade in East Asia.* Boston, MA: Kluwer Academic Publishers.

Deardoff, A.V. 2001. "Fragmentation in Simple Trade Models." *North American Journal of Economics and Finance* 12: 121–137.

Del Carpio, X., Nguyen H., and Wang L. Choon. 2012. "Does the Minimum Wage Affect Employment? Evidence from the Manufacturing Sector in Indonesia." *World Bank Policy Research Working Paper 6147.*

Kimura, F. 2008. "The Mechanics of Production Networks in Southeast Asia: The Fragmentation Theory Approach." In *Production Networks and Industrial Clusters: Integrating Economies in Southeast Asia*, edited by I. Kuroiwa, and Toh Mun Heng, 33–53. Singapore: Institute of Southeast Asian Studies.

Kimura, F., and M. Ando. 2005. "Two-dimensional Fragmentation in East Asia Conceptual Framework and Empirics." *International Review of Economics and Finance* 14: 317–348.

Lipsey, R. E. 2001. *Foreign Investment in Three Financial Crises, National Bureau of Economic Research Working Paper No. 8084.* Cambridge, MA: NBER.

Manning, C. 1998. *Indonesian Labour in Transition: an East Asian Success Story?* Cambridge: Cambridge University Press.

Manning, C., and K. Roesad. 2006. "Survey of Recent Development." *Bulletin of Indonesian Economic Studies* 42 (2): 143–170.

Manning, C., and K. Roesad. 2007. "The Manpower Law of 2003 and Its Implementing Regulations: Genesis." *Key Articles and Potential Impact* 43 (1): 59–86.

Soesastro, H., and M.C. Basri. 2005. "The Political Economy of Trade Policy in Indonesia." *ASEAN Economic Bulletin* 22 (1): 3–18.

Thee, K.W. 1994. *Industrialisasi di Indonesia: Beberapa Kajian.* Jakarta: LP3ES.

World Trade Organization (WTO). 1998. *Trade Policy Review: Indonesia 1998.* Geneva: Author.

WTO. 2003. *Trade Policy Review: Indonesia 2003.* Geneva: Author.

Industrialization and labour in Malaysia

Rajah Rasiah[a], Vicki Crinis[b] and Hwok-Aun Lee[a]

[a]Faculty of Economics and Administration, University of Malaya, Kuala Lumpur, Malaysia; [b]Faculty of Law, Humanities and Creative Arts, University of Wollongong, New South Wales, Australia

Although increasing globalizations spurred rapid industrialization in Malaysia, this article shows that the lack of significant technological upgrading and structural change has caused the premature plateauing of manufacturing, stemming from failures to coordinate policies, enforce standards, sustain high productivity growth and stimulate transition to higher value-added activities. Manufacturing as a whole has registered slow wage growth since the late 1990s, with labour markets characterized by heavy presence of low-skilled foreign workers, increased contract labour and outsourcing and declining worker organization. The focus on perspiration-based low-skilled foreign labour rather than on expanding professional and skilled labour has driven Malaysia down the low industrialization road. The Malaysian experience reflects a case of manufacturing's importance and direct contribution to the economy contracting before recording high levels of value added and sustained productivity growth, and with labour market practices constraining instead of facilitating positive change.

1. Introduction

For a long time, Malaysia was heralded as a model of a rapidly industrializing country for other countries to emulate (World Bank 1993). However, the lack of industrial deepening, and the onset of negative deindustrialization since the late 1990s have cast a different light on the Malaysian experience. The importance of manufacturing towards sustaining economic growth and development is well established, but conditionally on continuous productivity gains and in successful cases, on passage through positive deindustrialization. Heterodox economists identified manufacturing as the path to engender rapid growth and structural change because of its increasing returns (Young 1928).[1] Industrialization is viewed to drive its own growth, as well as that of the other sectors, including stimulating structural change from low value-added activities to high value-added activities and the consequent differentiation and division of labour to provide the opportunities for generating more and better jobs. To this argument, we take a related argument that was taken up by political economists concerned with the impact of differentiation and division of labour on the quality of jobs created. Piore and Sabel (1984), Pyke and Sengenberger (1992) and Zeitlin (1992) focused on the high road to industrialization. This article takes a leaf out of this argument by examining the Malaysian experience to evaluate the proposition that economies gripped by negative deindustrialization are incapable of supporting significant improvements in wages.

The aggressive promotion of export processing zones since 1972 assisted manufacturing industries in overtaking agriculture in Malaysia's GDP in 1988 (Malaysia 1991a).

Foreign direct investment (FDI) helped make Malaysia a major exporter of light manufactured goods. Electric−electronics, vegetable oils and fats and textiles and clothing were among the main manufactured exports generated by the Malaysian economy since the 1990s. Import-substitution policies targeted at heavy industries from 1981 drove the expansion of steel, transport equipment and cement manufacturing through protection, subsidies and government capitalization (Malaysia 1986). Transport equipment in particular has continued to enjoy strong government support.

Massive inflows of FDI into the manufacturing sector also caused tightening of the labour market by the mid-1990s (Ariff 1991; Rasiah 1995a). The focus of industrial policy shifted towards industrial deepening as the government attempted to take advantage of low unemployment levels (which reached 2.7% in 1995) to stimulate structural change into high value-added activities. Following the introduction of the Way Forward initiative by the government in 1991 targeted at making Malaysia a developed economy by 2020, a series of instruments were introduced to promote industrial deepening, alongside the Action Plan for Industrial Technology Development (APITD) of 1990 (Malaysia, 1991a).

Unfortunately, the effectiveness of these instruments to stimulate structural change from low to high value-added activities was attenuated by a combination of poor policy coordination and monitoring, counterproductive labour market practices and human resource constraints. Efforts to redistribute ownership and cultivate enterprise along ethnic lines have faltered, leading to both underachievement in Bumiputera participation in manufacturing, and efficiency losses more generally. In the absence of decisive and effective policy, firms resorted to importing foreign unskilled labour to sustain their operations, which aggravated further the situation by reducing the pressure to upgrade (Rasiah 1995b; Henderson and Phillips 2007). Imports of unskilled foreign labour and failure to stimulate upgrading technologically weakened the capacity of the manufacturing sector to support improvements in labour productivity and wages. Furthermore, Malaysia has sustained production substantially from extracting long work hours per week, rather than raising productivity per hour. At the same time, declining education quality inhibits the scope for technological absorption and innovation, while the industrial relations system has continuously diluted over time, instead of being harnessed for dynamic and coordinated gains in productivity and wages.

This article seeks to contribute to the debate on deindustrialization by showing that its premature occurrence has restricted both improvements in labour productivity and wages in Malaysia's manufacturing sector. The rest of the article is organized as follows. The next section discusses the main theoretical arguments on industrialization as an engine of growth. Section 3 discusses the premature deindustrialization experience of Malaysia. The subsequent section analyzes the impact of premature deindustrialization on labour productivity and wages. The final section finishes with conclusions and policy implications.

2. Theoretical considerations

The arguments on industrialization as the engine of growth and development arose largely from the advocates of industrial policy. Smith (1776) and Young (1928) had argued incisively on the capacity of industrialization to drive increasing returns activities. Veblen (1915), Gerschenkron (1962) and Abramovitz (1956) provided evidence to argue that successful industrializers have used industrial policy to stimulate rapid economic growth and structural change.[2] Rowthorn and Wells (1987) provided evidence to show that, as manufacturing matures, the shift towards services has been accompanied by continued improvements in productivity in a number of industries in the United States (positive deindustrialization) while it has declined in the United Kingdom (negative deindustrialization).

Industrialization – both the growth in share of GDP and its diversification into higher value-added activities – has been associated with the successful development of the Organization for Economic Cooperation and Development (OECD) countries in the initial years of rapid growth. East and Southeast Asia's successful developers – i.e. the flying geese stock of Japan, Hong Kong, Korea, Singapore and Taiwan enjoyed rapid industrialization throughout their high growth years (Hamilton 1983; Amsden 1989; Wade 1990; Rodan 1989).

Attempts to discuss the importance of industrialization will not be complete without a discussion of the trade and the structural orientation of industries that should be promoted. The 1950s' advocates of industrial development recommended a focus on inward-oriented heavy and capital goods as an integral part of final consumption goods manufacturing. Advocates of this approach argue that the department two goods (capital goods) are critical complementary inputs for the development of other industries (Kalecki 1976; McFarlane 1981). Britain, United States, Germany, Japan, South Korea and Taiwan very much enjoyed the development of both light manufacturing and complementary heavy industries, thereby making them versatile in entering a wide range of final goods industries. Yet, light manufacturing goods such as textiles and garments also grew rapidly in these countries. Because the expansion of these industries did not raise substantially the material living conditions of the masses, Adam (1975, 102) referred to them as 'banana republics that become pyjama republics'.

The focus on heavy industries behind import-substitution – in both large and small domestic markets – foundered in many countries because of failure to attain economies of scale and prevalence of clientelist approaches that removed competitive pressures and negated the translation of subsidies and grants into productive rents that drive firm-level technological catch-up. For example, poorly coordinated and corrupt import-substitution policies failed in Indonesia, the Philippines and in many Latin American countries (Rasiah 2010; Ofreneo 2008; Jenkins 1987; Evans 1997; Cardoso 2001).

However, Korea managed to achieve international competitiveness in the heavy industries of steel, shipbuilding and cars, and machinery and steel by using import-substitution for export promotion, while Taiwan managed to achieve competitiveness in machinery and metals, and electronics through deliberate promotional strategies and effective appraisal mechanisms (Amsden 1989; Fransman 1986; Amsden and Chu 2003). Governments in these countries enjoyed autonomy from clientelist groups to enforce stringent performance conditions on the manufacturers (Khan 1989). Hence, it can be argued that strategic industrial policy *a la* the Northeast Asian models have been successful. South Korea and Taiwan have also experienced a contraction in manufacturing's contribution to GDP with a trend expansion in services while manufacturing productivity has continued to rise, consistent with positive deindustrialization.

3. Premature plateauing of manufacturing

Although Malaysia has undergone considerable structural change, we present four arguments to support our claim that Malaysia has begun facing premature deindustrialization. First, the contribution of the manufacturing sector to GDP has started to contract since 2000, which has taken place when Malaysia's GDP per capita is still entrenched among upper middle-income countries. Second, the springboard of manufacturing growth, i.e. the light export-oriented electric–electronics and textile–garment industries, has faced a

Table 1. Sectoral GDP growth, Malaysia, 1990−2010.

Sectors	1990−1994	1995−1999	2000−2004	2005−2010
Agriculture	0.4	0.7	3.3	2.7
Mining	2.7	3.0	3.2	−1.7
Manufacturing	11.7	5.9	4.5	2.6
Electricity, gas and water	14.9	4.8	5.4	4.3
Construction	13.0	−1.7	1.6	4.9
Trade	12.8	3.8	4.2	8.4
Transport and communication	11.4	5.7	5.6	6.2
Finance[a]	16.0	9.6	5.9	8.2
Public administration	5.7	4.5	5.8	6.6
Others[b]	10.6	4.9	4.1	2.3
GDP	9.4	3.8	4.6	4.4

Note: [a]refers to finance, insurance, real estate and business services; [b]refers to community, social and personal services, producers of private non-profit services and domestic services of households including owner-occupied dwellings.
Source: ADB (2010).

slowdown over the period 2000−2010. Third, the import-substituting automobile industry that was promoted through heavy protection from 1981 has also begun contracting. Fourth, Malaysia's leading export-oriented manufacturing sectors have been continuously facing a downward slide in revealed comparative advantage.

Manufacturing enjoyed double-digit annual average growth since 1971 to overtake agriculture to become the leading propeller of GDP among the primary and secondary sectors in 1988 (see Rasiah 1995a). The swiftest growth in manufacturing was achieved over the period 1971−1994. However, average annual manufacturing growth fell from 11.7% in 1990−1994 to 5.9% in 1995−1999, 4.8% in 2000−2004 and 2.6% in 2005−2010 (see Table 1).

In contrast, the services sector recorded the largest expansion as its share in GDP grew from 31.6% in 1990 to 48.5% in 2010 (see Table 2). However, because the inter-sectoral dynamics of structural change has not evolved sufficiently well and with manufacturing value-added growth slowing down since 2000 before a structural shift to high value-added activities, the expansion in services is unlikely to produce the complimentary impact of driving GDP growth. Apart from investment forays into infrastructure,

Table 2. Structure of GDP, Malaysia, 1970−2010 (%).

Sectors	1970	1975	1980	1985	1990	1995	2000	2005	2010
Agriculture	29.0	27.7	22.9	20.8	15.2	12.9	8.6	8.4	10.4
Mining	13.7	4.8	10.1	10.5	11.8	6.2	10.6	14.4	10.9
Manufacturing	13.9	16.4	19.6	19.7	24.2	26.4	30.9	29.6	24.6
Construction	3.5	3.8	4.6	4.8	3.5	4.5	3.4	2.7	3.3
Utilities	0.3	2.5	2.7	0.7	2.8	3.1	2.5	2.4	2.3
Services	39.6	45	40.1	43.5	42.5	46.9	44.0	42.5	48.5
GDP	100	100	100	100	100	100	100	100	100

Source: Malaysia (1971−2011).

Table 3. Sectoral employment structure (%), Malaysia, 1970–2010.

Sector	1970	1975	1980	1985	1990	1995	2000	2005	2010
Agriculture	53.5	49.3	39.7	35.7	26.0	19.0	16.0	12.9	11.6
Mining and quarrying	2.6	2.2	1.7	1.1	0.6	0.5	0.5	0.4	0.3
Manufacturing	8.7	10.1	15.7	15.1	19.9	25.7	27.1	28.7	28.3
Construction	2.7	2.9	5.6	6.9	6.3	8.9	9.2	7.0	6.4
Services*	20.5	22.5	23.6	26.2	34.5	35.1	37.2	51.0	53.3
Total employment ('000)	3340	3928	4817	5625	6686	8024	8547	10,895	11,956

Note: *includes gas, water and electricity.
Source: Malaysia (1971–2011) and Osman, Pazim and Rasiah (2011).

telecommunications and banking services development abroad, the services are yet to become a major foreign exchange earner.

Similarly, the contribution of manufacturing, which had risen from 24.2% in 1990 to 30.9% in 2000, fell to 24.6% in 2010 (see Table 2). The evidence obviously shows a declining trend in the relative contribution of manufacturing to Malaysia's GDP growth since 2000. In addition, a shift is observed in the share of agriculture, which fell in significance from the 1960s until 2005 (Osman, Pazim, and Rasiah 2011), has begun to rise again from 8.4% in 2005 to 10.4% in 2010.

From its 60% contribution in 1957 (Osman, Pazim, and Rasiah 2011), agriculture remained the main employment generator in Malaysia until around 1990 when services took over as the lead job creator (see Table 3). Manufacturing surpassed agriculture around 1995 to become the next leading employment creator in Malaysia, but its overall contribution has started to fall from 2005. The infusion of foreign unskilled labour into manufacturing helped raise the share of employment in manufacturing, which rose significantly to 28.7% in 2005 before falling slightly to 28.3% in 2010.

Rapid inter-sectoral structural change also took place with exports. Agriculture accounted for 57% of Malaysian exports in 1970 but its share in total exports fell dramatically since to reach a trough of 3.7% in 2000, before rising again to 10.8% in 2010 (see Table 4). Manufactured exports enjoyed the biggest expansion rising from 11.1% of total exports in 1970 to reach its peak of 90.1% in 2000 before falling to 76.2% in 2010. The relative slowdown in manufacturing has allowed the agriculture and mining sectors together to increase their share in total exports from 9.8% in 2000 to 23.3% in 2010.

Table 4. Sectoral export structure, Malaysia, 1970–2010 (%).

Sector	1970	1975	1980	1985	1990	1995	2000	2005	2010
Agriculture	57.0	49.8	39.9	30.2	19.1	9.3	3.7	7.1	10.8
Mining	21.4	18.6	30.0	29.6	15.9	5.0	6.1	9.3	11.5
Manufacturing	11.1	20.9	21.8	32.7	58.8	84.2	90.1	81.6	76.2
Others*	10.5	10.6	8.3	7.4	6.2	1.4	0.1	2.0	1.6
Total (MYR billion)	5.6	10.2	30.7	42.5	88.7	204	427	552.1	638.5

Note: *includes unclassified agricultural, mining and manufactured goods and services.
Source: Malaysia (1971–2011).

Table 5. Manufacturing value-added growth (% per year), Malaysia, 1979–2010.

Sector	1979–1985	1985–1990	1990–1995	1995–2000	2000–2005	2005–2010
Food	5.5	6.6	12.2	10.7	3.0	11.0
Beverages	−0.3	2.4	−3.0	5.5	20.0	
Tobacco			15.2	−13.7	4.4	16.7
Textiles and garments	4.7	12.8	17.1	6.8	−11.5	−1.3
Footwear (except rubber)	NA	NA	10.2	7.3	−2.7	14.3
Wood	−4.5	13.1	16.4	3.8	−0.3	1.0
Furniture and fixtures	NA	NA	35.8	19.3	2.6	−1.7
Printing, publishing and allied	NA	NA	17.9	5.1	4.5	2.1
Paper	NA	NA	20.3	15.0	−3.3	7.0
Leather	NA	NA	29.4	−2.4	2.9	4.4
Rubber	4.2	25.0	13.6	7.6	−1.6	4.6
Chemical	2.8	7.9	12.5	12.0	12.3	−27.3
Petroleum and coal	NA	NA	25.3	37.4	11.1	11.2
Non-metallic mineral	3.6	7.4	16.7	4.4	1.3	8.4
Basic metal	9.8	5.0	8.7	10.2	4.4	13.6
Fabricated metal			23.9	9.9	1.7	7.6
Machinery	9.0	6.6	26.0	25.3	16.5	2.7
Electrical machinery and electronics	8.0	16.4	26.8	12.1	0.5	1.3
Transport equipment	9.0	15.0	17.6	6.5	4.6	10.6

Source: Computed from Malaysia 1986–2011.

While manufacturing became the largest real sector since 1988, its share in GDP began to fall after 2000. Table 5 shows average annual growth in value addition experienced by the manufacturing industries in Malaysia. Foreign capital became the prime driver of manufactured exports as large waves of foreign capital relocated textile and garment industries and electric–electronics assembly and processing plants in Malaysia since the 1970s, and subsequently from the second half of the 1980s following massive inflows from Japan and the Asian Newly Industrialized Economies (NIEs) that helped expand export manufacturing further.

Although manufacturing expansion began from the 1970s, government efforts to stimulate industrial widening and deepening only began with the introduction of the Industrial Master Plan (IMP) in 1986 (Malaysia 1986), and the Second Industrial Master Plan (IMP2) in 1996. The first IMP targeted incentives to attract foreign capital and to stimulate training, while the IMP2 continued this with the addition of incentives and grants for clustering and R&D activities (Malaysia 1996). Serious shortages in human capital and the failure of the meso-organizations created from 1991 to stimulate knowledge-based

activities such as designing and R&D restricted the capacity of IMP2 to stimulate industrial deepening (Rasiah 2010).

Ethnic considerations in government policies increased since the 1970s. The Industrial Coordination Act of 1975 required large-scale establishments to allocate at least
30% of equity to Bumiputeras. Export-oriented manufacturers, which were largely foreign-owned, were exempted from this rule. However, many domestically oriented
medium-scale Malaysian Chinese-owned companies, not qualifying for the exemption on
export grounds, kept their operations below the size threshold to avoid having the divest
their holdings, thus curtailing economies of scale (Lee 2007). Mandated transfers, as
expected, did not spur much capability building or innovative activity. Malaysia's early-
1980s heavy industries programme, under which the national automobile maker Proton
was established, also targeted the cultivation of Bumiputera ownership and enterprise.
These ventures largely struggled or failed, beset *inter alia* by poor selection and weak
monitoring. The manufacturing investment climate was liberalized from the mid-1980s,
although pockets of ethnic preferential policies have remained, such as in automobiles.

Massive FDI inflows into the manufacturing sector from the late 1980s helped reduce
the pressure on the government to create jobs (see Ariff 1991; Rasiah 1995a). The focus of
industrial policy shifted towards industrial deepening as the government attempted to take
advantage of low unemployment levels, which reached 2.7% in 1995. The APITD of 1990
helped provide the groundwork for the opening of the Human Resource Development
Fund (HRDF), Malaysian Technology Development Corporation (MTDC), the Malaysia
Industry Government High Technology (MIGHT), the cluster-based IMP2, the Multimedia
Super Corridor (MSC) and the Multimedia Development Corporation (MDec) in the 1990s
to support technological deepening (Malaysia 1991b, 1991c). The Malaysian Institute of
Microelectronics Systems (MIMOS) was also corporatized in the 1990s.

More generally, deficiencies in coordination and performance standards have hin-
dered value addition in the manufacturing sector, in spite of various initiatives to set
Malaysia in this direction. Hence, firms approached the government to import foreign
labour to sustain their operations, which aggravated further the situation by reducing the
pressure to upgrade. Government focus on unskilled labour over the 1980s and the 1990s
undermined firm-level initiatives to upgrade. These developments led a number of
authors to warn that the Malaysian industrialization project may have stalled (see Best
and Rasiah 2003; Henderson and Phillips 2007).[3]

The failure of the meso-organizations to stimulate the production of human capital
and knowledge stocks to spur upgrading led to a slowdown in manufacturing growth since
2000. The government introduced the Third Industrial Master Plan (IMP3) in 2006 which
attempted to continue its focus on clustering with the addition of support for services.
However, the IMP3 neither enjoyed the positive elements of clustering contained in
IMP2 nor addressed the latter's weakness of not comprehending complementary activities
effectively (see Rasiah 2011). Manufacturing value added grew only by 2.6% annually on
average in the period 2005–2010. The fastest-growing industries in 2005–2010 were
beverages and footwear, and the resource-based industries of petroleum and coal, and
metals (see Table 5). The textile and garment industries faced a contraction in
2000–2010, recording an annual average growth of −11.5% in 2000–2005 and −1.3%
in 2005–2010. The electric–electronics industry, which is Malaysia's largest
manufacturing industry, recorded an annual average growth rate of 0.5% in 2000–2005
and 1.3% in 2005–2010. While the contraction of the textiles industry appears as an
unavoidable result of the termination of the Multi-Fibre Agreement (MFA) and rising
competition from China, India, Vietnam and the least developed countries (LDCs),[4] the

Table 6. Manufacturing trade balance, Malaysia, 1979–2008.

Sector	1979	1985	1990	1995	2000	2005	2008
Food and beverage	−0.171	−0.327	0.594	0.641	0.520	0.594	0.159
Textiles and garments	−0.058	0.106	0.082	0.122	0.271	0.082	0.302
Wood	0.913	0.874	0.660	0.491	0.417	0.660	0.854
Chemicals	−0.710	−0.721	−0.635	−0.428	−0.176	−0.635	0.174
Petroleum and coal	NA	NA	0.512	0.382	0.379	0.512	0.052
Rubber and plastics	0.470	0.113	0.218	0.177	0.106	0.218	0.734
Non-metallic mineral	−0.335	−0.518	−0.464	−0.420	−0.156	−0.464	0.155
Basic metal	0.570	0.252	−0.492	−0.517	−0.393	−0.492	−0.393
Machinery (inc electrical)	−0.069	−0.071	−0.093	−0.019	0.104	−0.093	0.087
Transport equipment	−0.652	−0.624	−0.598	−0.502	−0.518	−0.598	−0.407
Professional and scientific	−0.477	−0.451	−0.385	−0.279	−0.150	−0.385	−0.322
Others	NA	NA	0.357	0.024	0.223	0.357	0.288

Note: Formula used: (Export − Import)/(Export + Import).
Source: Malaysia (1983–1991, 2010); ADB (2008).

contraction and slowdown in other manufacturing industries is a consequence of slow upgrading.

The discussion on premature deindustrialization will not be complete without an analysis of trade performance. The indices examined are trade balance (TB), imports in domestic demand, export intensity of output and the shares of exports in overall exports. The TB index denotes the relative significance of exports against imports and the estimations are shown in Table 6. The TB index varies between −1 and 1 with negative balances denoting that imports exceed exports. It can be seen that food and beverage, wood and petroleum and coal products have enjoyed the highest trade balances over the period 1990–2005. The data show that the TB improved for most industries over the period 1990–2000 and started to worsen over the period 2000–2005. However, other than food and other industries, the remaining industries recorded improvements in their TB in 2005–2008. The withdrawal of MFA quotas in 2004 suggests that textiles and garments are likely to face further contraction. The machinery industry enjoyed improvements over the period 1990–2000 with its TB recording a positive index only in 2000 and 2008, suggesting that the strategic instruments used to promote the industry following the launching of the IMP3 of 2006 has not materialized.

The transport equipment industry enjoyed strong protection since the promulgation of the Heavy Industries Corporation of Malaysia (HICOM) in 1980 and subsequent launching of Proton (Alavi 1996). The government approved further domestic automobile manufacturers in Perodua, Naza Motors, Modenas and Inakom. However, the TB account of the transport equipment industry has shown little improvement (see Table 6). The export value of automotive products from Malaysia rose from US$121 million in 1990 to only US$369 million in 2000 and US$1154 million in 2008. The commensurate export figures for Indonesia rose from US$22 million in 1990 to US$369 million in 2000 and US$2783 million in 2008 while those of Thailand rose from US$108 million in 1990 to US$2417 million in 2000 and US$16,227 million in 2008 (WTO 2009: Table 11.60). Clearly, exports from Thailand and Indonesia have grown significantly faster than exports from Malaysia over the period 1990–2008.

Table 7. Composition of manufacturing export, Malaysia, 1979–2008.

Sector	1979	1985	1990	1995	2000	2005	2008
Food and beverage	0.123	0.127	0.101	0.088	0.044	0.059	0.038
Textiles and garments	0.072	0.100	0.049	0.036	0.027	0.019	0.021
Wood	0.043	0.028	0.122	0.070	0.041	0.035	0.021
Chemicals	0.034	0.033	0.014	0.021	0.030	0.041	0.088
Petroleum and coal	NA	NA	0.193	0.073	0.098	0.141	0.067
Rubber and plastics	0.016	0.009	0.064	0.054	0.039	0.053	0.027
Non-metallic mineral	0.010	0.011	0.022	0.016	0.014	0.016	0.011
Basic metal	0.307	0.140	0.033	0.029	0.025	0.031	0.017
Machinery (inc electrical)	0.321	0.497	0.341	0.533	0.624	0.541	0.597
Transport equipment	0.033	0.043	0.025	0.029	0.008	0.010	0.020
Professional and scientific	NA	NA	0.014	0.016	0.020	0.023	0.018
Others	NA	NA	0.023	0.035	0.030	0.031	0.075

Note: Formula used: export of the industry divided by total manufactured exports; NA – not available.
Source: Malaysia (1983–1990); Computed from ADB (2008).

The results suggest that domestic capabilities seem to have developed more in resource-based industries enjoying natural endowments in the country. However, given that these industries are dependent on finite non-renewable resources, the government will have to gradually reduce overdependence on these industries. A sustained long-term strategy of industrial deepening cannot be built in these industries.

Machinery (mainly electric–electronics products) has dominated manufactured exports from Malaysia over the period 1990–2008 (see Table 7). Petroleum and coal products enjoyed the next highest share of exports. However, while the share of machinery and petroleum products showed an increase over 2000–2005 and subsequently a fall in 2005–2008, machinery recorded the opposite, falling in 2005 before rising in 2005–2008. While the relative contraction in exports in the 1990s was a consequence of massive expansion in electric and electronics exports, the fall after 2000 was caused by the termination of the MFA and increased exports from China and LDCs such as Cambodia (see Rasiah 2009a).[5]

While local suppliers grew,[6] the number of electronics MNCs in Malaysia engaged in designing and R&D activities constituted only 1.0% of the total in 2007 (see Rasiah 2010, 310). As most firms failed to evolve their technological capabilities to designing and R&D activities in the face of rapid expansion in China and Vietnam, the supplier base began to contract from the late 1990s (Grunsven 2006; Rasiah 2010). The lack of engineers and scientists in particular has been a glaring problem that has slowed down productivity growth in the industry. For example, Malaysia had only 729 researchers per million people when there were 7059 in Singapore and 6028 in Korea in 2007 (UNESCAP 2009, 97).

The trend decline in manufacturing labour productivity growth, with the key export-oriented industries and inward-oriented industry of transport equipment recording either a sharply declining or negative growth rates over the period 2000–2008, is a consequence of falling competitiveness arising from slow upgrading. Beverages and tobacco enjoyed the highest productivity growth in 2005–2008. While the share of electronics exports from Singapore and Thailand in global exports rose from 7.6% and 1.9%, respectively, in 2000 to 2.0% and 8.1%, respectively, in 2006, the commensurate shares from Malaysia fell from 5.4% in 2000 to 4.7% in 2006 (see Rasiah 2009b).

Taken together, the evidence is overwhelming that manufacturing has started to fall in significance from the mid-1990s with the contraction being the most serious since 2000. Critically, manufacturing industries have faced a slowdown or a fall in trade performance and productivity since 2000. The chronic contraction trends suggest that manufacturing growth in Malaysia has indeed plateaued and is facing negative deindustrialization since 2000.

4. Implications for employment, productivity and wages

Having established the long-term slowdown in manufacturing growth, in this section, we provide evidence to show that its premature slowdown has restricted both labour productivity and wage growth in the sector in Malaysia. Because of the paucity of comparable data, we use the period 1988 until 2010 in this section with the periodization defined on the basis of growth in mean wages in the manufacturing sector. We then evaluate labour policies and labour market outcomes, which have been inconsistent and counterproductive, specifically in failing to chart a clear and effective passage towards higher skills, higher wages and improved work conditions. Instead, Malaysia has entrenched dependency on low-skilled foreign workers. Labour policy regarding foreign labour has suffered from inconsistency, tendency to react to circumstances, lack of worker protection and poor monitoring against non-compliance and abuse (Devadason and Meng 2014).

Average annual employment enjoyed positive growth in all industries over the periods 1988–1990 and 1990–1997 (Table 8). Tobacco, textiles, footwear, and petroleum and coal experienced negative growth over the period 2001–2005. The number of industries

Table 8. Annual average growth of employment, Malaysia, 1988–2010 (%).

Sectors	1988–1990	1990–1997	2001–2005	2005–2010
Food and beverages	2.38	4.19	6.06	6.05
Tobacco products	24.32	13.37	−8.26	−18.01
Textiles	8.30	2.63	−0.70	−4.96
Footwear (except rubber footwear), other wearing apparel and made-up textile goods	18.14	0.41	−0.18	−1.93
Wood products	18.78	8.11	3.38	−3.09
Furniture and fixtures	12.55	17.69	6.97	−4.66
Printing, publishing and allied industries	5.86	8.50	10.72	2.53
Paper and paper products	15.61	9.05	5.50	7.82
Leather and leather products	69.03	2.83	3.41	0.41
Rubber products	12.26	3.20	7.47	−0.08
Chemicals and chemical products	11.62	7.46	8.85	−9.50
Products of petroleum and coal	0.00	16.29	−2.84	9.96
Non-metallic mineral products	17.26	10.07	3.11	3.31
Basic metal industries	18.84	11.04	5.33	7.87
Fabricated metal products	18.54	13.57	8.73	5.48
Machinery except electrical machinery	30.24	16.67	2.88	3.47
Electrical machinery and electronics	28.61	11.36	3.79	−1.50
Transport equipment	31.00	13.74	5.88	7.48

Source: Computed from various issues of manufacturing survey reports.

Table 9. Annual average growth of labour productivity, Malaysia, 1988–2010 (%).

Sector	1988–1990	1990–1997	2001–2005	2005–2010
Food and beverages	6.63	2.74	−3.91	4.66
Tobacco products	−25.57	1.56	−0.14	42.31
Textiles	4.64	13.87	−10.57	6.79
Footwear (except rubber footwear), other wearing apparel and made-up textile goods	3.87	5.63	−4.81	0.63
Wood products	2.62	4.75	−0.38	4.25
Furniture and fixtures	9.72	10.57	−6.00	3.12
Printing, publishing and allied industries	17.62	7.07	−4.59	−4.55
Paper and paper products	8.69	4.46	−11.56	−0.76
Leather and leather products	−12.04	13.26	−1.70	3.95
Rubber products	10.19	9.09	−3.97	4.68
Chemicals and chemical products	−6.95	5.43	5.48	−19.69
Products of petroleum and coal	33.37	5.93	28.15	1.08
Non-metallic mineral products	−0.32	3.28	−7.58	4.97
Basic metal industries	7.48	3.53	4.34	5.43
Fabricated metal products	6.20	6.27	−4.87	2.00
Machinery except electrical machinery	6.47	8.60	−3.05	−2.62
Electrical machinery and electronics	4.97	11.79	−0.91	0.04
Transport equipment	11.26	4.57	−12.41	3.24
Total manufacturing	6.53	5.87	−1.46	1.75

Source: Computed from various issues of manufacturing survey reports.

facing negative employment growth increased further over the period 2005–2010. Employment in tobacco, textiles, footwear, wood, furniture and fixtures, rubber, chemicals and electrical machinery contracted over the period 2005–2010.

Attracted by the provision of financial incentives and imports of foreign labour, manufacturing enjoyed significant labour productivity growth until 1997. All manufacturing industries enjoyed positive labour productivity growth over the period 1990–1997 (Table 9). Except for petroleum and coal products, the remaining manufacturing industries experienced negative labour productivity growth so that overall manufacturing labour productivity actually declined over the period 2000–2005. Apart from inward-oriented and resource-based industries, labour productivity of several export-oriented industries recorded negative or low annual average growth over the period 2005–2010.

Petroleum and coal, basic metals and chemicals were the only manufacturing industries to record positive labour productivity growth over the period 2000–2005 (see Table 9). Although labour productivity of most industries grew positively over the period 2005–2010, overall manufacturing labour productivity only grew by 1.8% on average per annum over this period. Labour productivity of the key industry, electric–electronics industry, grew at an annual average of 11.8% in 1990–1997 but grew by −0.9% in 2000–2005 and 0.04% in 2005–2010. The strong technological synergies offered by multinational corporations in the late 1980s and early 1990s appear to have been undermined by a lack of effective rooting policies for local firms to upgrade to the technology frontier (Rasiah 2009b).

The clothing and textile industry expanded during the MFA quota period (1974–2004) in Malaysia. The total export value of the textile and clothing industry for the year 1998 amounted to MR\$ 9.6 billion (4.7% of total exports) and was the third largest foreign exchange earner after the electronics and palm oil industries. In the previous years, the amount of export value in the textile and garment industry more than doubled. But in 2012, the industry had the same value as it did in 1998 and in 2012 registered a 12.4% contraction.[7] The decline is the result of the end of the MFA. In addition, most of the small garment factories have not introduced higher levels of technology but have relied on a combination of foreign workers, labour intensification and home-based workers to meet the increased competition and just-in-time production. Home-based production has expanded in the urban areas because working class Malaysian women were unable to work long hours in the factories but instead opted to take on homework for the manufacturing industries (Crinis 2013). According to the 2012 *Informal Sector Work Force Survey Report*, the largest share of women in informal employment are working in manufacturing activities (28% of total), followed by human health and social work (24%) and food and accommodation (19%; DOS 2013). Home workers, particularly in garments and textiles, account for a considerable majority of women in informal manufacturing. The dual workforce of low-skilled factory and home workers has kept wages low.

Unlike the clothing and textile industry, a study of two electronic firms showed that factory women with access to long-term employment had the opportunity to increase their skills since the 1990s when technology became more automated, incorporating flexible production techniques evident in the components sub-sector (Mohamad 1999). However, the employment pattern in this industry is unstable and is highly susceptible to over-production. Hence, national workers applying for jobs in the electronic factories have declined because the wages were too low. Instead of training workers and limiting the number of foreign workers, the government allowed manufacturers to resume foreign worker recruitment.[8] As a result, the industry has remained low-tech and labour-intensive due to the dependence on low wages and transient nature of employment.

In the manufacturing industries, foreign workers are employed on one to three year contracts (can be extended to five years), provided with accommodation and in some cases transport. The employment contract specifies the name of the employer and conditions, such as wages and terms of work, including hours of work and overtime. In Malaysia, the lowest paid category of workers on the government's 'Doing business in Malaysia' website are production workers (Crinis 2013). Before the minimum wage introduction, foreign workers were paid MYR18–26 per day. For the first 3 months, workers were paid MYR18 per day and then the rate went up to a ceiling rate of around MYR26 per day. Migrant workers do not bargain for higher wages because they fear losing their jobs. They increase their wages by working as much overtime as allocated. During the Global Economic Crisis (GEC), the number of foreign workers declined by 300,000 because expiring work permits were not renewed and the government restricted further intake of migrant workers. By the end of 2009, manufacturers had to increase wages to entice Malaysian workers. During the period of labour shortage, the wages of manufacturing workers rose from MYR450 (USD130) a month in 2008 to MYR650 (USD185). In response to pressure from manufacturers, the Malaysian government once again allowed electronics and textile firms to resume recruitment of male and female foreign workers (Crinis 2012).

Table 10. Annual average growth, real wages, Malaysia, 1988−2010.

Sector	1988−1990	1990−1997	2001−2005	2005−2010
Food and beverages	2.45	−0.23	0.01	1.66
Tobacco products	−14.92	−13.66	6.93	18.20
Textiles	5.77	3.06	−2.01	0.07
Footwear (except rubber footwear), other wearing apparel and made-up textiles	7.56	1.96	−1.61	−1.33
Wood products	1.29	−1.36	1.30	1.91
Furniture and fixtures	5.76	3.34	1.07	0.50
Printing, publishing and allied industries	3.12	0.01	−1.28	−4.22
Paper and paper products	2.74	3.51	−1.54	−0.01
Leather and leather products	−4.99	6.66	0.42	1.01
Rubber products	3.14	3.64	0.48	3.14
Chemicals and chemical products	1.23	2.19	2.96	−5.71
Products of petroleum and coal	−2.69	−0.80	0.70	−0.88
Non-metallic mineral products	−1.21	0.76	0.76	2.46
Basic metal industries	−1.54	1.58	0.74	5.43
Fabricated Metal products	−1.78	1.69	0.25	1.18
Machinery except electrical machinery	−1.20	2.78	−0.02	−0.83
Electrical machinery and electronics	1.24	4.29	1.41	1.82
Transport equipment	−2.87	3.74	−0.92	0.42
Total manufacturing	−1.17	0.92	0.55	1.31

Source: Computed from DOS (various issues), *Industrial Surveys*.

Real wage growth in the manufacturing sector in Malaysia never reached double-digit figures owing to a preponderance of specialization in low value-added activities and the use of anti-union labour policies by the government (Jomo and Todd 1994; Rasiah 1995b). Real wages grew most in the 1990s despite the inflow of foreign labour imports into the manufacturing sector because of a saturated labour market. However, real wages grew little after 2000 as investments and labour productivity in manufacturing began to fall.

In addition to the regulatory environment facing workers in Malaysia that has remained hostile, low labour productivity growth further undermined the capacity of labour to enjoy high wages in the manufacturing sector. Most industries recorded negative or low growth in real wages since 1988 (see Table 10), which reflects the low wage nature of manufacturing in Malaysia. Real wages in the manufacturing sector grew, on average, annually by only 0.6% and 1.3% in 2000−2005 and 2005−2010, respectively. Except for tobacco, which enjoyed significant growth in domestic demand, other manufacturing industries experienced either low or negative growth since 2001.

It is clear that real manufacturing wages grew little over the years owing to little tech-nological upgrading (Table 11). The strategy to import foreign unskilled labour has accentuated the problem further as it has removed the pressure for firms to raise wages. National policies to transform the country to developed status since 1991 has also been ineffective as not only have the country been unable to mobilize human capital

Table 11. Foreign workers in Malaysia, 2007.

Country	Domestic	Construction	Manufacturing	Services	Plantations	Agriculture	Total
Indonesia	294,764	211,016	206,780	41,012	290,454	103,974	1,148,000
Nepal	31	4493	172,311	1904	2584	8080	189,403
India	126	7382	28,446	60,049	22,451	23,575	142,029
Myanmar	61	14,857	29,906	6	1484	7911	54,225
Vietnam	31	5251	104,948	2951	79	645	113,905
Bangladesh	21	40,497	128,664	21,843	14,207	12,006	217,238
Philippines	10,443	1640	2858	1103	4562	2577	23,173
Thailand	426	1122	793	15,532	53	530	18,456
Pakistan	2	4947	3140	1708	971	6045	16,813
Cambodia	7458	173	2582	240	207	95	10,755
China	18	2284	959	3137	221	14	6633
Sri Lanka	883	106	1580	731	91	295	3686
Laos	1	13	16		1	1	32
Uzbekistan		6	1	4			11
Total	314,265	293,787	682,984	150,220	337,365	165,748	1,944,358

Source: Immigration Department (cited by Khamis Ar Majid, Labour Minister 2008).

domestically and from abroad, but the meso-organizations created to stimulate R&D and other forms of knowledge networks have translated little into firms participating in knowledge-intensive activities. Only a handful of firms have benefited from hiring the limited human capital available to participate in R&D and designing activities. Hence, Malaysia has remained confined to the low industrialization route.

The manufacturing sector has also lacked the supply of quality labour as the quality of education has declined over the period 1999–2011. For example, in the Trends in Mathematics and Science Survey (TIMSS) international standardized test, the share of Malaysian eighth graders attaining the 'high performance' benchmark plummeted from 39% in 1999 to 18% in 2007 and 12% in 2011 for mathematics, and from 24% to 18% and 11% in the respective years for science.

Standing (1992) found, from a broad survey of Malaysian manufacturing establishments, that unionized firms are more likely to engage in training and technological change. This is not surprising; firms are more likely to train workers who are likely to remain for the long term, which in turn derives significantly from workers being organized and having a greater stake in their workplace. Pressure from unions for higher wages and better benefits can also stimulate productivity gains. Malaysia's trends in unionization and utilization of contract labour, however, militate against such potential productivity- and wage-enhancement. Union density has continuously declined, from an already low starting point of 12% in 1980, to 7% in 2010 (Figure 1). The share of contract workers – a transient, precarious, largely foreign and migrant labour pool – grew through the 2000s. Furthermore, while the number of private sector unions has grown, their average size has dwindled in recent decades, constricting their bargaining power and effectiveness in representing workers' interests (Figure 2)

Wage growth has also been suppressed by massive inflows of foreign unskilled labour into manufacturing since 1990. Figure 3 and Tables 11 and 12 show massive official

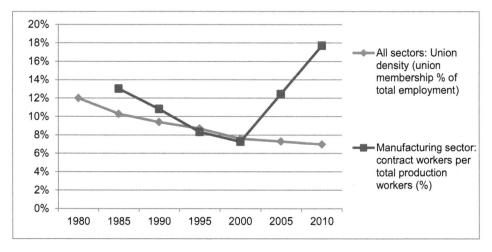

Figure 1. Union density and contract worker utilization in manufacturing, Malaysia, 1980−2010 (%). Sources: Authors' calculations from *Labour and Human Resource Statistics, Labour and Manpower Report*, MTUC (www.mtuc.org.my), *Yearbook of Statistics*, and *Annual Survey of Manufacturing Establishments*.

inflows of foreign workers over time and their source countries, based on immigration records. Truer estimates of the total number of foreign workers must include both documented and undocumented, which by the same token are harder to obtain. In 2012, the 6P biometric registration and amnesty programme registered 2.3 million foreign workers, or about 16% of the total employed population in Malaysia. However, it is believable – even mentioned by the government in May 2012 – that the figure is closer to four million, which staggeringly amounts to about a quarter of total employed. Notwithstanding the range of estimates, it is safe to say that the share is large and immensely impacts on the orientation and capacity of Malaysia's manufacturing sector and the economy at large.

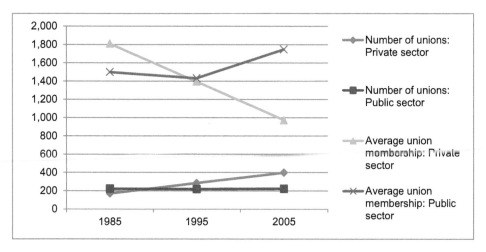

Figure 2. Number of unions and average union membership, Malaysia, 1985−2005.
Note: Public sector includes government departments and statutory bodies.
Sources: Authors' calculations from *Labour and Human Resource Statistics, Labour and Manpower Report*, MTUC (www.mtuc.org.my).

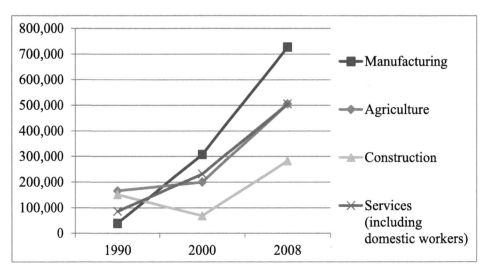

Figure 3. Foreign workers by sector, Malaysia, 1990–2008.
Source: Athukorala and Devadason 2012.

The educational profile of foreign and Malaysian workers evinces the overwhelming disparity in qualifications. In 2010, 60% of foreign workers had primary schooling or less, compared to 16% of Malaysian workers.[9]

Inflows of foreign labour have influenced productivity negatively in the sector. Since 1995, over 90% of foreign workers have been engaged in low-skilled jobs, compared to

Table 12. Foreign workers in manufacturing industries, 2007 and 2010.

Country 2007	Manufacturing 2007	Country 2010	Manufacturing 2010
Indonesia	206,780	Indonesia	198,643
Nepal	172,311	Bangladesh	170,332
Bangladesh	128,664	Nepal	135,764
Vietnam	104,948	Myanmar	92,135
Myanmar	29,906	Vietnam	68,433
India	28,446	India	13,866
Philippines	2858	Pakistan	2217
Thailand	793	Filipina	1915
Pakistan	3140	Cambodia	2353
Cambodia	2582	China	935
China	959	Thailand	893
Sri Lanka	1388	Sri Lanka	1382
Laos	16	Laos	16
Uzbekistan	1	Uzbekistan	0
		Others	2
Total	682,984		688,886

Source: Malaysian Bar Council; Malaysian Textiles Manufacturing Association.

less than 50% of Malaysian workers. Between 1985 and 2008, the number of foreign workers in low-skill production jobs increased by 81 times (from 5500 to 447,400). Over the same period, the number of foreigners increased 4 times at management and professional levels, 19 times among technical and supervisory staff and 21 times for clerical and general workers. In 2008, 96% of foreign workers in manufacturing were classified as unskilled, compared to 73% in 1985 (Athukorala and Devadason 2012).

The preference for low-skilled foreign labour corresponds with production characterized more by extracting perspiration rather than productivity. Comparison of weekly hours worked demonstrates the appeal and higher exploitability of foreign, especially low-skilled, workers, and confirms the entrenchment of a high exertion model in Malaysia. In 2009, foreign workers reported an overall average of 55 hours of work per week, compared to 46 hours for Malaysian workers – which clearly correlates with 48 hours as the legal definition of full-time employment.[10] The disparity is greater in those who are less skilled and more heavily worked. Among workers without formal education, 20% of foreigners worked more than 70 hours per week, compared to 54 hours for the corresponding fifth of longest working Malaysians.

An inertia and dependency has set in that is difficult to break, with abundant access to low-skilled foreign labour and scant market incentive to disrupt a still profitable system. Past experience, however, strongly suggests that promotion of productivity per hour yields higher development dividends, in view of the shift in industrialized economies towards fewer hours while maintaining positive deindustrialization. The International Labour Organisation (ILO)'s databases permit some comparison, based on GDP per hour. South Korea increased real GDP per hour (in 2005 dollars), from $4.7 in 1980 to $9.7 in 1990, before progressing further to $25.4 in 2010. In contrast, Malaysia registered an estimated GDP per hour of $5.3 in 2000, close to South Korea's of 1980, but only raised this to $7.1 in 2010. From 2000 to 2008, South Korea's average hours worked per week dropped from 49 to 44, while Malaysia's held at 49.[11]

The MTUC unsuccessfully tried to persuade the government to stop the inflow of foreign labour on the grounds that it depresses the wage structure and weakens incentives to attract Malaysian workers (Crinis 2008). By 2012, foreign workers exceeded national workers in a number of manufacturing industries. Foreign workers make up about 80% of the workforce in the clothing industry (Crinis 2012).

Foreign workers are subjected to levels of abuse ranging from wage deductions, injury and premature repatriation, and many injustices are overlooked because there are few labour inspectors (around 300) in a workforce of almost 14 million.[12] The burgeoning presence of foreign workers is inextricable from the chronic decline in union density in Malaysia, and an increasing utilization of labour contracting in the 2000s, as shown in Figure 3. These trajectories attenuate the capacity for stable employment and worker representation, which can contribute positively to upskilling and upgrading.

Most migrant workers are not organized in the electronic, clothing and textile industry due to government restrictions and initial union inaction towards short-term contract workers. First, the government limited the rights of workers to join unions in the export industries in the 1970s because of the risk of increasing labour costs and undermining international competitiveness. The union movement in Malaysia was unable to reach the large numbers of workers in the electronic industry because the government and employers preferred the Japanese model of in-house unions. While the MTUC continued to lobby the government to lift the ban on unions in the electronic industries, the US employers threatened to re-locate if the bans were lifted. After more than 30 years, workers were allowed to form regional unions in 2010.[13]

Second, the MTUC initially argued that migrants were a source of labour that under-mined unionized workers job security and their terms of employment.[14] It was not until 2008 that the MTUC sent a report to the ILO on the denial of Freedom of Association for migrant workers and worked towards making groups of migrant workers aware of their rights under national labour laws.[15] After this the MTUC started to lobby for contract workers as well as foreign workers and called for the government to assess labour market needs before issuing more work permits for overseas workers. Nonetheless employers continued to hire foreign workers because they were flexible, could work longer hours and could be repatriated when the contract ended. In more recent times, the MTUC has supported worker associations such as Gefont, a Nepalese Association helpline to reach foreign workers.

The MTUC also called on the government to at least set a minimum wage for the low-est paid workers (both nationals and foreign workers) to meet the cost of living which had increased over the 2000s due to increases in food, rents, petrol prices and water privatiza-tion.[16] But according to MTUC sources, the government listened to employers who argued that a minimum wage would reduce competition and FDI would move to another 'low-cost' location if a minimum wage was introduced.[17]

Not only have some employers preferred non-unionized foreign unskilled workers because of the attraction of low wages, they have also been able to bind foreign workers contractually over longer periods to reduce job hopping. The Human Resource Develop-ment Act of 1992, which was targeted at forcing firms to train national workers, became ineffective as companies, instead of providing training, resorted to hiring foreign workers. To make matters worse for labour, the government has confined the minimum wage legis-lation that was gazetted in parliament in 2012 to only national workers.

The Malaysian government eventually introduced minimum wages of MYR900 (USD291) for Peninsular Malaysia and MYR800 (USD259) for Sabah and Sarawak in Janu-ary, 2013. However, opposition from SMEs deferred its enforcement until the end of 2013.[18] For the larger companies who had to pay the minimum wage increase, the government allowed employers to deduct money from migrant wages to recover the expenses made for employing foreign workers. Despite the fact that the government stopped the practice of allowing employers to deduct the levy in 2009 after the Nike and Hytex incidents, it allowed employers to resume this practice (Crinis 2013). It appears that some workers were better off before introduction of the minimum wage legislation. Hence, the Minimum Wage Act offers little support for wage improvements in the manufacturing sector.

4.1. High-skilled labour outflows

In addition to the increase in unskilled migrant labour in Malaysia, skilled Malaysian workers have sought higher paying jobs outside Malaysia. Factors driving the brain drain are Malaysia's race-based affirmative action policies, as well as the fact that workers can make more money in Australia and Singapore. A recent estimate of Malaysia's Ministry of Human Resources indicates that there are 350,000 Malaysians working abroad, over half of which had tertiary education, and the Malaysian Employers Federation argues that there are 785,000 Malaysians working in overseas countries (Hugo 2011). Despite the government's array of programmes to lure professionals to Malaysia, few have returned (Roasa 2011).

Emigration from Malaysia is highly slanted towards ethnic Chinese, which accounted for more than two-thirds of emigrants to Australia (Hugo 2011, 156). The proportion of Chinese Malaysians was similar in both the 1986 and 2006 Australian censuses. An important start of the inflow of Malaysians to Australia is students' immigration (Hugo 2011, 155). The selective policy of privileging Malay students in entry to tertiary education institutions within Malaysia has been a factor in ethnic Chinese and Indian Malaysian students being disproportionately represented in the student outflow to Australia.

In fact, Australia's immigration policies have been particularly focused on skilled migration rather than unskilled migrants. This selectivity of migration is also reflected in the occupations which Malaysian migrants hold in Australia (Hugo 2011, 161). Malaysians have a higher level of labour force participation than the total Australian population (67.3% compared with 64.6%). In fact, 49.5% of employed Malaysians held skilled occupations, compared with only 28.7% of the total Australian workforce. There is a strong concentration in professional occupations which employ 4 out of every 10 Malaysian workers compared with 2 out of 10 in the total workforce. Emigration of Malaysians clearly represents a significant loss of human capital to Malaysia. As a result, Malaysian companies often face difficulty trying to find skilled workers and tend to bring in technically skilled labour to cater to higher levels of technology especially in the textile and electronic industries. These workers often earn higher wages than the Malaysian counterparts. In addition, there is little monitoring of the immigration of skilled workers and the introduction of technology; most companies are left to their own devices to upgrade and the managers of those companies often seek labour perspiration rather than investing in machinery and skilled labour.

The introduction of different forms of labour outsourcing also means that migrant workers are divided between those employed by contractors and sub-contractors. The latter do not receive the same benefits as former and are often undocumented. Workers arrested are held in detention until they are authorized by their Embassy to return to their country of origin. Some estimations show that there are around 60,000 migrants in detention depots across Malaysia (NST, 18 April 2014). The Home Ministry estimates that one detainee costs the government MYR35 per day, not including health costs (NST, 9 January 2014). The government blames the high number of 'illegals' on Malaysia's vast land and sea borders but critics also cite outsourcing companies, officials and employers as adding to the numbers of undocumented workers in Malaysia.

5. Conclusions

The evidence in this article shows that Malaysia is experiencing premature deindustrialization since the late 1990s. While it is typical for manufacturing's share in GDP to rise and fall as economies grow, Malaysia's experience can be classified negative as it is associated with the slowing down of productivity growth and export performance. Not only the trade performance of manufacturing in Malaysia has been falling, but manufacturing labour productivity has also slowed down.

Manufacturing's premature contraction has aggravated further real wage growth in the sector. Although the Malaysian government intervened – offering strong incentives and indirect subsidies to export-oriented industries, such as electric–electronics and textiles and clothing and protection, and direct subsidies to the import-substitution industries, such as steel and automobiles – the lack of human capital development and poor performance of meso-organizations has restricted technological upgrading in the sector. By the late 1990s, it became clear that government strategies to stimulate upgrading in the country had run out of steam as labour productivity growth in most manufacturing industries either contracted or slowed down. Mired in ethno-patronage politics and preoccupied with raising ethnic corporate ownership over upgrading technological capabilities, the incentive system in Malaysia lacked the mechanism to attract performers, as well as an appraisal system to transform the rents productively. Hence, the low industrialization road experienced by Malaysia got worse when Malaysia's labour productivity and trade competitiveness in a number of industries began to fall with real wages either slowing down or contracting since 2000.

While the successful industrializers, such as the United States, Germany, Japan, Korea and Taiwan, experienced a sustained rise in real wages even after deindustrialization set in, Malaysia's premature deindustrialization process has undermined its manufacturing sector's capacity to support a similar experience. Large imports of low-skilled labour have further aggravated the situation.

The Malaysian experience serves as a good example of promotional strategies lacking in the instruments to ensure industrial deepening of nascent economies. Liberal invitational strategies can engender the conditions to stimulate early manufacturing, but they are not sufficient to sustain rapid growth and structural change towards high value-added activities. Like most clientelist political alliances, ethno-patronage politics can be seriously rent dissipating as they compromise performance.

Acknowledgements

The Crinis research is part of a collaborative study funded by the Australian Research Council (ARC), 2007 to 2011.

Notes

1. The original argument on industrial policy can be traced to Smith (1776).
2. Countries such as Netherlands, Switzerland and New Zealand developed without much industrialization.
3. Rasiah (2011) offered conclusive evidence to show that the manufacturing sector have been facing negative deindustrialization since 2000.
4. Particularly from Cambodia (Rasiah 2009a).
5. A number of Malaysian firms have even relocated manufacturing in Cambodia to access developed markets (see Rasiah 2009a).
6. American multinationals initiated such efforts for their own self-expansion (Rasiah 1995a).
7. Malaysian Knitting Manufacturers Association, Statistic, 'Malaysian Exports of Textile and Apparel' http://www.mkma.org/ (accessed 7 November 2013).
8. Migration News 'Malaysia: New Migrants' March 1999, Volume 6, Number 3.
9. Authors' calculations from the 2010 *Labour Force Survey Report*.
10. Calculations from the 2009 (1st Quarter) Labour Force Survey.
11. Authors' calculations from online ILOSTAT and LABORSTA databases.
12. Bar Council (personal communication, Andrew, September 2013).
13. Malaysian Trades Union Congress, 'Regional Unions for Electronic Workers', Labour Bulletin, January 2010.
14. Malaysian Trades Union Congress, Reduce Dependency on Migrant Labour MOHR Should Play a More Central Role, 'Labour Bulletin', April 2007.
15. Malaysian Trades Union Congress, MTUC Report to ILO of Freedom of Association for Migrant Workers, 'Labour Bulletin', April 2008.
16. Malaysian Trades Union Congress, CPI Figures, Are They Reliable? 'Labour Bulletin', 25 June 2010.
17. Malaysian Trades Union Congress, Abdullah Badawi Sidelined and Ignored the Needs of 7 Million Workers, 'Labour Bulletin', March 2009.
18. Federal Government Gazette, Minimum Wage (Amendment), 28 May 2013. http://www.mkma.org/Notice%20Board/2013/MWOAmendment28Mei2013Statement.pdf (accessed 7 November 2013).

References

Abramovitz, M. 1956. "Resource and Output Trends in the United States Since the 1870." *American Economic Review* 46 (2): 5–23.

Adam, G. 1975. "Multinational Corporations and Worldwide Sourcing." In *International Firms and Modern Imperialism*, edited by H. Radice, 89–103. Harmondsworth: Penguin.

ADB. 2008. *Asian Development Outlook.* Manila: Asian Development Bank.

ADB. 2010. *Asian Development Outlook.* Manila: Asian Development Bank.

Alavi, R. 1996. *Industrialization in Malaysia.* London: Routledge.

Amsden, Alice. 1989. *Asia's Next Giant: South Korea and Late Industrialization.* New York: Oxford University Press.

Amsden, Alice, and Wan-Wen Chu. 2003. *Beyond Late Industrialization: Taiwan's Upgrading Policies.* Cambridge: MIT Press.

Ariff, K.M. 1991. *The Malaysian Economy: Pacific Connections.* Kuala Lumpur: Oxford University Press.

Athukorala, Premachandra, and Evelyn Devadason. 2012. "The Impact of Foreign Labor on Host Country Wages: The Experience of a Southern Host, Malaysia." *World Development* 40 (8): 1497—1510.

Best, M.H., and R. Rasiah. 2003. *Malaysian Electronics at the Crossroads.* Vienna: United Nations Industrial Development Organization.

Cardoso, F. Hernandez. 2001. *Charting a New Course: The Politics of Globalization and Social Transformation.* New York: Rowman & Little.

Crinis, Vicki. 2008. "Women Labour Activism and Unions." In *Women and Labour Organizing in Asia: Diversity, Autonomy and Activism*, edited by Kaye Broadbent and Michele Ford, 50–65. London: Routledge.

Crinis, Vicki. 2012. "Global Commodity Chains in Crisis: The Garment Industry in Malaysia, the Before, the Now and the Hereafter." *Institutions and Economies* 4 (3): 61–83.

Crinis, Vicki. 2013. "Vietnamese Clothing Workers in Malaysia: Global Production, Transnational Labour Migration and Social Reproduction." In *Women Workers and the Household in International Political Economy*, edited by Juanita Elias and Samanthi J. Gunawardana, 162–177. London: Palgrave.

Dermawan, Audrey. 2014. "Home Ministry Hopes to Make Deportation of Illegals Easier: Zahid." *New Straits Times*, April 18, 2014.

Devadason, Evelyn, and Chan Wai Meng. 2014. "Policies and Laws Regulating Migrant Workers in Malaysia: A Critical Appraisal." *Journal of Contemporary Asia* 44 (1): 19–35.

DOS. 2013. *Informal Sector Work Force Survey Report.* Putrajaya: Department of Statistics.

DOS. various issues. *Industrial Surveys.* Putrajaya: Department of Statistics.

Evans, Peter. 1997. *Embedded Autonomy: States and Industrialization.* Princeton, NJ: Princeton University Press.

Fransman, Martin. 1986. "International Competitiveness, Technical Change and the State: The Machine Tool Industries in Taiwan and Japan." *World Development* 14 (12): 1375–1396.

Gerschenkron, Alexander. 1962. *Economic Backwardness in Historical Perspective*. Cambridge, MA: Belknap Press.

Grunsven, Leo. 2006. *Theorizing Differential Dynamics of Mature MNC-Driven Export Manufacturing Complexes in Southeast Asia*. Utrecht: Royal Dutch Geographical Society.

Jenkins, R. 1987. *Transnational Corporations and Uneven Development*. London: Routledge.

Hamilton, Clive. 1983. "Capitalist Industrialization in East Asia's Four Little Tigers." *Journal of Contemporary Asia* 13 (1): 35−73.

Henderson, Jeffrey, and Richard Phillips. 2007. "Unintended Consequences: Social Policy, State Institutions and the 'Stalling' of the Malaysian Industrialization Project." *Economy and Society* 36 (1): 78−102.

Heng, Sim Bak. 2014. "RM 19m to House and Deport Illegals." *New Straits Times*, January 9, 2014.

Hugo, G. 2011. "Malaysian Migration to Australia." *Malaysian Journal of Economic Studies* 48 (2): 147−174.

Jomo, K.S., and Patricia Todd. 1994. *Trade Unions and the State in Peninsular Malaysia*. Kuala Lumpur: Oxford University Press.

Kalecki, Michal. 1976. *Essays on Developing Economies*. Hassocks: Harvester.

Khan, Mushtaq. 1989. "Clientelism, Corruption and the Capitalist State: A Study of Bangladesh and Korea." PhD thesis, Cambridge University.

Lee, Hwok-Aun. 2007. "Industrial Policy and Inter-ethnic Income Distribution in Malaysia: Industrial Development and Equity Ownership, 1975−1997." In *Industrial Policy in Malaysia*, edited by K.S. Jomo, 216−244. Singapore: Singapore University Press.

Malaysia. 1986. *Sixth Malaysia Plan, 1986−1990*. Kuala Lumpur: Government Printers.

Malaysia. 1991a. *Action Plan for Industrial Technology Development*. Kuala Lumpur: Ministry of Science, Technology and Environment.

Malaysia. 1991b. *Second Industrial Master Plan, 1991−1996*. Kuala Lumpur: Ministry of International Trade and Industry.

Malaysia. 1991c. *Sixth Malaysia Plan, 1991−1996*. Kuala Lumpur: Government Printers.

Malaysia. 1986−2011. *Industrial Surveys* (Various Issues). Kuala Lumpur: Department of Statistics.

Malaysia. 1996. *Eighth Malaysia Plan, 1996−2000*. Kuala Lumpur: Government Printers.

McFarlane, Bruce. 1981. *Australian Capitalism in Boom and Depression*. Kuala Lumpur: APCD.

Mohamad, Maznah. 1999, "The Management of Technology, and Women, in Two Electronic Firms in Malaysia." In *Positioning Women in Malaysia*, edited by Cecelia Ng, 95−166. London: Macmillan.

Ofreneo, Rene. 2008. "Arrested Development: Multinationals, TRIMs and the Philippines' Automotive Industry." *Asia Pacific Business Review* 14 (1): 65−84.

Osman, R.H., O. Pazim, and R. Rasiah. 2011. "Development of Agriculture." In *Malaysian Economy: Unfolding Growth and Social Change,* edited by R. Rasiah. Shah Alam: Oxford University Press.

Piore, M., and C. Sabel. 1984. *The Second Industrial Divide*. Cambridge, MA: MIT Press.

Pyke, F., and W. Sengenberger (eds.). 1992. *Industrial Districts and Local Economic Regeneration*. Geneva: International Labour Organization.

Rasiah, Rajah. 1995a. *Foreign Capital and Industrialization in Malaysia*. London: Macmillan.

Rasiah, Rajah. 1995b. "Labour and Industrialization in Malaysia." *Journal of Contemporary Asia* 25 (1): 73−92.

Rasiah, Rajah. 2009a. "Garment Manufacturing in Cambodia and Laos." *Journal of the Asia Pacific Economy* 14 (2): 150−161.

Rasiah, Rajah. 2009b. "Growth and Slowdown in the Electronics Industry in Southeast Asia." *Journal of the Asia Pacific Economy* 14 (2): 123−137.

Rasiah, Rajah. 2010. "Industrialization in the Second-Tier NIEs." In *The New Political Economy of Southeast Asia*, edited by R. Rasiah and D.J. Schmidt, 44−102. Cheltenham: Edward Elgar.

Rasiah, Rajah. 2011. "Is Malaysia Facing Negative Deindustrialization?". *Pacific Affairs* 84 (4): 715−736.

Roasa, Dustin. 2011. "Malaysia at Economic Crossroads as It Fights the Great Brain Drain." *The Guardian*. Accessed April 10. http://www.theguardian.com/world/2011/apr/21/malaysia-fights-brain-drain

Rodan, Garry. 1989. *The Political Economy of Singapore's Industrialization: National State and International Capital*. Basingstoke: Macmillan.

Rowthorn, Robert, and John Wells. 1987. *Deindustrialization and Foreign Trade.* Cambridge, UK: Cambridge University Press.

Smith, Adam. 1776. *An Inquiry into the Nature and Causes of the Wealth of the Nations.* London: Strahan & Cadell.

Standing, Guy. 1992. "Do Unions Impede or Accelerate Structural Adjustment? Industrial Versus Company Unions in an Industrialising Labour Market." *Cambridge Journal of Economics* 16: 327–354.

UNESCAP. 2009. *Statistical Yearbook for Asia and the Pacific.* Bangkok: United Nations Economic and Social Commission for Asia and the Pacific.

Veblen, T. 1915. *Imperial Germany and the Industrial Revolution.* New York, NY: Macmillan.

Wade, Robert. 1990. *Governing the Market: Economic Theory and the Role of Government in East Asian Industrialization.* Princeton, NJ: Princeton University Press.

World Bank. 1993. *The East Asian Miracle.* Washington, DC: World Bank and Oxford University Press.

WTO. 2009. *International Trade Statistics.* Geneva: World Trade Organization.

Young, Alyn. 1928. "Increasing Returns and Economic Progress." *The Economic Journal* 38 (152): 527–542.

Zeitlin, J. 1992. "Industrial Districts and Local Economic Regeneration: Overview and Comment." In *Industrial Districts and Local Economic Regeneration,* edited by F. Pyke and W. Sengenberger, 279–294. Geneva: International Labour Organization.

Globalization of industrialization and its impact on clothing workers in Myanmar

Myo Myo Myint, Rajah Rasiah and Kuppusamy Singaravelloo

Faculty of Economics and Administration, University of Malaya, Kuala Lumpur, Malaysia

This article examines the impact of foreign capital inflows and export expansion on employment and wages in the clothing industry in Myanmar. Although economic sanctions since 2003 by the United States affected foreign capital inflows, the evidence shows that clothing exports have steadily recovered since 2005. While wages in the industry are still low, they have improved over the period 2006–2012. Foreign firms showed higher mean wages, export-intensity and technological capabilities than national firms. The statistical results show that foreign equity has a positive impact on export-intensity and technological capabilities. Also, wages and employment were positively linked to export-intensity and technological capabilities. Hence, despite the exploitative nature of capitalist integration, the clothing industry shows that not only has wages and employment grown, the statistical results suggest that they will grow further.

1. Introduction

Although Hirschman (1958, 1970) had argued convincingly about the positive role export markets offered poor countries in their efforts to develop by providing the scale essential to stimulate backward linkages, it was not until the stark consequences of static import-substitution policies that had not clearly monitored technological upgrading target until the 1980s in countries, such as China, India, Indonesia and Brazil, that the debate on export-oriented industrialization was clear. On the one hand, Wallerstein (1979), Frobel, Heinrich, and Kreye (1980) and Henderson (1989) had argued that foreign-capital-led, export-oriented industrialization models merely created low-value-added jobs that were both transient and exploited on low wages in such economies. On the other hand, Warr (1987, 1989) and Jomo (1990) argued that export-processing zones simply created temporary jobs that were strongly subsidized through incentives by host governments. While developing economies openly invite foreign industrialists, they do contribute to the growth of local economy in the recipient country and provide opportunities required by them. However, the extent of transfer of technological know-how into local economy is still debated. Interestingly, the private sector contributed over 85% of Myanmar's GDP in 2005 (Than and Thein 2007).

Following the successful economic catch up of South Korea, Taiwan and Singapore, which became high-income economies by the 1980s, the debate shifted to whether these economies are unique cases that cannot be imitated either because of their conditions, or developed through geopolitical considerations, and if so, whether the changed liberalizing economic environment will allow similar policies (World Bank 1993). While we contend that economic development is a difficult process that requires governments to make tough decisions and governance capacity to affect it, governments seeking to achieve it must follow a routine that is highly disciplined with a strong focus on transforming economic activities from low- to high-value-added and target strong investment in public goods that generate national synergies. While this shall be the ultimate objective of the Myanmar government, we address a small objective in this article to see if increased flows of foreign direct investment (FDI) and exports have been accompanied by improvements in wages and working conditions in the clothing industry.

The rest of the article is organized as follows. Section 2 discusses the important theories that are important in locating the analysis. Section 3 presents the methodology and data. Section 4 examines FDI inflows. Section 5 analyses the impact of FDI on the labour process in the clothing industry. The article presents the conclusions in Section 6.

2. Globalization of Myanmar's clothing industry

The role of FDI in stimulating economic growth through employment creation and exports is now evident (see Rasiah 1995), though some still question its relevance. FDI inflows and exports, and with that learning from inflows of knowledge from abroad, have significantly globalized Myanmar's clothing industry since the late 1990s. While power, and oil and gas have been the prime destination of FDI inflows, though small, the share going to manufacturing has slowly grown from 6.9% in 2011 to 7.9% in 2013 (see Table 1). The number of manufacturing approved projects rose sharply from 64 in 2011 to 293 in 2013. However, the projects going to industrial estates have remained the same

Table 1.   Approved foreign direct investment and enterprises, Myanmar, 2011–2013

Sector	2011			2013 (November)		
	No.	US$ million amount	%	No.	US$ million amount	%
Power	5	18,873.7	46.69	7	19,284.4	43.71
Oil and gas	104	13,815.4	34.18	115	14,372.2	32.57
Manufacturing	64	2794.5	6.91	293	3480.03	7.88
Industrial estate	3	193.1	0.48	3	193.1	0.44
Mining	160	1753.9	4.34	68	2833.73	6.42
Livestock and fisheries	25	324.3	0.80	26	347.4	0.79
Other agriculture	7	173.1	0.43	12	191.9	0.44
Transport and communication	16	313.2	0.77	16	313.9	0.71
Hotel and tourism	45	1064.8	2.63	51	1797.9	4.07
Real estate	19	1056.4	2.61	22	1229.1	7.90
Other services	2	37.7	0.09	12	41.9	0.09
Construction	6	23.7	0.06	2	37.8	0.09
Total	456	40,424.07	100.0	627	44,123.6	100.0

Source: Directorate of Investment and Company Registration, Ministry of National Planning and Economic Development.

Table 2. Clothing firms, Myanmar, 2000–2011.

Year	State-owned enterprises	Foreign JV With MTI/ UMEH	With private	100% foreign firms	National private firms	Total
2000	1	–	5	18	248	272
2001	1	7	5	23	194	230
2002	0	6	4	27	180	217
2003	0	6	4	27	165	202
2004	0	4	4	22	112	142
2005	0	2	4	21	115	142
2006	0	2	4	21	126	153
2007	0	2	4	21	139	166
2008	0	2	2	21	145	170
2009	0	2	2	21	140	165
2010	0	2	2	21	145	170
2011	0	2	2	21	155	180

Source: MGMA (2012).

at 3 with the share of FDI inflows falling slightly from 0.48% to 0.44%, respectively, in 2011 and 2013. The number of investments has declined only in mining and construction sectors although their contributions have increased, especially in mining.

The clothing industry, which is labour-intensive and export-oriented, has experienced a decline in FDI inflows since the Americans imposed trade sanctions on Myanmar in 2003. Prior to the sanctions, half of the exports of garment industry products were to the United States and over 80% of the United States imports from Myanmar were clothes (Kudo 2005). Kudo (2005) further claimed that by 2004, about 25% of the garment factories involving a workforce of about 60,000 had closed. The anticipated lifting of sanctions in 2014 did not materialize so far, and hence, FDI inflows into the clothing sector have not increased significantly over the last few years. Nevertheless, the rising demand from other countries, including Japan, has helped sustain exports from the industry.

Nevertheless, since a decline from the peak of 2003, when there were 27 wholly foreign-owned firms, they have remained at 21 over period 2005–2011. National private firms fell from 248 firms in 2000 to its trough of 112 firms in 2004, before rising again to 155 firms in 2011 (see Table 2). Completely state-owned enterprises ceased to exist from 2002, while joint ventures with government-related agencies and private firms remained at two firms each in 2011. Overall, the number of wholly foreign-owned and joint-venture firms remained stagnant between 2008 and 2011. With the upward turnaround in the number of local private firms beginning 2009, the total number of clothing firms in 2011 registered the highest since 2004. The composition of firms is still dependent on national private firms more than those by FDI.

3. Theoretical considerations

The literature on FDI has long shifted from a focus on investment and employment creation to include spillover effects (including technology). On the one hand, while there is now some evidence of spillovers and technological rooting at host sites in developing economies (Rasiah 2004), the maquiladoras of Mexico have painted a negative dent on such accounts (Gibbs 2004). On the other hand, some argue that the global division of labour in the clothing industry has undergone considerable transformation, though uneven, which offered the potentials for technological upgrading (Rasiah and Myint 2013). The focus in this review is on the implications of FDI inflows on labour markets in poor economies.

Frobel, Heinrich, and Kreye (1980) had postulated that a new international division of labour had evolved with the poor countries becoming the new global 'sweatshops' for the rich countries through the spread of tax- and union-free export-processing zones that hire cheap unorganized labour. This argument rested on the view that capital seeking to extend valorization relocated operations from the developed economies to low-cost poor economies. This division of labour was argued to have facilitated production specializations in which the rich countries exported goods produced by high-skilled labour, and knowledge and capital-intensive production techniques, while the poor economies exported goods produced by low-skilled labour.

To Frobel, Heinrich, and Kreye (1980), the new international division of labour was conditioned by its drivers in the rich countries, while the poor countries were merely absorbed into the division of labour. The clothing industry was considered to have experienced such a fate in the 1970s–1980s, as the multi-fibre arrangement (MFA) quotas were partly used by the rich countries to promote investments in non-Communist countries and friendly allies, which enjoyed a fairly good basic infrastructure and political stability. As the advantages of low-cost labour evaporated from the newly industrialized countries (NICs) of East Asia (i.e. South Korea, Taiwan, Hong Kong and Singapore) and the second-tier industrializing economies of Malaysia and Thailand, a further differentiation of the division of labour in the clothing industry began to take shape since the 1990s. The expiration of the MFA in 2004 and the introduction of preferential access clause to the least developed countries (LDCs) that met certain conditions (e.g. International Labour Organization [ILO] covenants in Cambodia) opened the way for a relocation of clothing manufacturing to the LDCs, such as Bangladesh, Cambodia, Laos and Myanmar (UNCTAD 2005; Rasiah 2009).

At the same time, the theorizing of the changing global division of labour took on a new dimension since the 1990s as Gereffi (1994, 2003) advanced the concepts of 'producer-driven commodity chains'[1] and buyer driven commodity chains.[2] Gereffi (2003) and Rasiah (2012) also recognized the emergence of 'triangle manufacturing' in which contract firms from South Korea, Hong Kong, Taiwan, China, Singapore and Malaysia organize work in different countries (e.g. Bangladesh, Cambodia, Indonesia, Philippines and Vietnam) to meet retail buyers demand in the developed countries. These contract manufacturers not only took advantage of low-wage costs offered by the LDC sites but also the preferential access quotas these countries enjoyed in major markets. By outsourcing production to multiple suppliers, the contractors also placed the risk of losing orders onto the suppliers (Barrientos 2008).

Indeed, contract firms from the newly industrialized economies (NIEs) and Malaysia have increasingly connected into clothing value chains to organize production, including R & D related to production to deliver buyers' orders from a wide range of locations taking account of relative wage costs, transport costs and access to major markets, including Myanmar. This development has offered poor locations the opportunity to connect and participate in clothing value chains.

However, while further decentralization and relocation of clothing manufacturing into locations little governed by effective labour regulations have offered employment opportunities to thousands of workers, it has also aggravated further asymmetries between labour and management in the industry. Hence, trade union lobby groups in the developed countries have increasingly flagged the development as targeted at the exploitation of cheap labour, including the hiring of transient female and child labour. Mounting criticisms against such Race to the Bottom practices led to calls for a 'social clause,' which led several trans-national corporations (TNCs) to adopt voluntary 'Codes of Conduct' (CoC) to escape threats of consumer and labour boycotts in their home markets (Barrientos and Smith 2007; Barrientos 2008). However, because significant production has moved to poorly governed locations, it is not uncommon for many of the TNCs and their suppliers to escape such social audits.

Nevertheless, taking the cue from Rasiah, McFarlane, and Kuruvilla (2014), and especially the early works of Beresford (1989) and Beresford and Dang (2000) on Vietnam, we assume that employment is the first step towards appropriating benefits in the capitalist system, and that exploitation rather than super-exploitation is a necessary condition to reward workers for the sale of their labour power (Marx 1957; Luxembourg 2003). Also, as argued by Marx (1967) and Brenner (1977), the fundamental dynamism of industrial capitalism is that valorization is primarily drawn from relative rather than absolute surplus value. While Marx's articulation of these concepts was abstract as it is impossible to measure the organic composition of capital in precise terms, we simply focus here on the impact of foreign equity on wages and employment in the clothing industry in Myanmar. Also, while Myanmar's integration into the capitalist clothing production system would reflect an extension of absolute surplus appropriation by means for low-wage labour, once integrated, in as much as it would be exploitative, the material conditions of workers are likely to improve if capital continues to invest and reinvest once relative surplus value appropriation sets it. And as argued by Hirschman (1970), national governments have a strong role to ensure that the conditions of accumulation quickens a shift from absolute to relative surplus value appropriation in the industry. Hence, in addition to employment, we track changes in wages and working conditions against inflows of FDI into the clothing industry in Myanmar.

However, while critics are right in the sense that working conditions in the LDCs are inferior to those in more developed economies, and often violate the principles contained in the CoC, few studies have actually examined if FDI inflows into particular industries have been accompanied gradually with improvements in these conditions – including wages, skills and autonomy enjoyed by subsidiaries in the global value chain. Exceptions to such studies on Myanmar include Rasiah and Myint (2013). Hence, we examine in this article if inflows of FDI into clothing manufacturing have resulted in improvements to the labour process in the industry in Myanmar.

4. Methodology and data

In the absence of detailed information on FDI inflows by firms in the clothing industry, we use an analytic framework that interpretively analyses the link between FDI inflows and the unfolding labour processes in the clothing industry. Nevertheless, the data available are adequate to make the link between capital inflows and their consequences on the labour process in Myanmar. Indeed, it is the connectivity offered through linking with global value chains – both the subcontract firms from abroad and national firms – that has facilitated employment generation and exports from the industry in Myanmar.

We rely on a meta-physical methodology that uses a survey data collected in 2012. We obtained 72 observations out of the 100 sets of questionnaires distributed through the

Table 3.   Breakdown of sample by ownership and size, clothing firms, Myanmar, 2011

	Employment size			
	<500	≥500	Total	% population
National	22	29	51	32.7
Foreign*	12	9	21	87.5
Total	34	38	72	40.0
% population	23.9	100.0	40.0	

Note: *Foreign equity of 50% or more.
Source: Compiled from Authors' survey (2012).

Myanmar Garment Manufacturing Association (MGMA). A sampling frame on the basis of ownership and employment size was used. We ensured that all key questions were answered through follow-up interviews.

The sample data collected for this article are shown in Table 3. We sought data of 100 firms on the basis of ownership and data from the MGMA. We finally obtained 72 firm responses that answered all the critical questions used in this article. The responses exceeded the minimum allowable response rate of 67.5%, and hence, the missing values were just excluded.

The sample comprised 32.7% of the national firms and 87.5% of the foreign firms in the population. By employment size, the sample comprised 23.9% of firms with workforce of less than 500, and 100% of firms with employment of 500 and more. The workforce size category was chosen on the basis of advice given by the MGMA officials who distinguished high volume producers with steady export market orders from the other firms.

The key variables used in the multivariate analysis were measured as follows:

Foreign ownership (FO) = foreign equity/total equity.
Wages = total payroll of non-management workers/workers in US dollars.
Employment = total workforce in actual numbers
Export intensity = exports/total output

In addition, we estimated technological capability (TC) by normalizing and training expenditure in payroll (embodied in labour), the deployment of cutting edge processes (automation, time-motion studies and order lead time embodied in processes) and adaptive engineering expenditure in sales (embodied in machinery, production layouts and products). The normalization was undertaken using the usual formula:

$$(X_i - X_{min}) = (X_{max} - X_{min})$$

where X_i refers to the observation examined, X_{min} the minimum value of the variable and X_{max} the maximum value of the variable. The three proxies were then added to constitute TC. The purpose of estimating TC was to examine how technical change influenced employment and wage growth.

$$\text{Hence, TC} = (\text{TE}, \text{PT}, \text{AE})$$

where TE, PT and AE refers to training expenditure in payroll, use of automation, time-motion studies and actual lead time, and expenditure incurred in the adaptation of machinery and product enhancement in sales, respectively.

The following equations were run:

$$X/Y = \alpha + \beta_1 A + \beta_2 FO + \beta_3 TC + \beta_4 W + \beta_5 E + \mu \tag{1}$$

$$TC = \alpha + \beta_1 A + \beta_2 FO + \beta_3 W + \beta_4 E + \mu \tag{2}$$

where A, FO, W and E refer to age (in years), foreign ownership, wages and employment. Because of collinearity problems between FO, TC, wages and employment, separate regressions were estimated. For foreign equity to demonstrate a positive impact on exports and technological capabilities, the sign for FO must be positive. Also, for export intensity and technological capability to generate positive effect on wages and employment, W and E shall have positive signs. Age was included as a control variable.

5. Impact on labour market variables

In this section, we analyse the relative influence of foreign equity on employment and wages, and the relationship between these variables and export intensity and technological capabilities, respectively, using the 72 firm survey. Because the data collected are cross-sectional for the year 2011, we do not generate any causal relationships. Nevertheless, the results are indicative of the influence of foreign equity on wages, employment, export intensity and technological capabilities.

The descriptive statistics of the data collected is presented in Table 3. We chose to drop the answers on skills as there was a wide inconsistency in reporting as in some firms skilled workers carried the requisite qualifications while they did not in other firms. This distinction became all the more difficult to interpret as we found during the interviews several skilled sewers who could neither speak English nor possessed any skill certificates.

5.1. Univariate analysis

The minimum, mean and maximum firm-based wages of non-management staff in 2011 were US$29.2, US$57.1 and US$90.0 monthly, respectively (see Table 4). The minimum, mean and maximum firm-level employment were 125,674 and 2800, respectively. The minimum, mean and maximum firm-based export intensities were 20%, 75.4% and 100%, respectively. Since the TC variable was normalized, it is a relative measure of embodied technology among the 72 clothing firms. Since the firm at the technology frontier will have a maximum possible score of 3 owing to the three proxies (one each) used,

Table 4. Descriptive statistics, clothing firms, Myanmar, 2011

	Monthly wages			Employment			X/Y			TC		
	N	F	O	N	F	O	N	F	O	N	F	O
SD	7.8	9.9	8.5	551	516.2	554.9	26.7	14.7	25.9	0.43	0.44	0.44
Mean	56.5	50.4	57.1	744	515	671	68.7	90.5	75.4	1.62	1.75	1.66
Max	70.0	90.0	90.0	2800	2600	2800	100	100	100	2.78	2.76	2.78
Min	29.2	50.0	29.2	150	125	125	20	50	20	0.77	1.19	0.77

Note: N, F and O refer to national, foreign and overall, respectively.
Source: Computed from Author survey (2012).

the mean of 1.7 denotes being to the simple mean of 1.5. However, the range between the firms is high as the minimum and maximum values were 0.8 and 2.8, respectively.

By ownership, the mean wages, X/Y and TC of foreign firms were higher than the national firms. Foreign firms also paid the highest wage while a national firm paid the lowest wage in 2011. While the minimum X/Y of foreign firms was 50%, it was 20% among national firms. A national firm showed the highest TC, and another showed the lowest TC. National firms enjoyed the highest mean employment and enjoyed being the largest employer. Overall, foreign firms show higher means among the critical variables of wages, X/Y and TC suggesting that exposure to foreign capital in the clothing industry has generated positive benefits for Myanmar.

Also, the mean wages of clothing workers in 2011 were also significantly higher than the mean wages reported for similar workers in Myanmar over the years 2006 and 2010 suggesting that the material conditions of the workers have improved over time (see Rasiah 2009; Rasiah and Myint 2013). In addition, while foreign firms offered higher wages and technological capabilities than national firms, the mean differences were not very high. It appears that national firms have caught up with the practices of foreign firms, which can only be argued to be a consequence of demonstration effect and competing in export markets.

5.2. Multivariate analysis

The statistical results from the survey produced interesting results. The results passed the model fit (F-stats and χ^2-stats) tests for interpretation (Table 5).

Not only are the key variables highly significant and show the right signs, the constants are either insignificant or are only significant at the 10% level. The latter suggest the absence of endogeneity problems with the results. First, the foreign capital has not only been strongly correlated with export intensity and technological capabilities, the coefficients are positive and highly significant. Clearly, then foreign capital has been strongly influential in expanding clothing exports from Myanmar. Technological capabilities positively influence clothing exports (see Table 5). Also, the rising foreign capital also raises technological capabilities.

Second, wages are positively correlated with both export intensities and technological capabilities. Hence, not only has one pillar of globalization, i.e. exports, improves wages, rising wages also has a positive impact on technological capabilities. In other words, firms hire higher paid workers to participate in export markets, and to introduce higher technological capabilities.

Third, clothing employment rises with export intensities and technological capabilities. Whilst the first finding confirms Hirschman's (1958, 1970) argument that export markets provide the scale for the expansion of employment, the second finding shows that technological capabilities does not reduce employment in clothing firms in Myanmar.

Overall, while national capital has been the prime employment generator, foreign capital shows higher mean wages, export intensity and technological capabilities generally confirming the mean differences found in the descriptive analysis. National firms enjoy a higher mean in only employment. Also, FO is positively and strongly correlated with X/Y and TC, suggesting that the participation of foreign equity generates positive impact on export orientation and technological capabilities. In addition, both wages and employment are positively correlated with export intensity and technological capabilities.

Table 5. X/Y, TC and CO, clothing firms, Myanmar, 2011

	OLS: X/Y			Tobit: TC		
A	0. 03 (1.28)	0.193 (1.904)*	0.069 (0.739)	0.022 (0.198)	0.059 (0.415)	−0.042 (−0.262)
FO	0.412 (6.9?)***			0.453 (5.157)***		
TC	0.185 (2.543)**					
W		0.497 (4.567)***			0.555 (3.012)***	
E			0.223 (6.437)***			0.293 (4.655)***
C	0.328 (1.5?)	−0.385 (−1.832)*	−0.812 (−1.867)*	0.304 (1.824)*	−0.710 (−1.046)	−0.283 (−0.700)
N	72	72	72	72	72	72
R^2	0.149	0.301	0.423			
F-stats	26.122*	13.711***	23.987***			
χ^2-stats				−27.558***	−34.635***	−27.721***

Note: Figures in parentheses refer to 't' and 'z' statistics; ***, **, and * refer to statistical significance at 1%, 5% and 10%, respectively.
Source: Computed from Authors' survey (2012).

6. Conclusions

Consistent with the orientation of Beresford's (1989) work, this article followed the argument advanced by Marx (1967), Luxembourg (2003) and Brenner (1977) that exploitation is an integral component of capitalist relations and that relative surplus appropriation is the engine of industrial capitalism. While the analysis avoided the abstractions that Marx, Luxembourg and Brenner had used so as to deal with real data, it suggests that the results are consistent with the argument they had advanced, that capitalist integration through the inflow of foreign equity and link with export markets will be destructive initially but shall eventually offer the opportunity for local accumulation. While the cross-sectional data did not allow a direct assessment on the changes to the material conditions of workers, the comparison with evidence from past works shows significant improvement in mean wages.

While national capital has been the prime employment generator, foreign capital shows higher mean wages, export intensity and technological capabilities. National firms enjoy a higher mean in only employment. Also, FO is positively and strongly correlated with X/Y and TC, suggesting that the participation of foreign equity generates positive impact on export orientation and technological capabilities. In addition, both wages and employment are positively correlated with export intensity and technological capabilities. In other words, increased integration into global capitalist markets, however exploitative they may be, has positive outcomes on wages and technological capabilities. Also, increasing technological capabilities also suggest positive improvements in wages.

However, the evidence amassed did not allow for an assessment of other working conditions, role of unions and skills. While the highest incidence of unionization recorded in Myanmar by industry was reported in the clothing industry, we did not have evidence on their effectiveness. Similarly, the significant role of firms' participation in training was reported in our survey suggesting that skills have improved, but we did not have reliable data to draw conclusions on this. Hence, future research should deal with these issues.

Acknowledgements

We are grateful to constructive comments from two referees. The errors that remain are ours.

Notes

1. In such chains, TNCs organize global production chains that are shaped by the capital- and technology-intensive nature of their products, such as automobiles (Gereffi 2003).
2. In such chains TNCs and distributors coordinate production through decentralized production chains, such as clothing (Gereffi 2003).

References

Barrientos, S. 2008. "Contract Labour: The 'Achilles Heel' of Corporate Codes in Commercial Value Chains." *Development and Change* 39 (6): 977–990.

Barrientos, S., and S. Smith. 2007. "Do Workers Benefit from Ethical Trade? Assessing Codes of Labour Practice in Global Production Systems." *Third World Quarterly* 28 (4): 713–729.

Beresford, M. 1989. *National Unification and Economic Development in Vietnam*. New York: St. Martin's Press.

Beresford, M., and P. Dang. 2000. *Economic Transition in Vietnam*. Cheltenham: Edward Elgar.

Brenner, R. 1977. "The Origins of Capitalist Development: A Critique of Neo-Smithian Marxism." *New Left Review* 104: 25–92.

Frobel, F., J. Heinrich, and O. Kreye. 1980. *The New International Division of Labour: Structural Unemployment in Industrialized Countries and Industrialization in Developing Countries*. Cambridge: Cambridge University Press.

Gereffi, G. 1994. "The Organization of Buyer-Driven Global Commodity Chains: How US Retailers Shape Overseas Production Networks." In *Commodity Chains and Global Capitalism*, edited by G. Gereffi and Korzeniewicz, 95–122. Westport, CT: Praeger.

Gereffi, G. 2003. "The International Competitiveness of the Asian Economies in the Global Apparel Industry." *International Journal of Business and Society* 4 (2): 71–110.

Gibbs, J. 2004. "The Exploitation of Women in Mexico's Maquiladoras" *Honors College Capstone Experience/Thesis Projects. Paper 172*. Accessed September 27, 2014. http://digitalcommons. wku.edu/stu_hon_theses/172.

Henderson, J. 1989. *Globalisation of High Technology Production*. London: Routledge.

Hirschman, A.O. 1958. *The Strategy of Economic Development*. New Haven, CT: Yale University Press.

Hirschman, A.O. 1970. *Exit, Voice and Loyalty*. Cambridge: Harvard University Press.

Jomo, K.S. 1990. *Growth and Structural Change in the Malaysian Economy*. Basingstoke: Macmillan.

Kudo, T. 2005. "The Impact of United States Sanctions on the Myanmar Garment Industry." *Discussion Paper No. 42*. Chiba: Institute of Developing Economies.

Luxembourg, R. 2003. *The Accumulation of Capital*. Translated by A. Scharzschild, and introduced by T. Kowalik. London: Routledge

Marx, K. 1957. *The Process of Production of Capital*. Vol. I. Moscow: Progress Publishers.

Marx, K. 1967. *The Process of Circulation of Capital*. Vol. II. Moscow: Progress Publishers.

MGMA (Myanmar Garment Manufacturing Association). 2012. *Unpublished Clothing Data*. Yangon: Myanmar Garment Manufacturing Association.

Rasiah, R. 1995. *Foreign Capital and Industrialization in Malaysia*. Basingstoke: Macmillan.

Rasiah, R. 2004. *Foreign Firms, Technological Capabilities and Economic Performance: Evidence from Africa, Asia and Latin America*. Cheltenham: Edward Elgar.

Rasiah, R. 2009. "Can Garment Exports from Cambodia, Laos and Myanmar Be Sustained?" *Journal of Contemporary Asia* 39 (4): 619–637.

Rasiah, R. 2012. "Beyond the Multi-Fibre Agreement: How are Workers in East Asia Faring?" *Institutions and Economies* 4 (3): 1–20.

Rasiah, R., B. McFarlane, and S. Kuruvilla. 2014. "Globalization, Industrialization and Labour Markets." *Journal of the Asia Pacific Economy* 20 (1): 2–13.

Rasiah, R., and M.M. Myint. 2013. "Ownership, Technological Capabilities and Exports of Garment Firms in Myanmar." *Technological and Economic Development of Economy* 19: S22–S42.

Than, M., and M. Thein. 2007. "Transitional Economy of Myanmar: Present Status, Developmental Divide, and Future Prospects." *ASEAN Economic Bulletin* 24 (1): 98–118.

UNCTAD. 1989. *TNCs and the Removal of Textiles and Clothing Quotas*. Geneva: UNCTAD.

Wallerstein, I. 1979. *The Capitalist World-Economy*. Cambridge: Cambridge University Press.

Warr, P. 1987. "Export Promotion via Industrial Enclaves: The Philippines' Bataan Export Processing Zone." *Journal of Development Studies* 23 (2): 220–241.

Warr, P. 1989. "Export Processing Zones: Economics of Enclave Manufacturing." *The World Bank Research Observer* 4 (1): 65–88.

World Bank. 1993. *The East Asian Miracle*. Washington DC: World Bank and Oxford University Press.

Growth and employment in de-industrializing Philippines

Rene E. Ofreneo

School of Labor and Industrial Relations, University of the Philippines Diliman, Quezon City, Philippines

The Philippines was rated in the early 1960s by the World Bank as second only to Japan in Asia's industrialization race. In the 1970s–1990s, the Philippines pursued export-oriented industrialization (EOI). However, the Philippines' industrial drive failed to take off and we trace this failure to the narrow program of EOI that Philippines pursued with the support of international financial institutions, which was myopic because it simply focused on how to open up the economy without a focus on industrial upgrading. There were no value-adding linkages with the domestic economy, home-grown export champions, program for upgrading and infrastructure and support institutions for national producers. The failure is due to the absence of systemic governance and policy coherence. Nonetheless, the Philippines has posted positive growth rates in recent decades, due largely to remittances of Filipino migrant but has helped transform the country into a service-sector-led economy without passing through industrial transformation.

1. Introduction

The Philippines is an archipelago buffeted regularly by at least 20 or more typhoons a year. Some are deadly and devastating. In the case of Yolanda (international code name: 'Haiyan'), a super-typhoon that hit the country in November 2013, the government reported 8000 dead, 2000 missing, millions displaced and damages to infrastructures costing around US$13 billion (NEDA 2013).

This paper, however, is about a different typhoon – one that refuses to go and one that has failed to ease mass unemployment and mass poverty in the Philippines through the decades. This is the failure of the economy to take off, industrially. Unlike its East Asian neighbors, the Philippine industrial sector has been stagnant and even shrinking while its agricultural sector keeps declining. As a result, the Philippines has become a service sector-led economy without passing through an industrial transformation.

The Asian Development Bank (ADB) is not happy with this strange structural outcome. In 2012, it released the study of Norio Usui, *Taking the Right Road to Inclusive Growth: Industrial Upgrading and Diversification in the Philippines*, which posited that Philippine growth, sustained by the remittances of overseas Filipino workers (OFWs) and earnings from the offshored call center-business process outsourcing (CC-BPO) services, is simply unsustainable sans a solid industrial base. The Usui book was given wide publicity by the Bank and was formally presented to government agencies such as the National Economic and Development Authority (NEDA), Department of Trade and Industry (DTI) and the Department of Labor and Employment (DOLE). The Usui book

Table 1. Sectoral composition of economy, Philippines, 1980 and 2009 (%).

Sector	1980	2009
Output share		
Agriculture	25.1	13.1
Industry	38.8	31.7
Manufacturing	25.7	21.3
Services	34.3	55.2
Employment share		
Agriculture	51.8	35.2
Industry	15.4	14.5
Manufacturing	10.8	8.9
Services	32.8	50.3

Source: Extracted from Table 2-1 of Norio Usui, ADB, 2012.

also added pressure to NEDA and DTI to speed up the program of crafting a "road map" to revive and strengthen Philippine manufacturing.[1]

The ADB's lament on 'stagnant industrialization' in the Philippines is not new, especially to critics of the industrialization policies pursued by the government in the last four decades. Further, they find the ADB study somewhat incomplete because the collapse of the agricultural sector was hardly discussed. A 2004 study by Focus on the Global South (Bello 2004) and a 2006 study by the Fair Trade Alliance (*Nationalist Development Agenda* 2006) pointed out that Philippine *de-industrialization* in the last four decades has been accompanied by *de-agricultural development*, both of which have been reaffirmed by the ADB-cited statistics on the sectoral distribution of output and employment (see Table 1).

The country, a net agricultural exporting country in the nineteenth and twentieth centuries, has become a net agricultural importing country since 1995, the first year of the Philippine membership in the World Trade Organization (WTO). It has, in fact, become the world's biggest importer of rice (Arceo-Dumlao 2008). While the country has been a successful global producer of banana and pineapple, it has failed to attain self-sufficiency in staple crops (rice and corn), fishery, vegetables and meat products; it has also failed to stabilize the market for its traditional export crops (coconut, sugar, tobacco and rubber).

On industrialization, Philippine manufacturing was hailed in the early 1960s by the World Bank as Asia's most dynamic, second only to Japan (Ofreneo 1993). However, the country's industrial dynamism disappeared during the last four decades (Usui 2012; Bello 2004; Fair Trade Alliance 2006). These decades happen to be the decades of 'structural adjustment program' (SAP) promoted by the economic technocracy in the name of EOI and national competitiveness.

This paper is organized around two questions:

- Why has the SAP-led EOI program failed in the Philippines while its Asian neighbors have successfully embarked on an export-led industrialization?
- What has been the impact or consequences of this industrial failure on the labor market, especially on the most vulnerable among the Filipino working population?

This paper tries to answer the first question by examining key policy differences in the industrialization drive of the Asian NICs vis-a-vis the Philippines. For the second question, the author tried to decompose the structure of the labor force based on the statistical data provided by the National Statistics Office (NSO) and DOLE's Bureau of Labor and Employment Statistics (BLES).

2. Switch from ISI to EOI

After acquiring political independence from the United States in 1946, the Philippines pursued industrialization as a national economic goal by instituting a program of import-substituting industrialization (ISI) in the early 1950s. The ISI measures consisted mainly of 'controls' – a ban on imported finished products and a strict rationing of foreign exchange earnings (mainly US dollars). These measures were in response to a serious balance-of-payments crisis during the early post-World War II rehabilitation period, 1946–1949. However, the government, through the leadership of Central Bank Governor Miguel Cuaderno, used the controls to promote 'new and necessary industries' at home (Ofreneo 1993; Constantino and Constantino 1978). The growth of these ISI industries was rapid. By the early 1960s, the Philippines, as pointed out, was hailed by the World Bank as second to Japan in Asia in the industrialization process, ahead of the Asian NICs. A World Bank (1962) report summed up the changes in the 1950s as follows:

> The major structural change since the war has been the growth of domestic manufacturing. Organized manufacturing (5 workers and over), which was limited to the processing of agricultural products before the war, expanded more than 10% per year during the 1950's. By 1960, it had become a significant segment of the economy, accounting for 12.7% of the net domestic product that year. A vigorous entrepreneurial class has emerged and the nucleus of a skilled labor force has been formed.

In the 1960s, the 'controls' were lifted, on the pressure of the International Monetary Fund (IMF) on the then President Diosdado Macapagal. However, the ISI regime remained firmly in place when the latter replaced the protection measures with new ones: high tariff walls and a long list of restricted imports (Ofreneo 1993; Constantino and Constantino 1978). Still, positive and substantial growth was somehow sustained by the economy in the 1960s and 1970s (see Table 2), although at a lower rate compared to the initial ISI period of the 1950s.

In 1972, the then President Ferdinand Marcos declared martial law to consolidate and centralize political power unto himself. At the same time, he instituted a new economic program dubbed as the labor-intensive export-oriented (LIEO) industrial strategy

Table 2. Average annual GDP growth by sectors, Philippines, 1951–2010 (%).

	1951–1960	1961–1970	1971–1980	1981–1990	1991–2000	2001–2010
GROSS DOMESTIC PRODUCT	6.2	4.8	5.7	1.7	3.0	4.7
Agriculture	4.8	4.2	3.9	1.1	1.8	3.0
Industry, of w/c	7.1	5.5	7.6	0.3	3.0	4.2
Manufacturing	9.4	5.7	5.9	0.9	2.5	4.1
Services	6.7	4.7	5.2	3.3	3.6	5.8

Source: NSO and BLES.

spearheaded by the then newly created NEDA. The justifications for the switch from the old ISI to the new EOI, initially baptized as LIEO, were two-fold: one, the ISI program was unable to mop up unemployment due to limited expansion of ISI industries, and two, the ISI program was unable to cure the recurring BOP problem because the country was largely import-dependent (on oil, machinery, industrial raw materials, etc.) and its export base was limited, confined to traditional export crops (sugar, coconut) and minerals consisting mainly of gold and copper (Ranis Mission Report 1974; Ofreneo 1993).

In 1973, the United Nations Development Programme (UNDP) and the International Labor Office (ILO), on the request of NEDA, organized an economic mission to inquire on the employment implications of the LIEO shift. The UNDP-ILO Mission Report, more popularly known then as the 'Ranis Mission Report' because it was headed by Gustav Ranis of the Yale Growth Center, criticized heavily the ISI policy regime for its weaknesses, namely unsustainable economic development, weak employment generation and unequal economic distribution (Ranis 1974). The Report proceeded to justify the need for an industrial shift towards the export market and the 'mobilization' of the rural sector through agricultural modernization. The latter essentially meant the propagation of the 'Green Revolution' or high-yielding rice technology developed by the International Rice Research Institute based in the Philippines. The Ranis Report described the post-war Philippine economy as 'dualistic', consisting of a small 'organized sector' and a large 'unorganized' sector. In a way, the Ranis Report amplified further the criticisms raised earlier by the study of Hicks and McNicoll (1971) – the dualism in a 'labor-surplus' economy and the poor employment generation under the 'excessive ISI' policy regime.

To make the EOI/LIEO program work, the government and the World Bank launched 'development financing', a borrowing program in support of infrastructure development, especially infrastructures for EOI/LIEO enterprises such as the establishment of export processing zones (EPZs) and modernization of ports and airports. These EPZs initially attracted investors engaged in the assembly and exportation of labor-intensive products such as garments, footwear, toys and fashion accessories; in the late 1970s, these EPZs became attractive destination for electronics investors–assemblers (Ofreneo 1993).

However, the World Bank was unhappy with the limited growth of the EOI industries in the 1970s. It nudged the government to deepen the EOI program by pushing for a series of 'structural adjustment loans' (SALs) in support of an SAP. The SAP consisted of policy measures aimed at the deeper and wider liberalization of the economy through the lowering of tariffs, the elimination of trade restrictions, the liberalization of the investment regime, the deregulation of major economic sectors (finance, industry, services and agriculture), and the privatization of government corporations, services and assets (Fair Trade Alliance 2006).

In 1986, a 'People Power' revolt ousted the Marcos dictatorship and ushered in a new government headed by President Corazon C. Aquino. However, the change in political governance did not alter the directions of economic governance. The implementation of the three intertwining SAP programs of privatization, deregulation and trade/investment liberation was even intensified (Fair Trade Alliance 2006). In particular, the Aquino Administration and the succeeding Administration of Fidel Ramos deepened the privatization program through the creation of a Cabinet Committee on Privatization and an Asset Privatization Trust, accelerated the tariff reduction program at a rate much lower than the Philippines' bound commitments to the WTO, and liberalized the foreign investment policy regime by simply coming up with a short negative list of areas foreign investors cannot enter.

Table 3. Manufacturing share, Southeast Asian economies, 1980 and 2009 (%).

	1980	2009	Change
In GDP			
Indonesia	13.0	27.4	14.4
Malaysia	21.6	25.5	3.9
Philippines	25.7	21.3	(4.4)
Thailand	21.5	34.2	12.7
In employment			
Indonesia	9.0	12.4	3.4
Malaysia	16.1	18.3	2.2
Philippines	10.8	8.9	(1.9)
Thailand	7.9	13.7	5.8

Source: Usui (2012).

3. De-industrialization and de-agricultural development

What has been the performance of the Philippines under the EOI/SAP policy regime? As can be gleaned from Table 2, the Philippines posted the lowest growth in the EOI/SAP decades of the 1980s, 1990s and 2000s. It was also in these decades when the late industrializers in Southeast Asia – Indonesia, Malaysia and Thailand began overtaking the Philippines by posting higher growth performance in manufacturing (see Table 3).

Philippine manufacturing registered a zero growth rate in the 1980s. One direct outcome of this faltering industrial growth is the declining share of the sector, particularly its manufacturing sub-sector, in total employment (see Table 4). This declining share of industry to total employment is a clear indication of de-industrialization. And since there has been a proliferation of garments firms in the 1970s–1980s and electronics and auto parts manufacturers in the 1980s–1990s (Ofreneo 1993), the industrial/manufacturing stagnation can only be explained by the collapse of the ISI industries, most of which cannot compete in a globalized and liberalized home market.

The stagnation of industry has been accompanied by the faster stagnation of the other 'real' or productive sector of the economy, the agricultural sector. The Philippines has become a net agricultural importing country beginning in 1995. The country has also become the world's biggest importer of rice and an importer of a whole range of agricultural products such as corn, coffee, meat, milk, wheat, onion, garlic, vegetables, etc. The value of its exports (sugar, coconut, banana, pineapple and a few agricultural products) cannot equal the value of its agricultural imports. For example, in 2010, the total value of its agricultural exports was US$4.097 billion while the total value of its agricultural imports

Table 4. Employment share by sector, Philippines, 1970–2010.

	1970	1975	1980	1985	1990	1995	2000	2005	2010
Agriculture	53.7	53.5	51.8	49.6	45.2	44.1	37.1	26.0	33.2
Industry	16.5	15.2	15.4	13.8	15.0	15.6	16.2	15.6	15.0
Manufacturing	11.9	11.4	10.8	9.7	9.7	10.2	10.0	9.5	8.4
Services	28.2	31.8	32.8	36.5	39.7	40.3	46.7	48.5	51.8

Source: National Statistics Office.

was US$7.331 billion, resulting in a deficit of US$3.234 billion (NEDA, *Philippine Development Plan 2011--2016*, 2011). In a way, the declining agricultural sector explains why rural insurgency in the Philippines, Asia's longest running, has persisted.

3.1. Bright segments of the economy

The only bright segments of the formal economy are the CC-BPO sector and the service industries such as retail/distribution that are booming due largely to the spending by OFWs and families. However, as pointed out by Usui (2012), these segments of the economy are not enough to make the economy sustainable in the long run.

Both the OFW-driven economy and the CC-BPO sector were never imagined by the EOI-SAP economic planners to become the country's life savers and GDP boosters. In the case of the OFW phenomenon, the Marcos Administration justified the 'manpower export' program crafted in the mid-1970s by the then Ministry of Labor and Employment (MOLE) to be a 'temporary' one, that is, to ease unemployment while the LIEO program had not taken off fully. But since the LIEO and its later version, SAP-EOI, has never taken off, the temporary manpower export program has become permanent and has expanded tremendously, from over 20,000 contract migrant workers processed by MOLE in 1975 to several millions today.

As to the CC-BPO sector, its phenomenal growth in the last ten years was fortuitous and unplanned. It was not even reflected in NEDA's economic blueprint of 1999–2004 (NEDA 1999), although the first offshored call center was established in the Philippines by the America Online in 1997 at the former US air base, at Clark. The CC-BPO sector has developed on Philippine soil because providers of customer service for America's top 500 companies have found it cheaper to offshore such service in a country with a good supply of English-speaking, ICT-literate and American-acculturated workforce who are paid a fraction of what American call center agents would normally get. Of course, advances in modern communications, e.g., internet and VOIP, have served as facilitating factors. In 2010, the CC-BPO sector employed over 530,000 workers (from a mere 3000 or so in 2000) and earned around US$9 billion (NEDA 2011). Although this job figure still constitutes less than 2% of the country's 40 million workforce, the dollar earnings of the sector have a relatively bigger multiplier impact compared to the leading EOI industry (electronics) because these earnings all go to wages, building rentals, interests and profits of Filipino CC-BPO corporate partners. In contrast, dollar earnings in the electronics industry amounting to US$22 billion in 2012 is reduced by the hefty import content valued at US$16 billion (NSO, Foreign Trade Statistics).

3.1.1. Why has the EOI growth model failed in the Philippines?

Now back to the original question: how come the Philippine industrialization drive has faltered? This paper argues that the EOI growth model implemented by the country's economic technocrats, from the Marcos regime to the present, is narrow and simplistic. It differs radically from the export-led industrialization drive pursued by the Asian NICs and other successful Asian countries.

3.2. EOI's limited domestic linkages and discriminatory treatment of home-grown producers

One of the early analyses of the weaknesses of the Philippine EOI program was done in the early 1980s by a member of the ILO Asian Regional Team for Employment or

ARTEP, Datta-Chaudhurri (1981). Datta-Chaudhurri observed that most of the EOI factories or investments established in the 1970s and 1980s were producing garments, footwear, toy and fashion accessory producers as part of the global value chains of the investing multinationals which set up these factories in the newly established Philippine EPZs to take advantage of the generous fiscal incentives and cheap labor in the country. It was an 'enclave' export-oriented economy with limited domestic linkages and limited job creation for the host country, he concluded.

Datta-Chaudhurri added that the design of the EOI program was discriminatory or damaging to the domestic industrial sector. It ignored the potential leadership role of the local entrepreneurial and industrial class in the export and industrialization drive. This feature is distinctly different from the experience of the Asian NICs, which tried to build up both their export and domestic industries. The success of the EOI program in Japan and in the Asian NICs can be seen in the rise of the big global but home-grown industrial champions such as Samsung of South Korea, which started in the 1970s as a mere electronics assembler for Sanyo. Japan and the Asian NICs did not promote export orientation in a one-sided manner, meaning it was promoted alongside the development of the domestic market, with foreign investors complementing, not easing out, the locals. The literature on the Asian NICs also shows that both the export and domestic industries even enjoyed government protection, although such protection is often hidden in a labyrinthian manner (Chang 2006).

The anti-ISI orientation by the proponents of the EOI-SAP program pushed them to design and implement measures that are even discriminatory and harmful to the home-oriented Philippine industries, most of which were simply labeled as 'rent-seeking' based on the high tariffs imposed on competing imported goods. The statistics on the decline of manufacturing can only mean a steep decline in domestic manufacturing since the policy regime was overwhelmingly slanted in favor of EOI manufacturing. Many ISI-nurtured industries wilted under the EOI-SAP program due to a business environment hostile to the locals. For example, under SAP, the Philippines adopted a program of unilateral trade liberalization that was ahead or advanced compared to the big Asian exporting countries such as China and Thailand (Bello 2004; Fair Trade Alliance 2006). This was compounded by corruption, the most venal expression of which was the inability of the government at the national and local levels to stop the widespread smuggling of products competing with the locally produced goods such as shoes, vegetables, textiles, paper, steel, cement, petrochemicals, plastics, ceramic tiles and vehicles of various shapes and sizes (Francia and Ramos 2011). And since smugglers and ecozone exporters pay minimal or no taxes, the full burden of taxation in the Philippines falls hardest on the unprotected domestic industrial and commercial sectors and the consuming public.

3.3. On EOI enclave economy and environmental degradation: An early analysis

Gareth Porter (1988), an American investigative journalist, and Delfin Ganapin, an environmentalist-scientist in the Philippines, wrote (*Resources, Population, and the Philippines' Future*) how the narrow EOI growth model failed to ease mass poverty and contributed to the degradation of the environment, a decade after the EOI program was instituted by the martial-law regime. They observed that the EOI-led industrial sector:

> ... remained an enclave – a modern sector with no linkage to traditional agriculture. It did little to increase Philippine manufacturing's labor absorption or to stimulate demand for domestically produced consumer goods. By 1978, the share of manufacturing in total

employment had declined from the 1971 level of 11.5 per cent to 11.4 per cent. Most of the urban working class remained, in fact, in the 'informal' sector — in the Philippines primarily unpaid family labor. By the early 1980s, the industrial sector had stagnated due to low domestic demand, and in 1983 it slid into a deep recession as the bill for the Marcos regime's profligate borrowing came due.

Another burden to the domestic-oriented producers is the relatively higher cost of doing business in the Philippines, which has the highest power cost in Asia today. The latter is blamed by the public on the wholesale privatization of the generation-transmission-distribution-marketing of electricity, which benefited a few oligarchic families and foreign power corporations (Tanada and Malaluan 2011). Thus, even the multinationals that set up manufacturing subsidiaries in the Philippines during the ISI decades of the 1950s and 1960s such as the drug, home appliance and pharmaceutical firms, shut down their local production facilities in the 1990s in favor of production consolidation in nearby Thailand and Indonesia (Fair Trade Alliance 2006). They have reduced their Philippine operations into import-and-distribute business just like what Ford Philippines did in 2012, when it closed down its assembly plant in the country.

Also, the EOI/SAP-obsessed economic technocrats failed to consult and flesh out with the local business community and affected industries on what are the appropriate transition measures needed in anticipation or preparation for a more liberal trade and economic regime as a consequence of full SAP program implementation. In the first place, ISI industries clamoring for protection or at least, an even playing field, are seen by the neo-liberal economic technocrats as rent-seekers bent on capturing extra profits through higher tariffs. The Fair Trade Alliance and the Federation of Philippine Industries (FPI) have stories on how official explanations were being made by the SAP implementers or government officials only after the injuries to the domestic producers had already been inflicted. Worse, there is even no active government support to cases filed by domestic industry against dumping and unfair trade practices, e.g., on dumping of tiles and cement, committed by some countries such as China, Thailand and Malaysia.

3.4. Banking on FDI with no long-term plans to remain in the country

With their investments focused on segments or parts of their global production, e.g., sewing garments, assembling toys, a big number of FDIs which came under EOI turned out to have no long-term plans, much less programs to deepen and upgrade production, in the Philippines. Some are literally footloose investments, flying in and out of countries. This is exemplified by the labor-intensive garments industry, which had a million or so workers in the 1980s and 1990s and which now has fewer than 100,000 workers today, primarily because many garments investors relocated to China, Bangladesh and other cheaper global sites in the 1990s and early 2000s in anticipation of the end of the quota system under the Multi-Fiber Arrangement or MFA (Ofreneo 2011).[2]

In the 1990s onwards, garment was eclipsed by the electronics industry as the country's leading export-led manufacturing industry. The industry employs around 500,000 workers and the 700 or so electronics firms can be found virtually in all the four government-run EPZs, two special economic zones (Clark and Subic), and in the various private industrial parks registered with the Philippine Export Zone Authority. Lately, however, the industry, which accounted for two-thirds of the country's annual export earnings in the 1990s and 2000s, has been declining. Its share in the total export earnings today is now less than 50% of the total.

Will electronics, therefore, follow garments in the exit door? After electronics, however, there is no other major export industry comparable to electronics and garments in size, either in terms of employment or export earnings.

3.5. Missing programs of technology scaling up and industrial deepening

Sustained industrialization growth requires a dynamic spiral of innovation, learning and technology upgrading. And yet, this was literally absent in the design and implementation of the EOI program for the Philippines. There is the naive expectation by the technocrats that FDI, in an open economy, would eventually help raise the technological base of the country. In the meantime, the focus of policy attention is how to generate jobs through the promotion of the 'labor-intensive' export industries, which literally means assembly work in the garments industry, electronics industry, footwear industry, stuffed toy industry and auto parts industry. Very little programs are developed or being developed in support of innovations on new products, new designs, testing of materials (in the case of electronics), and, yes, value-adding linkage formation through the development of upstream and downstream industries.

The absence of scaling up through innovation and learning is amply illustrated by the electronics industry, which got stuck in the assembly work, from the mid-1970s to the present. In contrast, the electronics industry of South Korea, Malaysia and Singapore zoomed upward at the higher stages of electronics processing and value-adding product application because of continuous efforts in technology and skills upgrading (ADB 2003). In the case of the supposedly 'liberal' Singapore, the government set up special technical training institutions and even engineering and polytechnic universities (Nanyang Technological University, Singapore Polytechnic, Ngee Ann Polytechnic, Temasek Polytechnic and Nanyang Polytechnic) just to address the requirement for engineering and technical people needed by electronics and other industries being nudged by the government to go higher up the value chain (Swee 1996).

The reality is that the role of the government is crucial in industry upgrading processes and in developing a strong domestic science and technical base, which allows an economy to be creative, flexible and responsive to changing market situations. Doane (2004) wrote that Japan and the Asian NICs have pursued innovation and technology development in varied ways but all focused their efforts on (1) moving the country up the technology ladder and developing 'high-tech industries and technology clusters', and (2) encouraging 'low and medium tech' areas through the preservation and transformation of indigenous skills and technical skills ('technology blending' and clustering). There is no space to discuss the specific details of the experiences of each of these countries in scaling up the technology laddering. But what is clear is that in each country, the role of a strong, visionary and developmental state is central. Japan and the Asian NICs single-mindedly pursued a program of industrial policy, which entailed government support in capacity building in strategic industrial areas (both domestic and export) which have the potentials of pushing industrialization at a higher and faster level even if initially these industries had no comparative advantage, e.g., car making in Japan during the 1950s and steel making in South Korea in the 1970s. In a way, what China has done in the last three decades is a replication on a grand scale of the industrial policy experience of Japan and the Asian NICs.

In the case of the Philippines, the visionary and developmental state was sorely missing. Armed with martial-law powers, Marcos expressed some interest in developing a strong industrial base through the launching of 11 'major industrial projects' (MIPs), which are similar to some of the industrial projects pursued by the Asian NICs in the 1970s such as a petrochemical complex, integrated steel, copper smelter, diesel engine manufacturing and so on. However, he allowed his economic technocrats and their IMF-World Bank backers to dictate the economic priorities under the narrow LIEO/EOI growth model. When he tried to make a strong push for his 11 MIPs in 1981, the economy was already facing a debt crisis and the World Bank itself quickly shot down the MIP idea by pointing out that these MIPs are 'highly capital-intensive and energy-intensive' (Ofreneo 1993).

A few years after the 1986 People's Revolt, Limqueco, McFarlane, and Odhnoff (1989) observed that the Filipino economic technocrats and foreign consultants such as Gustav Ranis totally neglected the development of the Philippine 'capital goods industry' in the name of a 'purely export-oriented strategy'. According to Limqueco, McFarlane and Odhnoff, a 'capital goods sector development' could have contributed to a more balanced and broadly based industrial structure, increased agricultural productivity and surpluses, generated a pool of skilled workers and assured the country of sustained growth through a balanced inter-sectoral growth among the sectors. Unfortunately, Limqueco, McFarlane and Odhnoff were not at the economic saddle of the Philippines.

3.6. Incoherence unlimited

In sum, the Philippine industrial debacle is directly traceable to the narrow EOI growth strategy framework promoted by the economic technocrats. ***The issue is not whether to go export-oriented or not.*** Japan and the Asian NICs all elected to go export-oriented. The overarching issue really is how export orientation was pursued in the context of the overall need of the country to push industrialization at a higher and faster level. As outlined above, the EOI framework of the Philippines is not exactly the same EOI framework pursued by Japan and the Asian NICs. Moreover, Japan and the Asian NICs have a more holistic view of how overall industrialization through technology scaling up should be pursued.

In this regard, Rasiah (2007, 2010) has come up with a 'systemic quad' model incorporating what he sees as the necessary upgrading or capacity-building elements in a successful industrialization process for a developing country. He pointed out that scaling up the industrialization-technology ladder involves an integrated approach involving four pillars: (1) basic infrastructure to promote systemic stability and efficiency; (2) institutions to provide systemic support for learning and innovation; (3) network cohesion to provide the systemic price, technological and social relationships necessary to drive interactive and interdependent coordination; and (4) integration in the globalized production system (e.g., value chains, competition, etc.). In short, it is not a question of whether to go global or not but to qualify the terms of global integration. Of course, in all of this, the role of government is central, especially in clarifying the vision of industrial development and in fostering cohesion through positive coordination and cooperation among public and private institutions and actors in what Rasiah (2007, 2009, 2010) calls as 'network cohesion'.

On FDI and the coordinating role of the government, Rasiah (2008a, 2008b, 2009) explains that governments of host countries have three major policy tasks: understanding the dynamics of FDI-local interface in the host country production sites; understanding the motives of multinational production establishment or relocation, especially in the context of a host country's domestic and export markets; and framing strategies to nudge the multinationals to drive learning and innovation in the host sites. In short, the government should and must provide the directions on how to deepen and broaden the industrialization process in a globalized economic environment dominated by the global corporations or multinationals. Of course, for the government to be able to do all this, it must not only have a clear industrial development vision but must also have the political will to pursue consistently this vision.

It is abundantly clear that the Philippine EOI growth model, as fleshed out and pushed by the Filipino economic technocrats and foreign consultants such as Gustav Ranis, hardly fits into the Rasiah systemic quad model. Nor does the Philippine EOI growth model fits with the usual Asian EOI model based on the experience of Japan, Asian NICs and now, China.

4. What has been the impact of a failed EOI on the labor market?

What are the economic, employment and poverty outcomes under a failed growth model? The official statistics and data speak for themselves. The most significant developments include the following:

4.1. Rise of a remittance-driven economy

Because of the failure of the local economy to produce good quality jobs, workers with marketable skills have applied for overseas jobs. The Philippine 'manpower export' program, originally launched in the mid-1970s as a 'stop-gap' employment program, has become huge and permanent (Ofreneo 2010). This is because the EOI/SAP program, meant to solve the problem of lagging growth never took off. The total number of OFWs and other 'Overseas Filipinos' was over 10 million in 2011 (see Table 5), or roughly 10% of the total resident population. OFW remittances, which exceeded US$20 billion or some 10% of GDP in 2011 (Bangko Sentral ng Pilipinas 2013), are the reason why growth in the country has been described as increasingly consumption-led. The OFWs and their families have disposable incomes that they spend on consumption goods like home appliances and services like education. Some one-fifth of the country's population is directly dependent on the OFWs for its daily needs.

4.2. Expansion of the services sector

The Philippines has become a services-led economy without having experienced an industrial revolution and without the benefits of agricultural modernization.

The sector has two major sub-sectors: formal and informal. On the formal side, the most prominent is the CC-BPO industry, which employs young, English-speaking and

Table 5. Overseas Filipinos and overseas Filipino workers, 2000–2011 (millions).

Year	Permanent	Temporary	Irregular	Total
2011	4.86	4.51	1.07	10.44
2006	3.55	3.80	.87	8.23
2000	2.55	2.99	1.84	7.38

Source: Commission on Filipino Overseas, DFA. (Details may not add up due to rounding off of figures).
Permanent – Immigrants or legal permanent residents.
Temporary – Persons whose stay overseas is employment-related and who are expected to return at the end of their work contracts.
Irregular – Not properly documented or without valid residence or work permits or overstaying.

Table 6. BLES-DOLE, formal and informal employment, Philippines, 1980–2010.

Year	Formal Sector Wage & salary workers	Informal sector		
		Own account workers	Unpaid family workers	Total informal sector
1980	42.4	36.9	20.7	57.6
1985	43.8	39.7	16.5	56.2
1990	45.5	38.8	15.7	54.5
1995	46.2	39.0	14.8	53.8
2000	50.7	37.1	12.2	49.3
2005	50.4	36.9	12.7	49.6
2010	51.8	29.8	11.7	41.5

Source: *Labstat Updates* 15, 19 (August 2010).

tech-savvy workers who enjoy entry wages at least twice the mandated minimum wage in Metro Manila. But the bulk of employment in the formal service sub-sector is in the traditional service industries such as food, education, real estate, distribution and entertainment, where many of the workers are often low-paid casual workers. These industries are also remittance-driven industries, buoyed up by the spending of families of OFWs.

The informal side of the service sector is huge. It is composed of numerous micro and informal income-generating activities undertaken by the poor, such as hawking, vending, unregistered repair and personal services, home-based outwork, and similar activities. But the informal economy is not all services. One must add here the informal work done by industrial home workers, unregistered construction activities, small-scale mining, agriculture work done by landless rural poor (those without any land rights), coastal or municipal fishing and so many other similar 'non-service' activities. Overall, the informal economy covers a large part of the services and agricultural sectors; however, it also covers the informal segments of industry.

How big is the informal economy? The DOLE has been publishing statistics indicating that the size of the informal labor sector is fluctuating between 41% and 58% of the employed labor force (see Table 6). It does this by simply adding up the total of the unpaid family workers (12.7% in 2005) and the non-employer own-account workers (36.9% in 2005). However, the Employers Confederation of the Philippines (Ortiz-Luis 2008) gives a higher estimate – a whopping 77% of the employed, or 25 million out of the 36 million employed in 2006 (see Table 7)!

4.3. High unemployment and underemployment

The growth of the informal economy is directly related to the high rates of unemployment and underemployment in the country.

In 2010, the labor force participation rate was registered at 64.3% meaning 39.9 million out of the 62 million working age population are in the active labor force. About 37.1 million (or 92.9%) of the LF are employed, meaning the remaining 2.8 million are unemployed or have no jobs (see Table 8). The statistics also show that there are 7.1 million underemployed, or with jobs but are still actively looking for additional jobs. There are 3.97 million 'unpaid' family workers. And there are 12.65 million who are working at less than 40 hours a week. What all these figures tell is that more than half of the employed do not actually have adequate and decent work.

Table 7.   Number of IS workers, Philippines, 2006 '000).

Indicator	2006
Underemployed	7467
Underemployment rate	22.7%
Own-account workers	12,134
Employer	1467
Self-employed	10,667
% of employed	32.3%
Unpaid family workers	4038
% of employed	12.3%
TOTAL	25,151
As % of employed	77%

Note: Estimation by ECOP.
Source: Sergio Ortiz-Luis, *Philippine Employer*, May 2008.

The problem is that this seems to be the pattern in the last 30 years or so and that there are no visible signs of improvement. For example, unemployment was recorded at a low rate of 4.9% in 1980 but increased to 7.3% in 2010. In between, it soared at 11.2% in 2000 (see Table 9). It was reduced to a single digit in 2005, when the NSO survey question was modified, making it terribly taxing for a respondent unemployed to answer[3] if he/she is unemployed.

As to underemployment, the rates are virtually the same over the last three decades. Although underemployment dropped below 20% in 2010, about 2.6 million still expressed desire to have additional hours of work or additional jobs.

The persistence of massive and chronic unemployment and underemployment are at the roots of the persistent and chronic poverty in the country. They are also the reasons why the informal economy has become a huge phenomenon in the Philippines.

4.4.   Chronic mass poverty

The growth of informal employment and the high unemployment/underemployment rates are also reflected in the massive and persistent poverty in the country. Officially, one out of every five Filipinos (and one of every four families) in 2009 was considered poor (see Table 10). However, per assessment by this author, the ratio is more one to one.

Table 8.   Labor force statistics, Philippines, 2010.

	Millions	%
Working age population (15 years old and above)	62	
Labor force in working population	39.9	64.3
Employed in labor force	37.1	92.9
Unemployed of labor force	2.8	7.1
Underemployed of employed	7.1	19.1
Unpaid family workers of employed	3.97	10.7
Working less than 40 hours a week of employed	12.7	34.1

Source: National Statistics Office.

Table 9.   Unemployment and underemployment rates, Philippines, 1980–2010 (%).

Year	Unemployment	Underemployment
1980	4.9	21.7
1985	6.8	21.8
1990	8.4	22.4
1995	9.5	20.0
2000	11.2	21.7
2005	7.7	21.0
2010	7.3	18.8

Source: National Statistics Office, Labor Force Survey, various years.

The official poverty data, worrisome as they are, are understated. This is especially true in Metro Manila or the National Capital Region (NCR), which has a population of 11.5 million and yet got a very low poverty record for 2009, officially placed at only 2.6%. This meant only 54,949 NCR families (or less than 300,000 people) were considered poor. And yet, any visitor who visits the NCR cannot fail to notice the large colonies of slums all over the metropolis (Abad 2011) In particular, a memo of the President Management Staff revealed that a 2010 census by the Metropolitan Manila Development Authority of informal settlers shows that there is a total of 556,526 informal settler families or households in the metropolis. At a conservative ratio of five (5) members to a household, this easily translates to close to three (3) million people. As is well known, informal settler houses have uncertain legal status, as they usually squat on private or government lands. Most of these houses are made of light materials like cardboard boxes, which are easily washed away when giant floods hit the city. And most of these informal settlers are poor and belong to the large informal sector of the metropolis.

Table 10.   Official poverty statistics, Philippines, 2003–2009.

Indicator	Year		
	2003	2006	2009
A. Among families			
Poverty incidence (%)	20.0	21.1	20.9
Subsistence incidence (%)	8.2	8.7	7.9
Magnitude of poor	3,293,096	3,670,791	3,855,730
Magnitude of food poor	1,357,833	1,511,579	1,453,843
B. Among population			
Poverty incidence (%)	24.9	26.4	26.5
Subsistence incidence (%)	11.1	11.7	10.8
Magnitude of poor	19,796,954	22,173,190	23,142,481
Magnitude of food poor	8,802,918	9,851,362	9,440,397
C. General indicators			
Income gap (%)	27.7	27.2	25.7
Poverty gap (%)	5.6	5.7	2.7

Source: National Statistical Coordination Board.

A deeper scrutiny of the NSO 2009 data on poverty also shows why the estimate is very low. The poverty threshold per individual Filipino was set at P46.00 a day (or roughly a little over US1.00 a day). In Metro Manila, this amount will not be enough to buy a poor person two simple meals, let alone three meals plus a certain amount for transport, utilities and all. A more realistic figure for poverty threshold should be the World Bank's US$2.00 a day global standard. At this level, half of the population, based on the NSO data, shall fall under poverty.

4.5. *Unchanged social and economic inequality*

Social and economic inequality is also disturbing. Per a study by Africa (2011), former NSO Director, the income of the top 1% of the families in 2009 was equivalent to the aggregate income of the bottom 30 per cent. Africa observed that the present situation on inequality is virtually the same as it was in the 1960s. Further, he wrote that there is 'no visible middle class' in the Philippines.

The level of inequality in the country, from the 1980s to the present, can be seen in the Gini coefficient curve (see Figure 1). The curve has fluctuated within a narrow band, between .44 and .48, in the last three decades. With 1 as complete inequality and 0 as complete equality, the foregoing coefficients for the Philippines clearly indicate a highly unequal society.

4.5.1. *Informalization of the 'formals'*

Now what is happening on the narrow formal side of the labor market?

The quick answer is that the expansion of the informal sector or economy is complemented by the 'informalization' trend in the formal labor market. This trend is aided by

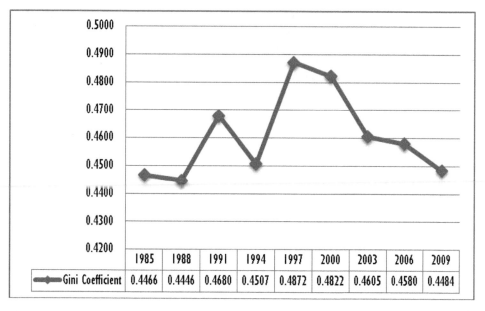

Figure 1.   Gini coefficient, Philippines, 1985–2009.
Source: National Statistics Office.

the reality of jobless growth in the organized sector due to the weak agro-industrial base of the economy and, yes, the availability of a large reserve army of flexible labor from the informal sector. This informalization is dubbed by trade unions as 'contractualization' or 'casualization', which generally means short-term and unprotected temporary hiring arrangements. A popular slang used for a short-term worker is '*Endo*',[4] whose employment contract has ended or bound to end in a short time.

The Philippine trade union movement, which is badly divided on many issues such as the minimum wage, is consistently united on their uniform denunciation of the flexibilization phenomenon that finds expression in various forms of flexible job hiring arrangements such as the outsourcing or subcontracting of work, deployment of agency-hired (third-party-managed) workers within the company's work premises and/or direct hiring of workers under short-term employment contracts. Unfortunately for the unions and many workers, the realities in the labor market are not too kind on them. Informalization or 'flexibilization' is widespread in the formal side of the services, industry and agriculture sectors.

Flexibilization also takes varied forms. But the common underlying thrust is to put workers under short-term employment arrangement, with the job contract ranging anywhere from one week to less than three years. The latter (three years) is the usual length or duration of a collective bargaining agreement (CBA), which explains why trade unionists complain that they have less and less workers to organize for collective bargaining purposes. Moreover, under the existing jurisprudence, non-regular workers are usually excluded from the scope of the CBA coverage. The following are the most forms of labor flexibilization:

- Hiring workers as temporaries or probationaries with no intention of regularizing them. Under the Labor Code of the Philippines (LCP), a company is allowed to subject workers to six-month probation, beyond which he/she is entitled to regularization if the job is 'regular and necessary' to the business. This encourages some companies and placement and manpower agencies to put short-term workers on a '5–5 arrangement',[5] meaning they are hired for only five months without any intention of regularizing these workers.
- Hiring workers as 'project employees'. Under the law, the tenure of project employees is co-terminus with the project they are assigned to, e.g., developing a cell site for a telecom company, whose completion is bound to happen on 'a day certain'. In the booming CC-BPO sector, most of the jobs are now under project-hiring arrangement.
- Hiring of trainees. Under the law, companies can hire trainees, anywhere between six months to two years, at compensation rates of 25% below the minimum wage. In one big electronics company with around 20,000 workers, the ratio of the apprentice-trainee is 19:1, meaning 19 apprentices-trainees for every 1 regular employee (Ofreneo and Hernandez 2010).
- Utilization of job/service contractors. Job contracting within company premises is the most common route these days towards flexibilization. The unions complain that agency workers, hired and deployed by third-party service contractors or 'manpower agencies', often outnumber the direct hires, especially in the retail, hotel and restaurant, and labor intensive manufacturing industries.

There are other flexible work and compensation arrangements (Kapunan and Kapunan 2006). They include the following: work on a commission basis, meaning workers are paid based on a percentage of the sales they make; 'boundary' system, which is common in the transport sector (drivers are supposed to turn over a fixed daily amount or 'boundary' to the transport owner (e.g., taxi) and appropriate to himself/herself whatever is the surplus; and piece-rate system, meaning workers are paid on the basis of results (quite common in the heyday of the garments industry). There are also seasonal workers, or those hired during peak demands for business, e.g., production of Christmas decorations for the Christmas season.

5. Conclusion

The narrow EOI growth model pursued doggedly by the neo-liberal technocrats in the last four decades has focused mainly on liberalizing the economy SAP-style sans a clear industrial and agricultural vision. The outcome has been disastrous for the economy and the Filipino working people. The growth model has failed to grow the jobs and welfare needed by a growing population. Mass poverty and inequality have persisted a quarter of a century after EDSA I and over a century after the Philippine Revolution for nationhood.

It is time to overhaul the existing growth model and clarify the industrial vision, if the Philippines wants to catch up with Asia.

Notes

1. In 2011, the DTI released an economic road map entitled *Enabling Business, Empowering Consumers*, which seeks to double exports and investments under the Aquino Administration (2011–2016). The DTI, through its Board of Investments (BOI), has made a commitment to revive manufacturing. It has asked the different industry associations to submit their respective 'industry road maps' as part of an overall program of rebuilding the country's industrial base.
2. Ironically, the garments industry, engaged in re-export manufacturing based on imported materials, contributed to the early demise of the country's ISI textile industry, which employed around 300,000 workers in the 1970s. There were limited linkages between the two sectors. But there were widespread accusations that EOI garments producers over-imported duty-free textile materials, which eventually found their way in the domestic market.
3. To be unemployed, one must be of working age, have no work, seriously looking for work, and should job be available today, prepared to assume the said job. If the answer is uncertain, some unemployed respondents are likely to be placed under the category 'not in the labor force'. In other countries, however, they probe into the phenomenon of idle workers who are not in the labor force by clarifying if the active search for jobs was due to discouragement from failed efforts in the past or expectation that no jobs are really available in the labor market. Labor economists call them 'discouraged workers'.
4. An indie filmmaker even produced in 2011 a movie entitled *"Endos"*, showing the employment saga of a contractual employee hopping from one job to another.
5. The term '5–5 labor market' was coined by Dr. Ofreneo in his report on the labor market situation in the garments situation in 1999. The report was part of the evaluation report by the Independent Monitoring Group on the 'Terms of Engagement' of the Levi Strauss with its contractor-producers in the Philippines. See Abrera-Mangahas et al. (1999).

References

Abad, J. 2011. "Report of the Technical Working Group (TWG) on Informal Settlers", Manila: Presidential Management Staff, Malacanang.

Abrera-Mangahas, A., V. Hernandez, R. Ofreneo, and N. Sancho. 1999. *Philippines Independent Evaluation Project for Levi Strauss & Co.'s Terms of Engagement*, Quezon City: Multiversity.

ADB (Asian Develoment Bank). 2003. *Asian Development Outlook 2003*. New York: Oxford University Press.

Africa, T. 2011. "Family Income Distribution in the Philippines, 1985-2009: Essentially the Same", Powerpoint Presentation at the Social Weather Stations, Quezon City, March 18.

Arceo-Dumlao, T. 2008. "Philippines Now the World's Top Rice Importer Despite Being Home to IRRI., In *Philippine Daily Inquirer*. Makati: PDI, April 25. newsinfo.inquirer.net.

Bangko Sentral ng Pilipinas. 2013. *Annual Report 2012*. Manila: BSP.

Bello, W. 2004. *The Anti-Development State: The Political Economy of Permanent Crisis in the Philippines*. Quezon City: Focus on the Global South.

BLES-DOLE (Bureau of Labor and Employment-Department of Labor and Employment). 2010. *Current Labor Statistics*. Manila: Department of Labor and Employment.

Chang, Ha-Joon. 2006. *The East Asian Development Experience: The Miracle, the Crisis and the Future*. Penang: Third World Network.

Commission on Overseas Filipinos. 2011. *Handbook on Overseas Filipinos*. Manila: COF.

Constantino, R., and L. Constantino. 1978. *The Philippines: The Continuing Past*. Quezon City: Foundation for Nationalist Studies.

Datta-Chaudhuri, M. 1981. "Industrialization and Foreign Trade: The Development Experiences of South Korea and the Philippines." In *Export-Led Industrialization and Development*, edited by Eddy Lee, 47–79. Singapore: ILO-ARTEP.

Doane, D. 2004. *Technology "Laddering", Blending and Clustering: Lessons and Experiences from Several Asian Countries*. Quezon City: Fair Trade Alliance.

Fair Trade Alliance. 2006. *Nationalist Development Agenda: A Road Map for Economic Revival, Growth and Sustainability*. Quezon City: Foundation for Nationalist Studies.

Francia, J., and E. Ramos. 2011. *Engaging the Dragon: Philippines-China Economic Relations*. Quezon City: Fair Trade Alliance.

Hicks, G., and G. McNicoll. 1971. *Trade and Growth in the Philippines: An Open Dual Economy*. Ithaca: Cornell University Press.

Kapunan, R., and R. Kapunan. 2006. *Labor-Only Contracting in a Cabo Economy*. Quezon City: C&E Publications.

Limqueco, P., B. McFarlane, and J. Odhnoff. 1989. *Labour and Industry in ASEAN*. Manila: Journal of Contemporary Asia.

NEDA (National Economic Development Authority). 1999. *Medium-Term Philippine Development Plan 1999–2004*. Mandaluyong: NEDA.

NEDA (National Economic Development Authority). 2011. *Philippine Development Plan 2011–2016*. Mandaluyong: NEDA.

NEDA (National Economic Development Authority). 2013. *Rehabilitation Assistance on Yolanda: Build Back Better*. Mandaluyong: NEDA.

Ofreneo, R.E. 1993. "Labor and the Philippine Economy." Doctoral dissertation, College of Social Sciences, University of the Philippines.

Ofreneo, R.E. 2010. "Migration and Development: When Will the Turning Point Come." In *Philippine Institutions: Growth and Prosperity for All*, edited by M. Sta. Ana, 263–284. Quezon City: Action for Economic Reforms and Friedrich Ebert Stiftung.

Ofreneo, R.E. 2011. "Garments: Seeking Protection Through Free Trade?" In *BusinessWorld* (released in two parts (May 23 and May 30)), edited by V. De Dios, S1/4–S1/5. Quezon City: BusinessWorld Publishing.

Ofreneo, R.E., and J. Hernandez. 2010. *Freedom of Association and Collective Bargaining in the Philippine Export Processing Sector*. Manila: ILO.

Ortiz-Luis, S. 2008. "The Practical Approach to Benefit the Majority." In *Philippine Employer*, edited by R. Ela, 13–17. Makati: Employers Confederation of the Philippines.

Porter, G. 1988. *Resources, Population, and the Philippines' Future*. Washington: World Resources Institute.

Ranis, G. 1974. *Sharing in Development: A Programme of Employment, Equity and Growth in the Philippines*, A UNDP-Organized Inter-Agency Mission Report. Geneva: International Labor Office.

Rasiah, R. 2007. "The Systemic Quad: Technological Capabilities and Economic Performance of Computer and Component Firms in Penang and Johor, Malaysia." *International Journal of Technological Learning, Innovation and Development* 1 (2): 179–203.

Rasiah, R. 2008a "Introduction: Critical Issues on Multinational-Driven Technological Capability Building and Localization." *Asia Pacific Business Review* 14 (1): 1–12.

Rasiah, R. 2008b. "Conclusions and Implications: The Role of Multinationals in Technological Capability Building and Localization in Asia." *Asia Pacific Business Review* 14 (1): 165–169.

Rasiah, R. 2009. "Technological Capabilities of Automotive Firms in Indonesia and Malaysia." *Asian Economic Papers* 8 (1): 151–169.

Rasiah, R. 2010. "Are Electronics Firms in Malaysia Catching Up in the Technology Ladder?" *Journal of the Asia Pacific Economy* 15 (3): 301–319.

Swee, Goh Keng. 1996. "The Technology Ladder in Development: The Singapore Case." *Asian-Pacific Economic Literature* 10 (1): 1–12.

Tanada, E., and N. Malaluan. 2011. *EPIRA at 10: Failed Assumptions and Unfulfilled Promises.* Quezon City: Focus on the Global South.

Usui, N. 2012. *Taking the Right Road to Inclusive Growth: Industrial Upgrading and Diversification in the Philippines.* Mandaluyong: ADB.

World Bank. 1962. *Economic Growth in the Philippines.* Washington: World Bank.

Online sources (websites):

http://www.census.gov.ph/content/foreign-trade-statistics-philippines-2012.

http://www.census.gov.ph/tags/labor-force.

http://www.bles.dole.gov.ph/learnstat/.

Industrialization, globalization and labour force participation in Thailand

Voravidh Charoenloet

Faculty of Economics, Chiang Mai University, Chiang Mai, Thailand

This article analyses the impact of globalization and industrialization on Thailand's labour market. While acknowledging the trend rise in wage employment in the labour force over the period 1971–2009, the article also shows that over half of the labour force has remained in non-wage employment, which has left a significant share of them vulnerable to the abuses of the capitalist system. The lack of technological upgrading has meant that employers have increasingly resorted to subcontracting work to informal homeworkers to compete in low value added activities. Outsourcing has also allowed employers to bypass the minimum wage legislation. Hence, we argue that it is important that workers from all forms of work are mobilized to strengthen the role of unions to ensure that there is a shift from the low to a high road to industrialization so that workers' rights are protected.

1. Introduction

Like most East Asian economies Thailand's labour force has undergone rapid transformation with an increasing rise in wage labour. While increased modernization had started a decline in farm labour, export-oriented industrialization became an important impetus for this development since the 1970s. Although Thailand did not introduce the usual instruments of industrial policy in a strict sense, industrial promotion through incentives was important in attracting foreign direct investment (FDI) and stimulating manufactured exports. However, while manufacturing has grown with Thailand becoming the leading exporter of automobiles from Southeast Asia, the latter has not evolved significantly to become Thailand's main employer. In fact, export-oriented industrialization in Thailand is still very much dependent on FDI with employment contracts largely renewable between one and three years.

Despite rapid expansion in wage employment over half of Thailand's labour force was still not in wage employment as late as 2009. Also, owing to frequent occurrence of economic shocks, self-employment, including farm labour, has often acted as shock absorbers whenever economic crises strike. The 1997–1998 Asian financial crisis and the 2008–2009 global financial crisis are examples. The consequences of these developments also mean that it is not possible to mobilize large numbers of industrial workers to support unions as not only is the government reluctant to support unionization but also the lack of longevity in employment makes unionization difficult. Much of the industrialization that has evolved puts Thailand on the low road.

Hence, this article seeks to analyse the persistence of non-wage labour and the precariousness of wage employment in Thailand's globalizing and industrializing economy. The next section contrasts the experience of the developed countries with selected Asian economies in general and Thailand in particular on the shift in the share of wage and non-wage employment over the years. The subsequent section analyses the expansion in wage labour in Thailand. This is then followed by the impact of export-oriented industrialization on the labour market. The final section presents the conclusions.

2. Historical backdrop of changes in labour force patterns

The development of wage labour can be observed throughout history and in particular prior to industrialization. In fact, it appeared under the manufacture and expanded further under the factory system during the industrial revolution in England. The long-term historical trend of decrease of farm employment is explained by the pushing-out effects inherent to farming activity than by the pulling effect of urban areas (Charoenloet et al. 2014). The pushing-out effects started in general by the private appropriation of land and the expulsion of peasants from the land they were cultivating. In eighteenth-century England, this has been the process of enclosure where landlords closed their land for the purpose of developing their own farming system and in particular for sheep breeding and therefore expelled peasants from the land. Marx referred to this as the process of proletarianization. It is believed that factory work would bring about the socialization process, where the working class would overcome their differences and developed common identity and political consciousness. This would set about the revolutionary process which provided the bypass of the capitalist system. Indeed, wage labour has been the dominant form of work in the industrialized countries. The rate of salarialization is around 80%–90% for developed countries between 1970 and 2005 (Table 1). On the contrary, independent labour or self-employed has been declining in importance.

In the European countries the ratio between independent workers and salaried workers ranged from 55% to less than 10% in 2000, which fell to 45% to 10% in 2008, which shows that the trend shows the expansion of wage labour at the expense of independent labour (Figure 1). Among the six developed countries shown in Table 1, with the exception of Germany over the period 1995–2005, this trend has also increased. If simply viewed from 1970 to 2005, the rise in the ratio is dramatic with Spain showing the most significant change. This trend is closely linked to economic growth and structural

Table 1. Wage labour in labour force, selected developed countries 1970–2005,

Developed countries	1970	1985	1995	2005
France	78.4	84.9	86.4	89.1
Germany	83.1	85.0	89.4	87.7
Italy	66.7	70.4	70.9	73.3
Japan	64.9	74.2	76.3	84.8
Spain	64.0	69.1	72.4	81.7
United States	89.8	90.9	91.4	92.5

Source: Eurostat yearbook 2012.

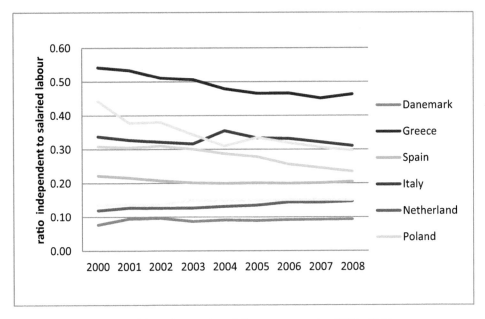

Figure 1. Wage labour in labour force, selected European countries, 2000–2008.
Source: Eurostat yearbook 2012.

transformation, and in particular, the decline of agriculture and the rise of manufacturing and modern services.

Wage labour has also expanded sharply in Asia as the globalization of capital has turned the continent into 'the factory of the world'. However, the proletarianization process is less of a reality in most of the Asian countries, with the exception of Japan and the East Asian newly industrialized economies of Hong Kong, Singapore, South Korea and Taiwan. In many Asian countries, including in Thailand, independent labour or the self-employed have remained important, while such an avenue has often acted as shock absorbers during economic crises, which are often accompanied by retrenchments (Rasiah, Yap, and Chandran 2014). Farmers constitute a large portion of the self-employed in the countryside of Thailand. It can be argued that modern institutions, such as, trade unions, labour laws and social protection have not been successful in promoting labour rights in many of the Asian countries, including Malaysia, the Philippines and Thailand.

Because the form of industrialization that has evolved in countries such as Cambodia, Bangladesh, Nepal, Indonesia, Pakistan and Thailand is heavily conditioned by the vicissitudes of volatile economic swings employment conditions are often transient with little worker protection. Hence, despite the rapid expansion of industrialization and factory employment, both salaried formal employment and independent and undocumented employment have coexisted in these countries. As shown in Table 2, salaried workers constituted less than half of all workers in Indonesia, Thailand, Cambodia, Pakistan, Bangladesh and Nepal.

Having located changes in historical perspective between developed and Asian economies, we turn to Thailand in the next section. With rapid integration into the global capitalist economy Thailand's workers have also been strongly exposed to the developments in export markets.

Table 2. Structure of employment in selected Asian countries, 2008.

| Country | Wage/salaried workers | Total self-employed | Status in employment | | | | | GDP per capita | Population living below 2 USD |
			Employers	Own account workers	Cooperative workers	Family workers	Not classified		
Indonesia	32.6	50.4	2.9	47.5	–	16.9	–	2253	53.8
Philippines	52.9	38.1	5.3	32.8	–	9.9	–	1847	45.0
Thailand	43.7	41.6	3.7	37.8	0.1	14.7	–	3868	11.5
Cambodia	12.9	41.2	0.2	41.0	–	14.7	–	651	68.2
Pakistan	37.4	35.3	0.8	34.5	–	27.2	–	1013	60.3
Bangladesh	13.9	63.6	0.3	63.3	–	21.7	0.9	494	81.3
Nepal	24.6	66.5	3.8	62.7	–	8.8	–	41	77.6

Source: Compiled from data provided in ILO (2010/11).

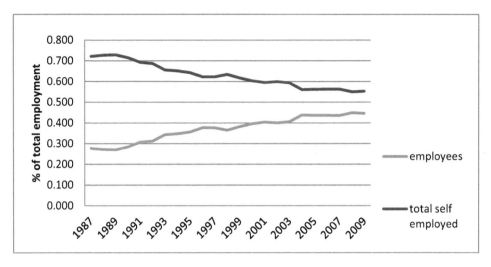

Figure 2.   Changes in the share of wage and non-wage labour, Thailand, 1987–2009 (%).
Source: Compiled from NSO labour surveys.

3.   Changes in labour force participation shares

Thailand too has experienced a trend decline in self-employment and a constant rise in wage employment. National survey data indicate that the share of self-employed in the labour force declined by 10 percentage points every decade with wage gaining as much of this fall. Wage labour rose from 12% in 1971 to 22% in 1981, 32% in 1991, 42% in 2002 and 45% in 2009. The data over the period 1971–1981 can be accessed from the National Statistical Office (NSO), while the data for the period 1987–2009 are shown in Figure 2.

The prime reason for the relative fall in the contribution of self-employment in the labour force is falling farm employment, which is a consequence of mechanization and modernization of agriculture. Wage employment has also risen as a consequence of a major expansion in industrial employment in manufacturing and growing demand for services. As shown in Figure 3, agriculture employment has continued to decline while that of industry and services has continued to rise. However, self-employment still accounted for over half of the labour force in Thailand in 2009, which is a distinctively different feature when compared to the experience of the developed economies.

4.   Expansion of wage labour in Thailand

Chinese migrants were the first batch of labourers to work as coolies and dock workers when Thailand first entered world trade specializing in primary exports (mainly rice). However the first major expansion in wage labour took place when public service was promoted under the nationalist military regime in the early 1950s. However, the labour force in Thailand was still significantly tied to agriculture till the late 1950s.

It was during aggressive promotion of industrialization that wage labour began to rise rapidly. Import substitution industrialization (ISI) was adopted in 1960 to modernize the country that created the private sector, which started hiring wage labour. By 1971 the private sector had expanded so much that it employed 70% of wage labour compared to 30% by the public sector. In 2009, the commensurate shares were 80% and 20%,

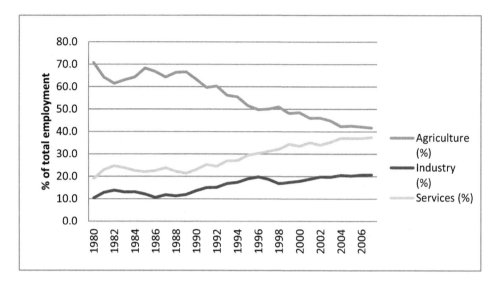

Figure 3.   Employment structure by sector, Thailand, 1980–2007.
Source: Compiled from NSO surveys.

respectively. Although public employment continued the rise its pace of growth slowed down since 1980 following the government's liberalization policies, including the privatization of state owned enterprise. Also, the introduction of export-oriented industrialization since 1985 drove large-scale hiring of factory workers (Rasiah 2010). The rapid growth in wage labour began to bear in the rise in its share in the labour force of Thailand. The share of wage labour in the labour force rose from 12% in 1961 to 22% in 1981, 30% in 1991, 40% in 2001 and 45% in 2009. The pace of growth in wage labour had significant slowdowns only during the crisis years of 1997–1998 and 2008–2009 (Figure 4).

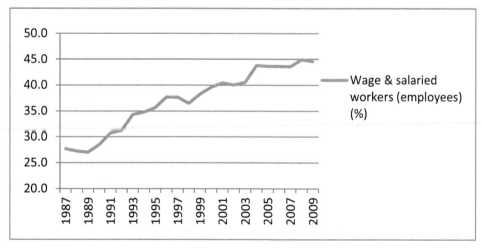

Figure 4.   Wage labour in labour force, Thailand, 1987–2009 (%).
Source: Compiled from NSO labour surveys.

5. The low road to industrialization

Since the adoption of the modernization programme in the 1960s, Thailand went through different phases of industrialization, which was documented in the country's five-year plans. Throughout the 1960s and 1970s Thailand was under an authoritarian regime, which saw social benefits traded-off for economic growth. Trade unions were abolished but workers could benefit from stable jobs and regular pay. The countryside provided the main source of cheap labour supply as young men and women migrated to the city to work in factories. Men went to the automobile industry, which paid higher wages, while women entered the clothing industry, which paid lower wages. Remittances were sent home and the close link between rural and urban was maintained. Unlike in the European countries, industrialization in Thailand did not bring about the process of proletarianization or the expropriation of peasants from the land. It is the unpaid family helpers who moved to sell their labour power keeping the head of households as independent labour in the farmland. The large reservoir of rural independent workers provided cheap labour for industrialization.

The ISI gave way to export-oriented industrialization (EOI) in 1985. The Board of Investment (BOI) extended its role since 1985 to promote FDI inflows, and foreign aid to develop the basic infrastructure in Thailand. Export processing zones became a major target of BOI's development plans since. While the state through the BOI was engaged aggressively in the promotion of industry, it did not participate in vetting, monitoring and appraising investment against incentives and grants. Some elements of industrial policy were visible but not interventionist enough to shift relative emphasis to manufacturing. In fact, Rock (1995) argued that Thailand's export success did not owe much to its industrial policy.

However, the shift towards EOI did not offer room for trade unions to participate in the labour process. Mounier and Charoenloet (2010) classified the labour regime under EOI as characterized by low wages, long working hours and low productivity (the 3Ls). To compensate for low productivity, the employers would implement long working hours with overtime added to the eight hour per day work-time and over six days a week). With very low wages, workers work long working hours to get decent income to support themselves. A study conducted by Workers' Right Consortium on the global trends for apparel workers revealed that clothing factory workers received the lowest wages, which grew slower than inflation. Such was the slow pace of wage growth in the clothing industry that real wages fell by 6.9% in the industry over the period 2001–2011. The availability of vulnerable migrant workers from Myanmar, Laos and Cambodia has made the situation even worse.

The 1990s saw the incorporation of Thailand as Southeast Asia's platform for the production of automobiles for export (Lauridsen 2008). This industry has expanded strongly to make Thailand the chief automobile exporter from Southeast Asia. However, while the skilled workers in this industry have enjoyed higher wages than the clothing and electronics workers, they do not represent the fate of most manufacturing workers. Also, even the automobile industry suffered from lay-offs following the Asian financial crisis of 1997–1998 and the global financial crisis of 2008–2009 (Rasiah, Cheong, and Doner 2014). The Asian financial crisis resulted in a contraction in Southeast Asian demand for automobiles, which triggered massive retrenchments. During the global financial crisis a sharp contraction in demand from the developed economies resulted in electronics and clothing factories retrenching workers. Foreign workers are the most vulnerable as they end up being retrenched first.

Whereas the rate of labour absorption into the labour force grew faster than population in the 1970s, by the 1990s this situation reversed as the labour market began to tighten to reflect

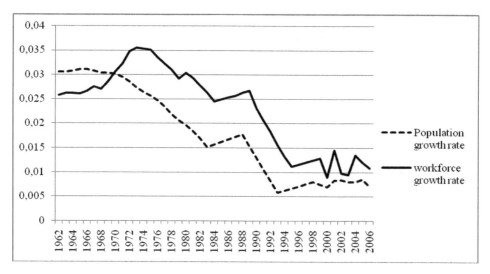

Figure 5. Annual growth rate, population and labour force, Thailand, 1962–2006 (%).
Source: NSO census and labour force survey.

serious labour shortages in a number of industries (Figure 5). It is estimated that there are 1.5 million foreign workers with around 900,000 of them regularized as legal workers. The majority of them are from Myanmar who mainly work in the building, fishery and sugar plantation industries where the conditions of work are deplorable.

While upswings and downswings are inherently part of uneven capitalist growth, the lack of effective social security mechanisms has left workers vulnerable to the EOI model. The lack of a dynamic industrial policy to expand human capital supply and a mechanism to stim-ulate structural change from low to high value added activities has meant that real wages in the light manufacturing industries of clothing and electronics have not grown much as Thailand's competitiveness in these industries have remained in low value added activities. Also, the large inflows of FDI and portfolio equity capital raised the value of the Baht thereby creating a massive asset bubble that quickly crashed. The rising value of the Baht led to rapid expansion in assets but also caused rising current account deficits, which precipitated a crash in the currency in June 1997 thereby triggering a contagion that also brought down the economies of Indonesia, the Philippines and South Korea (Rasiah 2000).

Further liberalization of the economy in the 1990s attracted greater competitive pres-sures from the new emerging low-cost countries, such as China, Vietnam, Cambodia and Bangladesh. Enjoying preferential access under the bilateral trading arrangements with the United States, and the 'Everything but Arms clause' with Europe, Bangladesh and Cambodia have become strong competitors in clothing exports (Rasiah 2009). Hence, the government introduced a minimum wage of 300 Baht (US$10) a day to stimulate indus-trial upgrading and change the labour regime from labour-intensive to technology and skill intensive operations.

However, the ad hoc manner with which the minimum wage was introduced and the lack of dynamic industrial policy instruments to promote the high road to industrializa-tion, competition from Bangladesh and Cambodia has resulted in the further casualization of clothing workers. Employers have continued to increase the hiring of informal workers to compete at the low end. Many firms have started to rely on flexible wages and employ-ment to cut production cost. In such a value chain, the big firm would keep its core production using permanent workers while outsourcing the low value added tasks to sub-contract workers (outworkers). A survey conducted by trade unions revealed that subcontract workers constituted 20%−30% of the assembly line and processing workers in the country. Other tasks, such as, cleaners and wardens have long been outsourced by both the public and private sectors. These workers do not come under the minimum wage regime and are often subjected to work violations. Within manufacturing the subcontracting of production is rampant in the clothing industry. For example, it is common to find a clothing firm from the newly industrialized countries producing for export garments under the original equipment manufacturing model. These firms themselves are contract producers who receive garment orders from big buyers. In the course of the production the subcontract firm would outsource part of the production to home-based workers.

The low road to industrialization path evolving in Thailand has also expanded demand for homeworkers as firms resort to the 'putting-out system' to keep production costs low. This arrangement has also been used effectively by low-cost firms during economic crises. After the Asian financial crisis of 1997−1998, the number of unemployed went up to 1.6 million, which amounted to an unemployment rate of 5.6% in 1998. Statistics from the NSO also shows a drop in the number of wage earners in manufacturing establishments as workers were laid-off because of the economic crisis while there was an increase in employment in trade and services but largely in the informal sector. Similarly, during the global financial crisis of 2008−2009 the labour force in Thailand grew only by 0.9%, 0.1% and 0.3% in 2008, 2009 and 2010, respectively, after having grown by 2.2% in 2007 (World Bank 2014). A sharp contraction in the export-oriented industries of electronics and clothing drove large number of national workers to the farms, while significant numbers of foreign workers were retrenched (Rasiah, Yap, and Chandran 2014).

In its last 2008 study, NSO registered homeworkers as contract workers, unpaid family workers and subcontractors. This classification puts homeworkers as independent labour working either permanently or temporarily, full time or part-time for somebody else. They are generally self-employed (employer, self-account or family workers) and hire their workforce through different contractual arrangements. The NSO survey involved 440,000 workers, which represents 1.1% of total employment and 3.6% of own account workers. Contract workers represent 85.7% of the sample, unpaid family workers 13.7% and subcontractors 0.6%. The distinction between contract workers and subcontractors is not very clear as they overlap extensively. Unpaid family workers have been included in the study of self-employment. Contract workers constitute the bulk of homeworkers who are not necessarily independent workers at home. Females represent 77% of contract workers in the sample.

Contract work is generally organized in labour-intensive activities such as silk and cotton weaving, garments and sewing, artificial flowers, wood carving, umbrella, basket-making and food processing. A merchant or a manufacturer contracts a worker or a group of workers in a village around proximate to his or her own business and gives them the inputs (rarely the machinery) to produce a good or more often a part to be assembled with other parts elsewhere or intermediate products (parts) to be assembled, with specification of quantity, quality and time limit. The product is then traded by the merchant or business owner who pays homeworkers a mean wage most of the time on a piece-rate basis. Sub-contracting also occurs when craftsmen accept for a time to work for a factory, including in the premises of the factory (e.g. furniture and construction). In this case they act as job-bers, that is, self-account or very small entrepreneurs who take a 'second hand job' and may recruit other wage workers to finish their orders. These forms of work offer a flexible workforce to merchants and entrepreneurs under a putting-out system.

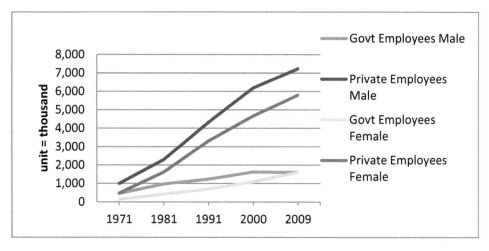

Figure 6. Public and private employees by gender, Thailand, 1971–2009 ('000).
Source: Compiled from NSO surveys.

The 2008 NSO study allows the characterization in detail of contract homeworkers, which showed that women accounted for 79% of total contracted homeworkers of which 60% were between 30 and 49 years of age, 75% married and 80% involved in craft related activities. Of the total, 52% are employed by enterprises and 37% by subcontractors who work 'second hand' for other enterprises or merchants, 79% of both male and female contract workers work at home and 19% in homes close to the merchants and entrepreneurs. Slightly over half (57%) of the contract workers work between five and eight hours a week, while 30% work more than eight hours a week. Because of the short working hours, contracted homeworkers generally undertake other work to supplement their incomes (Charoenloet et al. 2014).

Figure 6 shows the evolution of civil service and public employment in Thailand. Public employment growth gradually slowed down and stabilized since 2000. It is significant that the share of public employment, which is secure and includes conventional provisions of welfare for wage labour (leaves, health care, pension schemes), declined rapidly from 1980 onwards as a consequence of neoliberal politics. It accounted for a third of total employment in the 1970s but declined to around 20% by the end of 2000s. Meanwhile, female public employment increased from 24% of total public employment in 1971 to 50% in 2009. This trend will accelerate in the near future as the government pushes more and more civil servants out of the public sector as it has been the case for instance in higher education and health service. In fact, universities in Thailand have largely become self-financing following a withdrawal of state funds after the Asian financial crisis of 1997–1998.

In Thailand, the patterns of evolution of forms of work can be summarized as transitions from public to private employment, from wage labour to 'grey zones' and 'atypical forms of wage labour', as well as from self-employment to 'grey zones' where it is transformed into subordinated work without entering the canonical form of wage labour.

Most studies on labour relations in Thailand do not distinguish clearly between working for oneself – self-employment – and working from time to time for somebody else. Although independent labour may not be 'free' but could be 'subordinated' and turned into 'dependent labour'. So, to employ a dichotomy between 'free' versus 'not free', 'formal sector' versus 'informal sector', 'industry' versus 'agriculture', 'urban' versus 'rural' may fit less to the real world of work, which is a result of global production systems (Lucassen 2008). This brings into question the organizing of such systems, which takes into account the global space. Individual initiatives as promoted by the neoliberal ideology are not a solution, but one that needs collective action. Workers need to organize themselves through trade unions, though, that is not enough to build bargaining power in the globalized world. Efforts to build bargaining power for workers through trade unions may lead to the exclusion of the workers involved in the production process. Employers in Thailand have a history to retrenching the leaders of unions who mobilize workers to agitate improvements in working conditions of workers (Charoenloet 2002). Although workers have access to benefits through labour laws, which give social protection, such as, social security and workmen compensation fund, they are often abused by employers. The putting-out system of outsourcing work has become a convenient mechanism for employers to locate harmful and low wage paying tasks outside the domain of unions as they are subcontracted out to homeworkers.

This is because global production is not done only in factories or only by factory workers as significant aspects of production happens outside the factory through the 'informalization' of work. While the outsourcing of work to homeworkers has reduced the bargaining power of unions, homeworkers are also exposed to 'precarious' work as contract firms try to drive costs down. It is through effective link with trade unions that these workers can be helped. Organizing them is difficult because of the geographical distance between each or groups of workers. Yet, workers need to be organized and mobilized into groups based on common interests related to work. A forum is needed for them to facilitate the exchange of information and experience and how to cooperate to build a broader base for mobilization.

In Thailand, mainstream trade unions are organized vertically and are highly fragmented (Charoenloet 2000). Hence, serious efforts are needed to mobilize workers for trade unions because of two reasons. First, unions are built for factory workers with a common identity and interest. Second, the bargaining power of workers would increase when trade unions become members of broader federation and labour councils. Among workers registered under the social security department in Thailand, 9.5 million of a workforce of 36 million are wage workers in the private sector. However, of this large number, only 326,950 workers are members of trade unions. To make matters worse there are around 1200 trade unions with 90% of them concentrated in Bangkok and the Central Region (Labour Relation Department 2007). Also the 16 labour federations and 11 labour councils are just too many to mobilize workers under one stand. Not only is labour fragmented and weak but trade union elections have also been affected by the one union, one vote framework used.

It might be worth bringing back the past practice of organizing workers from different trade unions by taking account of industrial districts, which are commonly known as 'Industrial Zones Trade Union Workers'. Such an organization may try to accommodate different types of workers' demands and to organize horizontally, which is not recognized by present labour laws in the country. It is important that this practice is brought back as it will allow discussion of the real problems facing workers. Nevertheless, an interesting experience in organizing collective action has been undertaken by the 'Northern Labour Network'. Workers are redefined in more broadly beyond just factory work to include workers from all sectors. In the past, this was done through the creation of a broader coalition comprising trade unions in the Northern Industrial Zone, the federation of transnational migrant workers, the northern home-based workers network and the 'empowerment group' of sex workers. Such coalitions may need to be pursued in parallel with the creation of the workers educational centre and forum for exchange in order to raise social consciousness among workers to compliment the role of mainstream trade unions.

6. Conclusion

While Thailand's economy has grown significantly since the global forces of investment inflows and trade expanded strongly, especially since 1985, over half of the labour force has still remained in non-wage employment as late as 2009. The nature of work created by FDI driven export-oriented industrialization, which is exposed to the vicissitudes of volatile fluctuations in demand, has meant that the employment opportunities created are not permanent. Farming has often acted as the shock absorber whenever external shocks hit the economy as is the case with the 1997−1998 and 2008−2009 economic crises.

While some industries have benefited from global integration, e.g. automobiles, they do not constitute the main body of manufacturing activities in Thailand. It is here that the failure of the Thai state to stimulate industrial upgrading from low to higher value added activities despite introducing the minimum wage has led a number of employers to seek cost cutting measures to continue to compete in low value added activities. The dire consequences of such measures include the subcontracting of labour to homeworkers who are paid low rates for their work. The outsourcing of work in activities, such as, in the clothing industry, has undermined the bargaining power of workers as employers often do not observe labour laws governing the informal sector. The liberalization of the economy has increased casualization of work with the informal sector increasingly playing a major role.

The existing framework of highly fragmental industrial relations and with too many federations and councils has diluted the capacity of trade unions to effectively mobilize support to organize workers in Thailand. Despite their shortcomings, we argue that it is through the mobilization of workers through a centralized command that the rights of workers exposed to the abuses of low road to industrialization can be corrected. The government should take tripartism seriously so that workers, employers and the government work towards putting Thailand on the path of high road to industrialization.

Acknowledgements

This paper is based on a research project on labour and social protection in Thailand funded by the Thai Health Promotion Foundation. The author would like to thank the research team for its contribution and special thanks to Prof. Dr. Alain Mounier from the Centre of Education and Labour Studies (CELS) and Prof. Dr. Rajah Rasiah from the University of Malaya for their valuable comments. However, the paper remains the author's responsibility alone.

References

Charoenloet, V. 2000. "Industrialization and Labour Fragmentation in Thailand." In *Social Development in Asia, Social Indicators Research Series*, Vol. 5, 99–126. Eindhoven: Kluwer Academic.

Charoenloet, V. 2002. "Thailand and Industrial Restructuring: Government Policies and the Labour Situation Since 1997." *The Journal of Comparative Asian Development* 1 (2): 245–261.

Charoenloet, V., A. Mounier, P. Panichkul, and T. Tassanakunlapan. 2014. "Dynamics of Social Protection for Workers under the Present Employment Structure and Welfare System in Thailand." *A Research Funded by the Thai Health Promotion Foundation*. Bangkok, Thailand (in Thai).

Eurostat yearbook. 2012. *Labour Market*. Brussels: European Commission.

ILO (International Labour Organization). 2010/11. *World Social Security Report 2010/11*. Geneva: International Labour Organization.

Labour Relation Department. 2007. *Statistics of Trade Unions in Thailand for the Year 2007*. Bangkok: Ministry of Labour.

Lauridsen, L.S. 2008. *States, Institutions and Industrial Development. Industrial Deepening and Upgrading Policies in Taiwan and Thailand Compared*. Aachen: Shaker Verlag.

Lucassen, J. 2008. "Writing Global Labour History 1800–1940 : A Histography of Concepts, Periods and Geographical Scope". In *Global Labour History: A State of the Art*, 39–89. Bern: Peter Lang A.G, International Academic Publishers.

Mounier, A., and V. Charoenloet. 2010. " New Challenges for Thailand: Labour and Growth After the Crisis." *Journal of Contemporary Asia* 40 (1): 123–143.

Rasiah, R. 2000. "Globalization and International Private Capital Movements." *Third World Quarterly* 21 (6): 943–961.

Rasiah, R. 2009. "Garment Manufacturing in Cambodia and Laos." *Journal of the Asia Pacific Economy* 14 (2): 150–161.

Rasiah, R. 2010. "Industrialization in the Second-Tier NIEs." In *The New Political Economy of Southeast Asia*, edited by R. Rasiah and J. Schmidt, 44–103. Cheltenham: Edward Elgar.

Rasiah, R. 2012. "Beyond the Multi-fibre Agreement: How Are Workers in East Asia Faring?" *Institutions and Economies* 4 (3): 1–20.

Rasiah, R., K.C. Cheong, and R. Doner. 2014. "The Southeast Asian Experience with the Asian and Global Financial Crises." *Journal of Contemporary Asia* 44 (4): 572–580.

Rasiah, R., X.S. Yap, and V.G R. Chandran. 2014. "Crisis Effects in the Electronics Industry in Southeast Asia." *Journal of Contemporary Asia* 44 (4): 645–663.

Rock, M.T. 1995. "Thai Industrial Policy: How Irrelevant Was It to Export Success?" *Journal of International Development* 7 (5): 745–757.

World Bank. 2014. *World Development Indicators*. Washington, DC: World Bank Institute.

Globalization, industrialization, and labor markets in Vietnam

Angie NgocTran[a] and Irene Nørlund[b]

[a]Social, Behavioral and Global Studies Division, California State University, Monterey Bay, Seaside, CA, USA; [b]Department for Nutrition and Health, Faculty of Health and Technology, Metropolitan University College, København, Denmark

This paper investigates the dilemmas of reaching the Vietnamese goal of 'civilized and equitable' society expressed from central planning towards a 'socialist market economy under state guidance' with deeper integration into the global capitalist system, and their impacts on the labor markets. Using long-run statistical data, historical contexts and industrial policies, and fieldwork interviews (from 1980s to 2014), we focus on two important labor-intensive, export-based industries: the long-established textile/garment industry and the emerging electronics industry, which surpassed textile exports in 2013. Evidence shows that the 'high road' to industrialization model – with domestic linkages and skills upgrading – does not accompany growth in exports, as low-skilled assembly, mostly young female workers join the labor force with non-liveable wages and substandard working conditions. These two case studies delve into different stages of industrial policy, which is more defined in the textile/garment case and underdeveloped in the electronics case.

Introduction

In commemoration of Melanie Beresford's untimely death, this paper re-examines the key themes and arguments that she made in her 2008 article, 'Doi Moi in Review: The Challenges of Building Market Socialism in Vietnam,' and in her other scholarly works.[1] Her findings provide insights into our own research, which addresses the key themes of this special journal issue: the interconnections between global capitalist integration and industrialization, and their effects on the Vietnamese labor markets.

In the 2008 article, Beresford provided an insightful and prescient review of the 20-year period after Doi Moi, or the transformation from central planning towards a 'socialist market economy under state guidance.' She posed critical and timely questions: 'Is Vietnam still on the road to socialism? Or has it... effectively abandoned that path in favor of capitalism?' (Beresford 2008, p. 222) . Her arguments point to the inability of the Vietnamese state to provide crucial investment to support state enterprises – partly due to donor pressure – which led to foreign investors and the domestic non-state sector dominating the economic landscape. Still she argued for the possibility of state-led development which requires a clear and authoritative industrial policy, lest cronyism tip the balance (Beresford 2008, pp. 221–222).

Extending her inquiry, our overarching research question focuses on the dilemma faced by the Vietnamese government in fulfilling the Vietnamese Communist Party's stated goal of a 'civilized and equitable' society. In particular, we focus on these questions: How do political and economic forces influence industrialization (growth) and equity (distribution and impacts on the labor markets)? How have global integration and industrialization affected the Vietnamese labor markets? What are the conditions for 'high-road' industrial policy and the challenges to keep higher value-added inside Vietnam?

In honor of Beresford's interests in historical contexts and gender equity, we first present the context and literature review before analyzing the impacts of industrial policies on the textile/garment and the electronics industries. We examine these policies' impacts on the labor markets with attention to gender differences.

Historical context and literature review

Historical evidence shows that the global integration had started during the French colonial era (1880s–1954) (Nørlund, 1994). The liberation struggle (1945–1954) culminated in the 1954 Geneva agreement which divided the country at the 17th parallel, forming the Democratic Republic of Vietnam (DRV) in the northern part and the Republic of Vietnam (RVN) in the southern part. In the North, the construction of socialism started with the collectivization of agriculture and formation of a state-owned industrial sector around 1965, when the war with the USA escalated. In the South, already the center of commerce and industry during the colonial French period, the RVN government (with United States support as part of the anti-communist strategy) set out to develop a capitalist economy that was dependent on foreign capital, and that imported consumer goods, raw materials, and technical expertise from the United States and its East Asian allies – Japan, Taiwan, and South Korea – in the 1960s (Tran 2013).

After the USA–Vietnam war ended in 1975, Vietnam was reunified into the Socialist Republic of Vietnam (SRV). But post-war Vietnam faced two decades of an American trade embargo (1975–1995), which curtailed Western capital investment in Vietnam. Internally, the SRV government imposed the socialist model on the whole country, expanding the model of the north. From 1960 to 1979, the government implemented 'classic socialism' with the dominance of the state and cooperative sectors in the context of a planned and war-time economy. The DRV and later SRV were part of the former communist economic bloc (CMEA)[2] from 1954 to the disintegration of the bloc in 1989.

Under hard economic constraints, top–down government imposition was challenged by grassroots reform ideas and experiments (Fforde and de Vylder 1996). This 'fence breaking' process led to the Sixth Party Congress in 1986, which endorsed the more flexible approach with cooperation between plan and market and the development of an internal free market system and widespread decentralization (Beresford 1995, p. 8). The 1979–1989 period was called the 'transition period' with *Doi Moi* (renovation) process. The period witnessed Vietnam's isolation from the neighboring countries: China, Taiwan, Japan, South Korea and the Association of Southeast Asian Nations (ASEAN).

The 1989 disintegration of the Soviet Bloc and the collapse of the Eastern European market (Vietnam's major trading partners) led to a systemic shock for the Vietnamese economy, with loss of trade, dwindling aid, loans, and commerce from those sources (Beresford and Đặng 2000). Facing such difficulties, Vietnam opened itself to other markets, especially Japan, ASEAN, and the European Union. Since 1989, the Vietnamese state has called itself a 'market economy with socialist orientation' (Beresford 1988, 2008; Beresford and Tran 2004; Fforde and de Vylder 1996). After several years adjusting to the new global situation, the Vietnamese government accepted and endorsed the market-based economy at its Party Congress in 1992 (Fforde 2013).

Further global integration took place when the Clinton administration ended the 20-year US trade embargo in 1994 and established diplomatic relations with Vietnam in 1995. This led to the Bilateral Trade Agreement with the USA in 2000, the Vietnam–USA Textile Agreement in 2003, and Vietnam's accession to membership in the World Trade Organization (WTO) in 2007. This integration process opened the floodgate to foreign direct investment (FDI) in Vietnam from the United States and its Western allies. Trade between Vietnam and China increased when the two countries normalized their relations in November 1991, after Vietnam's withdrawal from Cambodia in 1989.

The labor laws, the Vietnamese General Confederation of Labor (VGCL) and their official labor newspapers continue to shape the labor markets and labor activism (Tran 2007a, 2007b). Originally, the progressive Vietnamese Labor Code – effective in January 1995 – encompasses all the work and pay conditions, nonwage benefits, special stipulations for female workers as well as the right to strike stipulated in Chapter 14. However, with increasing pressure from foreign investors, the revised Labor Code was ratified with a weakened Chapter 14, limiting ways in which workers can go on strike (Tran 2013). However, workers still appeal to their legal entitlements stated in the Labor Code to fight for their rights as explained further below. We now turn to the major industrial policies that impact the labor markets.

State-led development policies: equitization program and industrial policies

There are two different perspectives on the role of the state in development/industrialization. The first perspective includes arguments made by conventional neoclassical economists who, at least in theoretical debates, advocate minimal state intervention in the economy, limited to preventing 'market failures' and to maintaining macro-economic stability and (Ricardian's) static comparative advantage. Assessing Vietnam's market reforms and integration into the global market system, they advocated institutional reforms following the Washington-consensus, IMF, World Bank, and WTO policy directives (Nørlund, Tran, and Nguyen 2003; Vo and Nguyen 2009; Abbott, Bentzen, and Tarp 2009). In terms of global integration – WTO accession – Vo and Nguyen focused on 'FDI inflows' and discussed vaguely 'diversifying/differentiating export products... attracting efficient FDI/strategic partners.' However, they did not consider the conflicting consequences of 'attracting efficient FDI/strategic partners' which would curtail/limit/ hamper the development (or maturation) of the fledging domestic industries.

The second perspective adopts the state-led or developmental state industrialization framework (Tran 1996). Scholars have demonstrated that government industrial policies (in developed countries) to support strategic 'infant industries' and protect domestic markets had created *dynamic* comparative advantage for long-term economic development (Reinert 2007; Wade 2003).[3] Beresford argued that the Taiwanese model might be more appropriate to contemporary Vietnam than the Korean (chaebol) model (Beresford 2008, p. 235): seeing the possibilities of state-owned enterprises (SOEs) in key sectors providing inputs or buying outputs from thousands of small export-oriented factories in Vietnam. Due to pressure from the IMF, World Bank, and donor communities, not only state investment in strategic development areas was inadequate, but also institutional reform (equitization/ privatization) was ineffective (Beresford 2008, p. 230). Consequently, foreign investment and the domestic private sector benefit from the GDP growth by shifting to labor-intensive manufacturing with low costs in equipment and low labor costs (for low-skilled jobs)

(Beresford 2008, p. 233).[4] Empirical evidence supports her claim: in 2009, manufacturing continued to rank the highest in total FDI funds, with East Asian investors (Taiwan, South Korea, Malaysia, Japan, and Singapore), the USA and their island protectorates (the Cayman Islands and Samoa) topped the list of FDI investors in Vietnam (Tran 2013, pp. 129–230).

However, global fluctuations have impacted Vietnam, at times beyond their control. Nørlund, et al. argued that in the 1990s the government did encourage FDI in Vietnam's industrialization strategy, on the basis that the SOEs would continue to ensure the living standard of the urban workers. But the Asian Crisis at the end of the 1990s changed the state's strategy to emphasize private-sector development and a slowdown in the SOE reforms to equitize (Nørlund, Tran and Nguyen 2003). Tran found that Vietnam's position in the global supply chain has exposed firms to low value-added assembly operations, and workers to non-livable wages and retrenchments, substandard working conditions, and a vicious cycle of underdevelopment and poverty (Tran 2004, 2012). Evidence for impacts on the labor markets and linkage development potentials will be provided in the case studies below.

Equitization process and its impacts on the labor force

Under pressure from the IMF, the World Bank, and the international donor community in the second half of the 1990s, the Vietnamese state had to privatize SOEs, calling this process 'equitization' (Nørlund, Tran and Nguyen 2003).[5] This hyperbole is an ideologically correct way to express the transfer of public assets to the private sector in a socialist country. In principle, state managers determine the values of these SOEs and then sell shares to workers and other investors, creating joint-stock companies in the private sector. Smaller (often unprofitable) SOEs were absorbed into larger corporations. By 2005, only 4086 SOEs remained out of the initial 12,000 SOEs. Vinatex (case study below), one of the few remaining state corporations, was considered successful (Beresford 2008, p. 231). By 2008, the remaining 1824 state-owned enterprises were in monopolist public utilities and military and defense industries (Tran 2013, p. 132). While recognizing the remaining large SOEs as a success of the Vietnamese state who 'resist donor pressures in the interests of maintaining a consensus-driven policy approach,' Beresford acknowledged that the state had compromised with the neo-liberal financial institutions by not injecting new capital investment into the remaining large SOEs, thus foregoing its industrial strategy for the public sector (Beresford 2008, pp. 232–233). We update this argument with findings in the two case studies below to trace the impacts of industrial policies.

Overall, the impacts of the equitization process on the labor force were negative. This process led to the laying off of hundreds of thousands of former state workers who lost their wages and benefits. Labor protections were diminished with decreasing oversight from the VGCL and the Ministry of Labor, Invalids and Social Affairs (MOLISA). Many workers employed in state-owned enterprises were considered 'redundant' and were laid off: from 59% (of workers in state-owned enterprises) in 2000 to only about 19% in 2009, although most state managers have been able to keep their jobs (Tran 2013, p. 114). However, for public workers nationwide (not just factory workers), there was an increase from 3.7 million (in 2000) to 5.0 million (in 2009) (GSO 2006, p. 42, 2010, p. 61). This increase may be due to the state efforts to create jobs for workers in other state sectors such as education, health, banking, and civil service.

The boundaries between state and non-state sectors in Vietnam have become blurred as the equitized enterprises had been folded into the diverse subcategories in the domestic private sector (including joint-stock, limited liability companies). The labor force in the domestic private sector almost doubled its share of the industrial workforce between 2000 and 2009: from 29% in 2000 to 59% in 2009. Similarly, the FDI sector – including 100% of foreign capital and joint-venture capital – had doubled its share of the industrial work-force: from employing 11% in 2000 to 21% in 2009 (Tran 2013, p. 114).

Most laid-off state workers did not receive a one-time severance payment, full compensation and entitlements, as well as the ability to buy preferential shares. In sum, most workers ended up losing their shares to private investors, being forced to retire early and owning no means of production. In response to this injustice, state workers had engaged in all forms of protest, and appealed to the legal framework that promises benefits and compensation (Tran 2013).

Impacts of global integration and WTO accession

Most studies show contradictions facing market socialism in Vietnam. While agreeing that *Doi Moi* resulted in positive outcomes – including improvements in poverty reduction – the distribution of income and wealth from globalization and industrialization has been very uneven (Beresford 2008; Tran 2012; Abbott, Bentzen, and Tarp 2009; Nørlund, Tran, and Nguyen 2003; Nørlund et al. 2006). Beresford addressed the uneven distribution of the fruits of GDP growth in the early 2000s. There had been an increase in regional inequality as the income gap widened between urban and rural areas, and poor people had been unable to participate in the benefits of growth (Beresford 2008, p. 236). Class formation – defined as people's separation from the means of production – has been increasing (Beresford 2008, pp. 237–238).

Beresford was concerned about the proletarianization process in which people became heavily indebted through subcontracting arrangements. Moreover, she argued that the subordination of labor to capital was prominent in the rapid expansion of wage employment, especially in the domestic and foreign private sectors where most workers were women who received low wages, assembling products in export-oriented factories (Beresford 2008, pp. 234, 238). By 2014, this situation has not improved.

Vo and Nguyen – in their analysis of the social and economic consequences to Vietnam after two years of WTO membership – tempered the 'rosy' analysis of Vietnam's accession to the WTO. While there was an increase in job creation in labor-intensive industries, the 2008 inflation (of over 18%) hurt low-income assembly workers a lot more than did employees with income in high value-added services (Vo and Nguyen 2009, pp. 127–228). Poor households did not benefit from global integration with lower purchasing power parity and higher food prices. The actual poverty rate was around 15%–16% by the end of 2008 (Vo and Nguyen 2009, p. 128).

GDP, trade and foreign investment

While it is important to show the magnitude of the integration into the world economy by way of foreign trade and GDP (Rasiah 2007, Introduction; Table 1), these data are not enough to assess Vietnam's global integration. To gauge Vietnam's insertion into the global economy and its impacts on both labor and capital, it is important to measure the magnitude of imports in trade statistics, or to subtract total import from total export statistics to find the value of *net export*. These statistics may offer a more accurate assessment, showing that they indicate a smaller value-added accumulation that actually stays in Vietnam (Tran 2012).

Tables 1 and 2 show that the *net* export (export minus import, instead of the sum of imports and exports) can better reflect the impacts of global integration on Vietnamese

Table 1. GDP, trade, industry, share in GDP (1990–2012, selected years).

	1990	1995[a]	2000	2010	2012
GDP (in 1000 USD, in current US$)[b]	6,471,740	20,736,164	33,640,086	115,931,750	155,820,002
Export (in 1000 USD) in current FOB price)	2,404,000	5,448,900	14,482,700	72,236,700	114,631,000
Import (in 1000 USD, current price)	2,752,400	8,155,400	15,636,500	84,838,600	114,347,000[c]
Total Trade (in 1000 USD)	5,156,400	13,604,300	30,119,200	157,075,300	228,978,000
Share of Total Trade in GDP (%)	80%	66%	90%	135%	147%
Trade Deficit/Surplus (in 1000 USD)	−348,400	−2,706,500	−1,153,800	−12,601,900	+284,000
Share of NET Export in GDP (%)	−5.4%	−13%	−3.4%	−11%	+0.18%
Industry, value-added % of GDP)[d]	22.7%	28.8%	34.2%	38.2%	38.6%
Manufacturing in current prices (in USD)[e]	804,809,490	Not available	5,653,724,138	7,146,511,628	7,553,093,525
Manufacturing (% of GDP in current prices)	12%	Not available	17%	6%	4.8%

Notes:
[a]The addition of the 1995 statistics is because it marks the end of the US trade embargo and the start of trade relations with the US and its allies.
[b]World Development Indicators: http://databank.worldbank.org/data/views/reports/tableview.aspx.
[c]This GSO import statistics ($114.3 billion) is higher than the World Bank statistics ($113.8 billion). To be consistent, we use the higher GSO import statistics. The difference, $0.5 billion, may be due to different ways in which imports are calculated. The World Bank used the CIF price (or Cost, Insurance and Freight). *Taking Stock: An Update on Vietnam's Recent Economic Developments* The World Bank, Hanoi, 10 July 2013, p. 24.
[d]World Development Indicators: http://databank.worldbank.org/data/views/reports/tableview.aspx.
[e]GSO statistics (2006, 2010, 2012).
Source: World Development Indicators: http://databank.worldbank.org/data/views/reports/tableview.aspx (accessed on 7 February 2014); General Statistical Office (GSO) (2006, 2010), 2012.

Table 2. The VGTI, imports and exports (2000–2012, in US$ million) (textile and garment only, without shoes/footwear).

	2000	2001	2002	2003	2004	2005	2006	2007	2008	2009	2010	2011	2012[a]
Cotton	90.4	115.4	111.6	105.4	190.2	167.21	219.0	268	468	395	673.5	1061.5	877.2
Fiber	237.3	228.4	272.6	317.5	338.8	339.59	544.6	744	788	896	1301.9	1541.2	1408
Fabrics	761.3	880.2	1523	1805	1927	2399	2984	3980	4454	4212	5383.1	6791.1	7039.9
Auxiliary materials[b]	1194.7	1397.9	1513.4	1825.9	1724.3	1774.2	1952.0	2152	2376	1932	3583.7	3684.8	3159.7
Import[c]	2283.7	2622	3421	4054	4180	4680	5700	7144	8086	7435	10,942.2	13,078.6	12,484.8
Export	1891.9	1975.4	2732.0	3609.1	4385.6	4838.4	5834.0	7794	9121	9066	11,209.8	13,211.7	15,090.2
Net export	−391.8	−646.5	−688.7	−445.1	+205.6	+158.4	+134.4	+650	+996	+1631	+267.6	+133.1	+2605.4

Notes:
[a]Preliminary 2012 data, from the GSO Statistics which are consistent with the World Bank 2012 statistics.
[b]Auxiliary materials include machinery, parts, and other accessories.
[c]These statistics are the sums of imported cotton, fiber, fabrics and auxiliary materials. They exclude chemicals and dyes.
Source: *Statistical Yearbook* (2011, pp. 525, 533) General Statistics Office of Vietnam. 'Some main goods for exportation.' http://www.gso.gov.vn/default_en.aspx? tabid=472&idmid=3&ItemID=14610 (accessed on 26 November 2013).
GSO. 'Some main goods for importation.' http://www.gso.gov.vn/default_en.aspx?tabid=472&idmid=3&ItemID=14605 (accessed on 26 November 2013). *Taking Stock: An Update on Vietnam's Recent Economic Developments*, The World Bank (2013, pp. 22, 24).

society, with special attention to manufacturing, which accounts for the largest share of the wage-earning labor force. Table 1 shows that the net export in Vietnam has just started to be on the positive side in 2012; all net export values were negative before that.

The foreign sector played a crucial role when political relations with Western countries were reestablished in 1994–1995 after the collapse of the Soviet Union and its Eastern European bloc and the start of diplomatic relations between Vietnam and the USA. Industrial development was stagnant for a few years at the turn of the 1990 decade, but consistent *Doi Moi* policy in the early 1990s had given the private sector equal status to that of the state sector. Since then, foreign investments increased quickly, even with setbacks both during the Asian crisis (1997–1998) and during the recession from 2008. However, the level of investment quickly returned: FDI increased from US$428 million in 1991 to an annual level of investment for the following decade of US$2–3000 million. In 2005 investment passed US$3000 million, and after the accession into the WTO it reached the level of US$8000 million, and stabilized around US$11,000 million through 2012. The main investors have been Asian industrial nations, such as Japan, Taiwan, Singapore, and the Republic of Korea (GSO 2012, p. 173).[6]

Foreign trade showed a parallel experience. From a low level of trade in 1980s, it began to increase in the late 1980s and then reached to about six times higher in 2000. Between 2000 and 2010, trade increased fivefold; between 2010 and 2012, trade increased by 50%. Trade deficits increased from 1990 to 2010 (the high deficit in 2010 might be due to slow demand for products during the global financial crisis), but the trend changed and a small surplus was the result in 2012 (Table 1).

To assess the overall growth and trade picture since integrating into the world economy, we need to understand the impacts of value-added in trade and the possibility of industrial policy to transcend this challenge.

The garment/textile and electronics industries

Vietnam has integrated into the world trade market at an amazing speed. However, the country did not turn into a new growth economy like Republic of Korea or Taiwan. Instead, most value-added in Vietnam has been low and concentrated in light industry and foodstuffs.

The Vietnamese Textile and Garment Industries (VTGIs) continue to account for the largest share of the wage earning labor force since Vietnam joined the WTO in 2007 (Table 2). The VTGI employed over 2 million workers in 2010 (Tran 2012). In 2012, the total value of textile/garment export was $15.1 billion (GSO statistics and World Bank figure).[7] The USA has become the largest importer of Vietnamese textile and garment products, followed by the EU, Japan, and the Republic of Korea.[8]

While this trade figure puts Vietnam as the fifth largest exporter of garment and textile products in the world, the performance of the VTGI on keeping value-added in Vietnam is not spectacular. In 2011, the value-added that remained in the VTGI was only $2.16 billion USD (or 35%), and the domestic content ratio was about 46% (Tran 2012, pp. 127, 133). In 2012, GSO statistics show an increase in net export of the VTGI: from US$0.13 billion in 2011 to $2.6 billion in 2012 (Table 2). This suggests an increase in value-added.

Production of the textile and garment industries continues to depend on imports of raw materials and technology, mostly in low value-added, low-paying assembly work. Positive *net* export did not start until 2004 but with small and fluctuating magnitudes, until reaching 2012 with an impressive US$2.6 billion (Table 2). Vinatex and VITAS

(Vietnam Textile and Apparel Association) officials are knowledgeable about this low value-added problem and the bottlenecks that plague the VTGI. The Vinatex case study below explains the bottlenecks and the potential for state-led industrial policy.

As of August 2013, there are 4500 textile/garment factories in Vietnam, of which 650 FDI enterprises (14% of the total factories) but they accounted for 55% of the total turn-over of the textile and garment industries (Interview with Mr Nguyen Van Tuan, July 2013). This shows the high capacity of foreign-invested textile/garment factories.

Exports of high-tech products represent the most interesting increase compared to the long-term stronghold of the VTGI export. In terms of share of 2012 total export value (in FOB price), total US$20.5 billion of high-tech exports [including US$7.8 billion (6.8%) of electronics and computers, and US$12.7 billion (11%) of cell phones and accessories], compared to US$22.4 billion in the VTGI [including US$15.1 billion of textile/garment export (13.2%) and $7.3 billion of footwear export (6.3%)].[9] According to the South Korean Embassy (cited in the World Bank 2013, pp. 21–22), this rise in high-tech products was directly related to Samsung's expansion of cell phone factories in Vietnam with LG Electronics following suit.

There are two separate concerns about this rise in electronics export trend (compared to the textile/garment export): (1) similar to the VTGI export, the high export value of these high-tech products may include imported raw materials/components from South Korea. Thus more data about the value of these component imports are needed before we can ascertain the real value-added of high-tech exports and their impacts on Vietnamese labor market; and (2) the highly toxic work environment in electronics factories has different impacts on workers' health, compared to that of textile and garment factories.

Feminization of the labor markets

Further integration into the global economy has seen an increase in manufacturing workers as a share of the total labor force, noticeably since 2010. The share of manufacturing workers in the total labor force has increased steadily from 8% (1995) to 21% (2012) (Table 3).

Female workers are important to the FDI, domestic private, and the household/informal sector in modern-day global market. By 2012, over 52 million people joined the labor force (aged 15 years and older), which represents a 77% participation rate. Of those employed, most were low-skilled: only 15% were trained (GSO 2012, p. 1). Most young workers (both females and males under 30 years of age) were employed by foreign-owned and domestic private enterprises (GSO 2012, pp. 2–3). Female workers in the *formal* sector accounted for almost 70% of the total wage workforce (GSO 2012, p. 2).[10]

Feminization of the labor force in the FDI sector is also observed in the electronics sector (Vind 2008, pp. 1484, 1486). Most FDI enterprises (concentrating in both textile/garment and electronics sectors) have been hiring more female than male workers: 78% to 82% were women between 2005 and 2010. In non-FDI manufacturing factories, the trend is reversed: female workers accounted for 41% (2005), 38% (2010), and 24% (2012) (Table 3). This trend may underestimate *informal* female workers who are not counted in official statistics.

Wage differences by gender are related to the industrialization process and labor migration to metropolitan areas producing for the global market. Factors such as level of education, factory location (with export processing and industrial zones such as Red River delta, Mekong River delta, Central provinces, Southeast provinces, Hanoi, and Ho Chi Minh City), and economic sector (private, public) are found to significantly affect female

Table 3. Labor force, by sector (1995–2012, selected years).

Categories	1995[a]	2000	2005	2010	2012 (prelim)
Labor force (in million. Total employment over 15 years)	33.3[2001 SYB]	37.6[2005 SYB]	42.8[2009 SYB]	49.052 million in VTGI[b][2012 SYB]	52.62.5 million in VTGI[c][2012 SYB]
Of which: People in manufacturing (in mill people and percentage of total labor force	2.6 (7.8%)	3.9 (10.34%)No break-down by gender available[2005 SYB: industry/ manufacturing]	5.3 (12.3%)2.19 females2.08 males [2009 SYB]	6.65 (13.6%)2.53 females2.37 males [2012 SYB]	10.9[d] (21%)2.66 females2.51 males [2012 SYB]
Employment in textile enterprises (actual stats)	No break-down data	All: 122,759Of which: 85,162 females (69%)	All: 188,356Of which: 129380 females (69%)	All: 184,343Of which: 111,005 females (60%)	No gender break-down available
Employment in garment enterprises (actual stats)	No break-down data	All: 231,948Of which: 187,127 females (81%)	All: 511,278Of which: 419,504 females (82%)	All: 858,696Of which: 699,531 females (82%)	No gender break-down available

Notes:
[a]We cannot find any solid information for 1990 manufacturing – only for total industrial output. The early GSO books only had total industrial output value without breaking it down to sector level (such as Manufacturing and Mining). However, the later GSO books (such as 1999, 2001) do list 1995 output value by subsection. Therefore, we have omitted the 1990 data from this table and showed the breakdown for manufacturing in 1995 instead.
[b]Interview with Nguyen Van Tuan, the Vice General Secretary of Vietnam Textile and Apparel Association, VITAS, July 2013.
[c]Interview with Nguyen Van Tuan, January 2014.
[d]This statistic includes workers in industry and construction. Sources: GSO Statistical Yearbook 2001 for 1995 statistics (GDP p. 52, Manufacturing p. 234, Population p. 41, Export p. 370, Import p. 371).
Sources: Statistical Yearbook in 2001, 2005, 2009, 2012.

workers' wages. Overall, women receive less than men in the private sector (which includes both domestic and foreign investment) (Pierre 2012, pp. 35, 43). Men in higher level occupations tend to have smaller wage gaps, and greater gap in manual/unskilled jobs (Pierre 2012, p. 33). Consistent with the Vietnam Household Living Standards Survey (VHLSS 2012) data, in terms of mean hourly wage, female wage workers earn only 90% of males doing the same jobs. Wage workers from vulnerable groups such as unskilled youth, women, and ethnic minorities are paid less than others (Pierre 2012, p. 23).

Moreover, troubling trends emerge related to young workers migrating to work in factories in supplier factories in metropolitan areas. First, migrant workers have become younger in all major regions, including rural areas. In 2008, more than 85% of factory workers in the export processing zones (EPZs), industrial zones and joint-ventures were young female migrant workers (between 18 and 30 years of age) (Pierre 2012, p. 9). By 2011, most migrant workers congregated in the top three cities in the South: Binh Duong, Dong Nai, and Ho Chi Minh City, where most strikes erupted. On average, workers earned only about VND1.3−1.5 million per month (less than US$100) as of 2008 (Tran 2013, pp. 183−184, 187). Second, an increase in the supply of young Vietnamese workers means that they leave school earlier (Pierre 2012, p. 43). The long-term implication of this trend may adversely affect workers' knowledge, critical thinking, and other skill sets for future careers.

However, workers in these sectors do not play the role of victims. For state workers who were laid off from equitized factories, their sense of entitlement and expectation of receiving social welfare benefits and compensation continued to run high. State workers used the state media and the laws to appeal to relevant government officials to fight against SOEs that did not follow the law, such as not paying severance allowances to workers who were laid off in previously equitized/privatized SOEs. While results have not always been successful, many former state workers also reminded the state to uphold its responsibilities in both social contracts (the social welfare function) and legal contracts (Tran 2013). For migrant workers in factories making products for the global economy, the long-term positive effect of the minimum wage strikes victory − which they started at the end of 2005 and ended in the beginning of 2006 with a 40% minimum wage increase − has led to an annual minimum wage adjustment to costs of living. For instance, effective 1 January 2014, a new set of minimum wage increases has been applied to both FDI and private sectors (Tran 2013).[11]

Trans-Pacific Partnership trade negotiations

Integrating further into the global capitalist economy has forced Vietnam to further liberalize its textile and garment industries. Before discussing the VTGI/Vinatex and the electronics industry, it is important to understand the larger context of the ongoing trade negotiations between Vietnam and other countries such as the Trans-Pacific Partnership (TPP) agreement.[12]

Joining the TPP requires Vietnam to address the following issues: transparent public spending with open-tender process for all biddings; privatization of the remaining SOEs (no subsidies); intellectual property rights of pharmaceuticals and chemical companies; an independent labor union system (not just the VGCL); respect for labor standards and the environment; on trade and investment, no trade barrier (all tariffs have be to zero); and the 'yarn forward' requirement which stipulates that fibers may be produced in any country but each component starting with the yarn used to make the textile or apparel must be from the TPP area. Essentially, it requires all three steps to be done within the TPP region: spinning of the yarn/thread, weaving/knitting of the fabric, and assembly of the final product (Interview with Nguyen Van Tuan, Vice General Secretary of Vietnam Textile and Apparel Association – VITAS, and director of the Vietnamese Cotton Association, July 2013; Platzer 2013, p. 16). These requirements (similar to the Rule of Origin from the EU) would encourage Vietnam to develop backward linkages and move up the ladder to become a higher value-added producer (Tran 2012).

According to Mr Nguyen, joining the TPP agreement can alleviate the disadvantageous position of the VTGI: importing most raw materials from foreign countries, and 17.5% tariff rate exporting to the USA. If the TPP agreement were signed, Vietnam can negotiate with the USA and other member countries to open up their markets for Vietnamese products, and attract more investment in Vietnam.[13]

Internal evaluation of the values of major state-owned conglomerates exposed many problems.[14] In particular, the problem of funneling/transferring of state investment to unrelated enterprises/operations for personal interests, or the selling of state property to other companies, has become a systemic problem in the economy. Dr Lê Đăng Doanh (former Director of Central Economic Management Institute) called for the need to retrieve these lost state investment (or 'thoái vốn ngoài ngành'). He argues for strong and specific state policy to oversee and prevent this common practice.[15]

State industrial policies in Vietnam

Sengenberger and Pyke (1990) defined 'high-road' industrialization as based on efficiency enhancement and innovation: 'through economic gains that make wage gains and improvements in social conditions feasible, as well as safeguarding workers' rights and providing adequate standards of social protection.' The key to attain this is as follows: better organization and mobilization and utilization of productive labor (which then permits a better use of technology, not the other way around). To make labor more productive, labor standards are indispensable: to curb downward pressure on wages and working conditions, joint conflict resolution, joint resource utilization, cooperation for exchanging information; trusting relationships between firms, and between employers and work forces; 'a mutual understanding or agreement, not to undercut wages and violate laws, is required to maintain trust.' (p. 9)

On 'high-road' industrialization, Rasiah (2007, pp. 184–186) analyzed the importance of the 'dynamic cluster' of the systemic quad model, in which the government, a critical stakeholder, oversees the four pillars, underlying the dynamic clustering. They include the following: (1) the basic infrastructure; (2) the high-tech infrastructure, (3) the integration in global markets and value chains, and (4) the network cohesion. He argues for a strong role of all levels of government to provide stability (economic, political, and security); high-tech institutions that drive learning and innovations (technology diffusion, licensing, training and R&D); connection with global value chains with just-in-time internal integration (assembly, design, packaging, and logistics); and networked cluster which calls for interface and coordination between vertically connected economic agents such as industry-government offices/councils, chambers of commerce, and economic development board such as the one in Singapore.

The following two case studies assess an ongoing industrial policy in the VTGI, and potentials for the electronics industry (which surpassed textile/garment export in 2012 discussed earlier).

The case of Vinatex

Vinatex provides an example of an ongoing state industrial policy which still employs the highest number of wage laborers and ranks on the top three export products in Vietnam. The Prime Minister Decree 118/2013/ND-CP entitled: 'About the organization and the by-laws of Vinatex' (taking effect as of 1 December 2013) intended to use Vinatex as its industrial policy. The state aims to raise value-added and domestic content ratios, in terms of raw materials for the VTGI. The timing of this decree coincides with the international pressure from the TPP negotiation for the state to privatize their assets. It states the key objectives of Vinatex: to make profits and preserve state investment (as well as Vinatex's own sources) and develop a textile and garment corporation group (*tập đoàn*) using state-of-the-art technology and a four-stage supply chain, covering: fiber, weaving, dyeing/finishing and sewing. The emphasis on value-added is very explicit in the language of this decree: 'the need to raise value-added in the textile and garment products.'[16]

In 2013, Vinatex's share in VTGI is about 14%. The total value of the VTGI export in the first six months of 2013 was US$8.9 billion, a 14.5% increase compared to the same period in 2012. Of this figure, Vinatex's total textile/garment export accounted for US$1.28 billion (a 13% increase compared to the same period).[17]

Mr Nguyen (VITAS) has demonstrated some possibility for a successful industrial policy via Vinatex. He shows impressive knowledge about the whole supply chain – from raw cotton, to spinning, to weaving and knitting, to dyeing and finishing – and pointed out the weak backward linkages of the VTGI supply chain.

Throughout all the interviews and correspondence (in 2013 and 2014), he is very conscious of the different levels of the linkages, and of the need for industrial upgrading, akin to going up the ladder of a pyramid structure. By 2014, over 70% of Vietnamese manufacturing still occupies the lowest level: CMT (cutting/making/trimming or low value-added assembly jobs); 20% OEM (Original Equipment Manufacturing), 9% ODM (Original Design Manufacturing), and at the top: only 1% of Original Brand Manufacturing (OBM). The higher one goes up the ladder of the so-called pyramid, the higher value-added one accrues. Therefore, except for the lowest CMT level (which FDI suppliers provide fabrics to Vietnamese subcontractors), the other three (OEM, ODM, and OBM) can use Vietnamese fabrics or source fabrics from elsewhere.

Mr Tuan admitted in the August 2013 interview: 'the majority of materials used in the sector are imported from foreign countries.' Thus, even with such high export values, Vietnam does not accumulate the value-added of these import materials, but primarily the wages of Vietnamese workers who assemble these garment components.[18] In particular, the wage-based value-added for the workers and managers – although a tenfold increase in *net* export after the onset of the global financial crisis in 2009, from US$268 million in 2010 to about US$2.6 billion in 2012 – accounts for only 17% in the total US$15.1 billion total VTGI trade value (Table 2).[19]

Vinatex had been merging its member firms (to address the pressure to privatize), yet still holding onto the value-added logic of state-led industry policy.[20] As of 2011, Vinatex had 60 textile and garment privatized member companies, yet the state still controlled by owning the majority shares of Vinatex's big textile factories (such as Phong Phu) and garment factories (such as Viet Tien) (Tran 2012, p. 132).

The newly configured structure for Vinatex reflects state ambivalence in privatizing, yet still holding on to some parts of Vinatex to carry on its industrial policy. This structure shows three groups: (1) the first group is called: *công ty Mẹ - Tập Đoàn Dệt May Việt Nam* or verbatim translation: '*Mother company*-the Vietnamese textile/garment

Corporation Group' (from now on Corporation Group for short).[21] (2) The second group is called **Children** companies (*công ty Con*) of the corporation group with two subgroups (the Corporation Group owns 100% of some, and only 50% of some).[22] (3) The third group, joint-stock companies that are linked to the Corporation Group (*công ty liên kết của Tập Đoàn*), is supposed to have their own (non-state) budgets.[23] Clearly, the state maintains a strong grip on the first and second groups.

Equitization has been the key concern for Vinatex and is directly related to the recent Vinatex industrial policy and the ongoing TPP negotiations with other countries. Attempts to interview Vinatex officials by phone and email were not very successful. However, a phone interview with Ms Pham Huong (the former director of the international relations department, now the head of a retail operation: Vinatex Mart) revealed this ongoing concern. Ms Huong mentioned that no one from Vinatex was willing to talk because 'they were all busy with the privatization/equitization of Vinatex conglomerate.' Everyone was afraid to say something wrong and so passed the buck onto the generic 'leader of the conglomerate.' Ms Huong explained that the Vinatex leadership had been in the process of assessing the value of some major SOEs in the VTGI and had been waiting for the Prime Minister's decision (Interview with Ms Pham Huong, 30 July 2013).

The bottlenecks are in the processing of yarn produced in Vietnam and in the dyeing process, not the production of raw cotton as expected (Mr Nguyen Van Tuan, July 2013 and January 2014). In 2012, the VTGI created a whole commodity chain, from the raw cotton stage to final fabrics for use in manufacturing for export and domestic use. But only a small percentage of quality fabrics were available for garment manufacturing. Mr Tuan stated that in 2012, Vietnam produced 5000 tons of raw cotton and imported 415,000 tons (of which 50% came from the USA, 20% from India, and 30% from Brazil, Australia, and Africa). With 5.1 million spindles, Vietnam spun the cotton into 700,000 tons of yarn, of which only 35% (245,000 tons) were for domestic market and 65% (455,000 tons) for export (of which one-third went to China, one-third to Turkey, and the rest went to Malaysia, Taiwan, South Korea, and Japan). Ironically, this 65% of Vietnamese made yarn probably will return to Vietnam by way of imported finished fabrics which Vietnamese garment producers have to buy.

For the remaining 245,000 tons of yarn that stayed in Vietnam, 1.3 billion meter squared of raw fabrics were produced, and of that, 0.5 billion raw fabrics were exported (unclear to where) and 0.8 billion came out of the dyeing and finishing process successfully. Therefore, of the 6.8 billion of meter-squared fabrics needed for garment production, only 12% (0.8 billion) was domestically produced. Over 85% of the fabrics needed for garment export most likely came from outside of Vietnam, or produced by FDI textile factories inside Vietnam.

However, differential power relations in the global supply chains are beyond Vietnam's control. The corporate buyers (such as Walmart, Liz Claiborne, the Limited) and their suppliers/primary vendors (East Asian owners/managers) dictate where to source the fabrics for garment manufacturing in Vietnam for export (Tran 2011, 2004).

The electronics industry

While Rasiah's (2007) dynamic clustering framework explains well the cases of Japan Taiwan, Korea, and Singapore in the 1970s and 1980s, it does not adequately explain socialist Vietnam, joining the twenty-first century global supply chains. As a 'latecomer,' integrating into the global markets does not automatically lead to access to knowledge and technology transfer.

Vind's (2008) study provides a more relevant model to late-comers such as Vietnam. He interviewed 35 company managers (mostly from Japan and Korea, with only three from the USA) in Ho Chi Minh City, and examined how transnational companies can be a source of skill upgrading in the electronics industry in Ho Chi Minh City. His conceptual framework is the reverse product-cycle model and transfer of technological capability which argues that higher skills can be transferred when developing countries move from being *reproduction* factory in the 'mature stage' of the foreign company (requiring only operator dexterity), to *learning* factory in the 'growth stage' (requiring enterprise-specific and relation-specific skills), to *pilot* factory in the 'R&D stage' (requiring scientist and engineering skills) (Vind 2008, p. 1483).

He argues that this model is more relevant (as opposed to the OEM–ODM–OBM model) to Vietnam because the electronics industry in the twenty-first century is dominated by foreign companies – an accurate reflection of reality – and the most likely route for transferring capabilities is through the local (Vietnamese) companies which can act as suppliers to exporting foreign companies. Vind found that Vietnamese companies mainly provided labor-intensive assembly of components, such as coils, cable assemblies, and mini-motors used in mobile phones and digital cameras. He concluded that Vietnamese electronics industry occupied 'a marginal position in the global production networks of electronics' (Vind 2008, p. 1484).

Evidence shows that Vietnamese electronics industry continues to be low-skilled assembly (Ohno 2009; Vind 2008). Ohno argues that Vietnam's industrialization up to 2009 was basically Stage 1, in which they assemble and test electronic devices and components (Ohno 2009, pp. 26–27). All design, technology, production, and marketing are directed by foreigners. Vind found that most electronics factories in Vietnam are 'reproduction factories' with mature technology and a narrow role in basic component manufacturing (Vind 2008, p. 1490). Only low engineering skills are required in these 'reproduction factories' with standardized production, little design, R&D and creative work to be done in Vietnam (Vind 2008, pp. 1488–1489). There is no positive spillover, or very limited skills or other technology transfer from foreign to local firms. The Vietnamese companies cannot compete with the high salaries offered by the foreign companies to recruit the best engineers there, thus not much upgrading of the domestic electronics industry, resulting in limited absorptive capacity (Vind 2008, p. 1490).

The case of intel

In 2013, the electronics export – mobile phones – surpassed the VTGI export.[24] Recent evidence shows that the 'reproduction factories' arrangement is similar to the case of Intel in Vietnam. Intel allocated US$1 billion to build its largest assembly and test facility (doubling the second largest plant in Malaysia) to produce chipsets for laptops and desktop computers in Asia and the world. This facility – located in the Saigon High Tech Park – went into operation in Ho Chi Minh City in July 2010.[25] At full capacity, Intel plans to employ up to 1000 engineers and thousands of technicians. But upon finishing with its chip-making facility in Ho Chi Minh City in 2010, Intel can only hire 1000 staff due to few workers with good command in English and basic engineering skills (Forbes (CORPORATE AUTHOR) 2014; Saarinen 2012).

Thus far, skills' training only occurs at the engineering level, not the general workers. Only a small group of Vietnamese engineers receive advanced technical training, at home and abroad (Vind 2008; Boudreau 2014). Thus, minimal technical knowledge transfers to the local factories, and most are female, low-skilled production assembly workers (Vind

2008, pp. 1486–1487). Intel management has been promoting education, especially in engineering, mainly for a few skilled workers (Intel Vietnam Scholars). As of January 2014, they sent 73 students from Vietnamese technical and engineering universities to get bachelor's degrees at Portland State University, and provided scholarships to Vietnamese students to get master's degrees at the Royal Melbourne Institute of Technology (RMIT) in Vietnam. In promoting gender diversity, they funded 300 scholarships for female technical students at other institutions. They also sent Vietnamese engineering professors to the USA to change how they teach in Vietnam (Boudreau 2014). Moreover, Intel has been collaborating with the Vietnamese Ministry of Education to improve the English curricula for students and graduates (Saarinen 2012). Overall, similar to the case of the East Asian electronics companies, technical training in Intel focused on a selected few in engineering and technical fields.

Overall, the internal value-added remains very small. Most raw materials and parts are made outside of Vietnam: processor and other 'micro-circuit dies cut from semiconductor wafers' are made at Intel's other fabrication plants.[26] The majority of assembly workers are low-skilled, who make about US$152 per month for testing and assembling these raw materials into the final chips which are then shipped out for computers and other devices. Moreover, while Intel has used Vietnamese local suppliers for food, human resources, and security services, they still prefer partners in their global network who supply raw materials and even consider relocating to Vietnam to meet Intel's growing demands in producing new products.[27] This is not a good trend for 'high-road' industrialization and 'dynamic cluster' if the Vietnamese government does not go beyond providing only the basic high-tech infrastructure, and not improving the value chains and network cohesion with the local economy.

Conclusion

The Vietnamese government continues to face the dilemma in fulfilling the goal of a 'civilized and equitable' society. Since the introduction of the marked-based economy and deeper integration into the global capitalist system from about 1992–1994, total trade has increased and expanded. While the net added value of the investment and trade are limited; Vietnam is still mainly supplying low-skilled labor force in both the VTGI and the emerging electronics industry.

The situation is murkier in terms of equity and the effects of global integration on the labor markets. Troubling trends emerge with an increasing supply of young Vietnamese workers who leave schools early and migrate to work in insecure/precarious jobs in metropolitan areas. Without proper education and basic skill sets, their future careers look bleak after leaving these low-paying and low-skilled jobs. Gender differences continue to put female workers in a more disadvantageous position vis-à-vis their male counterparts in producing for the global market. Thus, gender consideration should be included in all industrial policies, especially in labor-intensive industries.

The textile and garment industries have been facing two-prong problems since the mid-1990s: first, ineffective industrial policy resulting in low quality Vietnamese-made fabrics for garment export; second, differential power relations in the global supply chains which put Vietnam in the CMT low value added assembly stage (Tran 2011, 2012). The Vinatex case study confirms that various forms of equitized state-owned factories should still be considered as a part of the state sector. Clearly, the state has found ways to circumvent the donor pressure to privatize all SOEs, and invest in linkage development, intending to climb up the ladder of CMT/OEM/ODM/OBM production as shown in the Vinatex case study. But state protection for the workers falls far short: it is not enough to create jobs for the workers, but also what types of jobs and whether workers have a chance to upgrade their skills and enhance their well-being.

The electronics industry has the potential to upgrade skills through local supplier linkages, if the local Vietnamese companies can act as suppliers to exporting foreign companies. However, both USA and East Asian electronics companies in Vietnam (tier-1 suppliers) are assembly plants and testing facilities, which use imported raw materials and do not connect to the local economy. The government has no policy to absorb transferring capabilities from these FDI companies to the local suppliers, other than collaboration in English education and engineering skills which benefit only a small number of employees. On the impacts of 'high-road' industrialization on workers, more research is needed on the labor regime of Intel subsidiary in Vietnam: how they pay workers and offer them an environment that facilitates creative energies, and how does Intel Vietnam subsidiary pursue a labor-friendly approach to production organization.

Our findings are consistent with Beresford's on the dominance of foreign investment in the private sector and the potentials of state-led development policies (being implementing by Vinatex). Moreover, ongoing TPP trade negotiation can provide a window of opportunity to engage in upward linkage development as discussed in the Vinatex case study. Still, lack of transparency on the effectiveness of industrial policies in these strategic industries limits our analysis of the real situations.

In conclusion, Beresford had exposed a prescient dilemma which continues to be relevant to the present. Evidence shows that Vietnam has not yet abandoned socialism, at least in terms of industrial policies and progressive labor laws. But it is the workers who constantly remind the state – and their institutions such as the labor newspapers and the unions – to uphold the socialist vision and social contract for their rights and entitlements.

Further research is needed on the effectiveness of state-led corporation industrial policy (the Vinatex case) and the Taiwanese small-scale linkage model (not yet developed in the electronics case) to move up the value-added pyramid and to improve workers' conditions. Last but not least, environmental considerations should be included in all industrial policies, especially in the toxic electronics, high-tech industry.

Acknowledgements

We would like to thank the very helpful feedback and comments of the participants in the Chiang Mai Workshop held on 9–10 January 2014. Appreciation also goes to Joe Lubow for the copy-editing assistance.

Notes

1. Towards Gender Budgeting in Vietnam (2005); Reaching for the Dream: Challenges of Sustainable Development in Vietnam (with Tran 2004); Economic Transition in Vietnam: Trade and Aid in the Demise of a Centrally Planned Economy (with Beresford and Đặng 2000); Authority Relations And Economic Decision-Making in Vietnam: An Historical Perspective (with Đặng and Beresford 1998).
2. Council for Mutual Economic Assistance (CMEA) established in 1949 to facilitate economic development of the former Soviet bloc.
3. Examples include: US NASA; Japanese car industry, Korean electronic and shipbuilding industries; Taiwanese electronic and textile industries.
4. Beresford also recognized the element of welfarism: the social welfare function continues to be served by the SOEs. In the same vein, Michael Karadjis argued that SOEs have allowed

workers to play a role in their decision-making process, and thus preventing them from becoming commodities in the post-*Doi Moi* period (Karadjis 2011, p. 47).

5.   Other initiatives have had a direct bearing on the form and extent industralization achieved in Vietnam such as the Grassroots Democracy Decree (1998), but given the scope of this paper, we could not go into detail. Overall, Beresford argued that this decree was potentially good, but uneven implementation (Beresford 2008, p. 240) (Nørlund, Tran, and Nguyen 2003, pp. 64–65).

6.   FDI statistics refer to implemented capital, which is considerably lower than the annually committed capital, but more realistic.

7.   The total export value includes two components: $15.5 billion (FOB value) for apparel export and $1.2 billion for textile export, totaling $16.7 billion (Interview with Mr Nguyen Van Tuan 2013).

8.   Vietnam News Agency, 2 August 2013. The estimated total export value for all sectors in 2013 is about US$133.5 billion (a 16% increase compared to that in 2012) with the USA and the EU being the top two export markets.

9.   In terms of value change in percentage: a steep increase in export of high-tech products such as electronics and computers (doubling from 30% in 2011 to 68% in 2012) and a slight increase in cell phones and accessories (98.4%–98.8%). At the same time, the value change of VTGI export decreased from 25.3% to 7.5% (World Bank, p. 22).

10.   The statistics may be larger if we include women working in the informal sector.

11.   2.700.000 VND/month for zone I; 2.400.000 VND/month for zone II; 2.100.000 VND/month for zone III; 1.900.000 VND/month for zone IV. http://thuvienphapluat.vn/van-ban/Doanh-nghiep/Nghi-dinh-182-2013-ND-CP-muc-luong-toi-thieu-vung-2013-213648.aspx (accessed 14 November 2013).

12.   The TPP member countries include: the USA, Vietnam, Singapore, Peru, New Zealand, Mexico, Malaysia, Japan, Chile, Canada, Brunei, and Australia (Voice of America, 2013).

13.   However, Mr Tuan stopped short of arguing for value-added/backward linkage logic in this forum, and said simply that the VTGI has been carrying out research, focusing on markets, materials, labor, equipment, management and the financial resources of its businesses, to push for the signing of the TPP agreement.

14.   Mạnh Bôn, "Tái cơ cấu DNNN vẫn như "đánh cờ nước một." http://vietstock.vn/2013/12/tai-co-cau-dnnn-van-nhu-danh-co-nuoc-mot-768-325404.htm

15.   Bích Ngọc, "Thoái vốn ngoài ngành: Định giá tài sản sai lệch,vô căn cứ," http://vietstock.vn/2013/12/thoai-von-ngoai-nganh-dinh-gia-tai-san-sai-lechvo-can-cu-768-325526.htm.

16.   Prime Minister Decree 118/2013/NDCP: "About the Organization and Activities of the Vietnamese Textile and Garment Conglomerate," signed on October 9, 2013. http://thuvienphapluat.vn/van-ban/Doanh-nghiep/Nghi-dinh-118-2013-NDCP, accessed 1 October 2013, pp. 2–3.

17.   "Vinatex công bố kết quả SXKD 6 tháng đầu năm 2013," *Vinatex*, 9 July 2013 http://www.vinatex.com/Portal/Detail.aspx?Organization = vinatex&MenuID = 72&ContentID = 9510, accessed 22 December 2013.

18.   Vietnam News Agency (VNA), "TPP agreement to benefit Vietnamese garments, textiles," 2 August 2013. http://en.vietnamplus.vn/Utilities/PrintView.aspx?ID = 37380, accessed December 2013.

19.   Given the scarcity of available statistical data, for now, we have to settle with a second-best analysis by assuming that the value-added based on wage approximates the difference between imports and exports (or *net* export).

20.   This refers to Beresford's use of the term "chaebol" in a more Vietnamese metaphoric way (2008, p. 231), and not in a strict sense as: "large firms that were outcomes of forced mergers between family-owned firms." (Amsden 1989).

21.   The Corporation Group (Vinatex) owns two production units – the Center for Waste Water Treatment and the Hai Phong Veston Factory – and seven units/departments including Textile/Garment Institute, Fashion Institute, Cotton Research and Nha Ho Agricultural Development Institute, Textile/Garment Health Clinic, Textile/Garment and Hanoi Fashion Vocational School, Technical and Economic School in Hochiminh City, and Technical and Economic Vocational School.

22.   There are two types of subsidiaries of Vinatex, ranging from 50%–100% capital owned by Vinatex. There are four limited responsibility companies with 100% legal capital owned by

Vinatex (three of these four are knitting factories). The stronghold on knitting is consistent with Tran's findings that the Vietnamese producers have been able to use 20-30% of Vietnamese knit fabrics in garment manufacturing for export (Tran 2012, p. 129). The other twelve subsidiaries are joint-stock companies with only 50% of their legal capital controlled by Vinatex. This joint-stock type of subsidiary is a mixed group, consisting of textile/garment factories, cotton/fiber companies, service companies such as infrastructure development, investment development, as well as recruitment services for employees to work overseas, and commercial services.

23. In the third group: the two major textile/garment corporations – Phong Phu Textile and Viet Tien Garment – were previously owned by Vinatex. They have been "privatized" and became joint-stock corporations, yet still "linked" to Vinatex. Furthermore, 26 other former large textile and garment SOEs have become independent joint-stock companies—at least on paper – that are also linked to Vinatex. While it remains unclear about the relationship between these 26 joint-stock companies and Vinatex, this newly configured structure suggests how the Vietnamese state struggles, on the one hand, with folding into the neo-liberal requests of further liberalization of the economy (the prevalence of the joint-stock companies), yet on the other hand, still holding on to state-led value-added industrial policy aimed at more equitable economic development and job creation which may be achieved by increasing domestic content used in manufacturing for export.

24. http://tuoitrenews.vn/business/16512/mobile-phone-becomes-vietnams-leading-export, 2 January 2014.

25. http://www.intel.com/content/www/us/en/jobs/locations/vietnam/sites/ho-chi-minh-city.html Set up since 1997, Intel Semiconductor Ltd., the sales and marketing office (at the OEM, developer and end-user levels) in Ho Chi Minh City, built US$1 billion assembly test facility to produce chipsets.

26. http://www.crn.com.au/News/301897,the-worlds-biggest-chip-shop.aspx.

27. http://english.thesaigontimes.vn/Home/business/other/22027/Intel-Expands-Production-In-Vietnam.html.

References

Abbott, Philip, Jeanet Bentzen, and Finn Tarp. 2009. "Trade and Development: Lessons from Vietnam's Past Trade Agreements." *World Development* 37 (2): 341–353.

Abbott, Philip, and Finn Tarp. 2011. *Globalization Crisis, Trade, and Development in Vietnam*, WIDER Working Papers 2011–20, New Directions in Development Economics. Helsinki, Finland: United Nations University. http://www.wider.unu.edu/publications/working-papers/2011/en_GB/wp2011-020/.

Abrami, Regina, and Nolwen Henaff. 2004. "The City and the Countryside: Economy, State and Socialist Legacies in the Vietnamese Labor Market." In *Reaching for the Dream: Challenges of Sustainable Development in Vietnam*, edited by M. Beresford and A. Tran, pp. 95–134. Copenhagen: Nordic Institute for Asian Studies Press.

Amsden, Alice. 1989. *Asia's Next Giant: South Korea and Late Industrialization*. New York: Oxford University Press.

Beresford, Melanie. 1988. *Vietnam: Politics, Economics and Society.* London: Pinter Publishers.

Beresford, Melanie 1995. "Interpretations of the Vietnamese Economic Reforms 1979-85." In *Researching the Vietnamese Economic Reforms: 1979-86*. Australian-Vietnam Research Project Monograph series #1, January 1995, 1–16. Sydney: Macquarie University.

Beresford, Melanie and Angie Ngoc Tran. eds. 2004. *Reaching for the Dream: Challenges of Sustainable Development in Vietnam*. Copenhagen: Nordic Institute of Asian Studies.

Beresford, Melanie. 2008. "Doi Moi in Review: The Challenges of Building Market Socialism in Vietnam." *Journal of Contemporary Asia* 38 (2): 221–243.

Beresford, Melanie, and Phong Đặng. 2000. *Economic Transition in Vietnam: Trade and Aid in the Demise of a Centrally Planned Economy*. Cheltenham: Edward Elgar.

Bích Ngọc. "Thoái vốn ngoài ngành: Định giá tài sản sai lệch, vô căn cứ." *Đất Việt newspaper*. Accessed August 2013. http://vietstock.vn/2013/12/thoai-von-ngoai-nganh-dinh-gia-tai-san-sai-lechvo-can-cu-768-325526.htm.

Boudreau, John. 2014. "Intel's Vietnam Success Begins With Building Paper Towers." *Bloomberg News* 15 January 2014. Accessed March 25. http://www.bloomberg.com/news/print/2014-01-14/intel-s-vietnam-success-begins-with-building-paper-towers.html.

Đặng, Phong, and Melanie Beresford. 1998. *Authority Relations and Economic Decision-Making in Vietnam: An Historical Perspective*. Copenhagen: Nordic Institute for Asian Studies Press.

Forbes (CORPORATE AUTHOR). 2014, "Intel Integrates Backward To Improve Vietnamese Education, Society." http://www.forbes.com/sites/michaelhorn/2014/03/04/intel-integrates-backward-to-improve-vietnamese-education-society/.

Fforde, Adam. 2013. "From 'Constructing Socialism' to 'doing Development': Growth and its Meaning in Contemporary Vietnam." Paper to the 5th International ADI Conference, Asian Dynamic Initiative, June 13–14. Copenhagen, Denmark: University of Copenhagen.

Fforde, Adam, and Stefan de Vylder. 1996. *From Plan to Market: The Economic Transition in Vietnam*. Boulder, Colorado: Westview Press.

GSO (General Statistics Office). 2006. *Statistical Yearbook of Vietnam 2005*. Hanoi: Statistical Publishing House.

GSO (General Statistics Office). 2010. *Statistical Yearbook of Vietnam 2009*. Hanoi: Statistical Publishing House.

GSO (General Statistics Office). 2012. *Report on the 2011 Vietnam Labor Force Survey*. Hanoi: Ministry of Planning and Investment.

Giesecke, J.A., N.H. Tran, G.A. Meagher, and F. Pang. April 2011. *Growth and Change in the Vietnamese Labor Market: A Decomposition of Forecast Trends in Employment over 2010-2020*. Melbourne, Australia: Centre of Policy Studies, Monash University.

Interview with Mr. Nguyen Van Tuan. July 2013. Vice General Secretary of Vietnam Textile and Apparel Association – VITAS, and director of the Vietnamese Cotton Association.

Karadjis, Michael. 2011. "State Enterprise Workers: 'Masters' or 'Commodities'?" In *Vietnam Update Series: Labour in Vietnam*, edited by A Chan, 46–90. Singapore: Institute of Southeast Asian Studies.

Nørlund, Irene. 1994. "Textile Production in Vietnam 1880-1940 Handicraft and Industry in a Colonial Economy." PhD diss., University of Copenhagen.

Nørlund, I. 1996. "Democracy and Trade Unions in Vietnam." *The Copenhagen Journal of Asian Studies* 11: 73–99.

Nørlund, Irene, Dang Ngoc Dinh, Bach Tan Sinh, Chu Dung, Dang Ngoc Quang, Do Bich Diem, Nguyen Manh Cuong, Tang The Cuong, Vu Chi Mai. 2006. *The Emerging Civil Society. An Initial Assessment of Civil Society in Vietnam*. Hanoi: CIVICUS.

Nørlund, Irene, Tran Ngoc Ca, and Nguyen Dinh Tuyen. 2003. *Dealing with the Donors: The Politics of Vietnam's Comprehensive Poverty Reduction and Growth Strategy*. Policy Papers, Institute of Development Studies, University of Helsinki, Helsinki, Finland, 4/2003.

Ohno, Kenichi. 2009. "Avoiding the Middle-Income Trap: Renovating Industrial Policy Formulation in Vietnam." *ASEAN Economic Bulletin* 26 (1), 25–43.

Pierre, Gaëlle. May 2012. *Recent Labor Market Performance in Vietnam Through a Gender Lens*. Policy Research Working Paper 6056 The World Bank, East Asia and Pacific Region, Poverty Reduction and Economic Management Unit & Human Development Unit, Washington, DC.

Platzer, Michaela D. 2013. "U.S. Textile Manufacturing and the Trans-Pacific Partnership Negotiations." Congressional Research Service. November 20, 2013. Accessed March 2014. http://fas.org/sgp/crs/row/R42772.pdf.

Rasiah, Rajah. 2007. "The Systemic Quad: Technological Capabilities and Economic Performance of Computer and Component Firms in Penang and Johor, Malaysia." *International Journal of Technological Learning, Innovation and Development* 1 (2): 179–203.

Reinert, Eric. 2007. *How Rich Countries Got Rich . . . and Why Poor Countries Stay Poor.* London: Constable.

Saarinen, Juha. 2012. "The World's Biggest Chip Shop." CRN Magazine, May 23. http://www.crn.com.au/News/301897,the-worlds-biggest-chip-shop.aspx.

Sengenberger, Werner, and Frank Pyke. 1990. "Small firm industrial districts and local economic regeneration: Research and policy issues." ILO Working Paper no. 1, International Conference on Industrial Districts and Local Economic Regeneration, Geneva, Switzerland, October 18 and 19. http://www.ilo.org/public/libdoc/ilo/1990/Q5390B09_302_engl.pdf.

Tran, Angie Ngoc. 1996. "An Analysis of the Developmental State: The Case of the Vietnamese Textile and Garment Industries." PhD diss. University of Southern California.

Tran, Angie Ngoc. 2004. "Linking Growth with Equity? The Vietnamese Textile and Garment Industries since Doi Moi." In *Reaching for the Dream: Challenges of Sustainable Development in Vietnam*, edited by Melanie Beresford and Angie Ngoc Tran, 235–182. Copenhagen: Nordic Institute of Asian Studies.

Tran, Angie Ngoc. 2007a. "Alternatives to the "Race to the Bottom" in Vietnam: Minimum Wage Strikes and Their Aftermath." *Labor Studies Journal* 32 (4): 430–451.

Tran, Angie Ngoc. 2007b. "The Third Sleeve: Emerging Labor Newspapers and the Response of Labor Unions and the State to Workers' Resistance in Vietnam." *Labor Studies Journal* 32 (3): 257–279.

Tran, Angie Ngoc. 2011. "The Vietnam Case: Workers Versus the Global Supply Chain." *Harvard International Review* 33.2 (Summer 2011): 123–150. http://library2.csumb.edu:2048/login?url=http://go.galegroup.com.library2.csumb.edu:2048/ps/i.do?&id=GALE%7CA261641040&v=2.1&u=csumb _main&it=r&p=AONE&sw=w.

Tran, Angie Ngoc. 2012. "Vietnamese Textile and Garment Industry in the Global Supply Chain: State Strategies and Workers' Responses," *International Journal of Institutions and Economies* 4 (3): 123–150.

Tran, Angie Ngoc. 2013. *Ties That Bind: Cultural Identity, Class and Law in Flexible Labor Resistance in Vietnam.* Ithaca, NY: Southeast Asia Program (SEAP), Cornell University Press.

Van Tuan, Nguyen. The Vice General Secretary of Vietnam Textile and Apparel Association, VITAS (Interviews in July 2013 and January 2014).

Vo, Tri Thanh, and Anh Duong Nguyen. 2009. "Vietnam after Two Years of WTO Accession: What Lessons Can Be Learnt?" *ASEAN Economic Bulletin* 26 (1): 115–135.

Viet Nam Household Living Standards Survey. 2012. Hanoi: General Statistics Office of Vietnam. Accessed December 2013. http://www.gso.gov.vn/default_en.aspx?tabid=483&idmid=4&ItemID=14844.

Vietnam News Agency (VNA). "TPP Agreement to Benefit Vietnamese Garments, Textiles." August 02, 2013. Accessed December 2013. http://en.vietnamplus.vn/Utilities/PrintView.aspx?ID=37380.

Vinatex. "Vinatex công bố kết quả SXKD 6 tháng đầu năm 2013." July 9, 2013. Accessed December 22. http://www.vinatex.com/Portal/Detail.aspx?Organization=vinatex&MenuID=72&ContentID=9510.

Vind, Ingeborg. 2008. "Transnational Companies as a Source of Skill Upgrading: The Electronics Industry in Ho Chi Minh City." *Geoforum* 39 (2008): 1480–1493.

Voice of America. 2013. "Hiệp định thương mại TPP có thể đạt được vào đầu năm 2014." December 11, 2013. Accessed December 22. http://www.voatiengviet.com/content/co-the-dat-hiep-dinh-thuong-mai-tpp-vao-dau-nam-toi/1808126.html.

Wade, Robert. 2003. *Governing the Market: Economic Theory and the Role of Government in East Asian Industrialization.* Princeton, NJ: Princeton University Press.

World Bank. 2013. *Taking Stock: An Update on Vietnam's Recent Economic Developments.* Hanoi: The World Bank.

Index

Page numbers in *italics* refer to figures. Page numbers in **bold** refer to tables.

Action Plan for Industrial Technology Development (APITD) 78, 83
agriculture share in economy *46*
Aquino, Corazon C. 114
Asian Development Bank (ADB) 111, 112
Asian Financial Crisis (AFC): China 18, 31; Indonesia 57–8, 60–1, 65; Thailand 130, 136, 138; Vietnam 146, 150
Asian Regional Team for Employment (ARTEP) 116–17
Asset Privatization Trust 114
Association of Southeast Asian Nations (ASEAN) 144
Australia 94–5
automotive deregulation 60

banana republics 5, 79
Beresford, Melanie 143–4
Berlin wall 4
Bhutan 4, 6
Bilateral Trade Agreement 145
birth rates in China 28, *28*
Board of Investment (BOI; Thailand) 136
Bolshevik revolution 4
broad-based economic expansion 52
Bureau of Labor and Employment Statistics (BLES; Philippines) 113

Cabinet Committee on Privatization 114
call center-business process outsourcing (CC-BPO) 111, 116, 126
Cambodia: introduction 3, 4; labour-intensive manufacturing 31; low-income groups in 6; Vietnam's withdrawal from 145; vulnerable migrant workers from 136, 137
capitalism: crony capitalism 52; in India 55; industrial capitalism 3–4, 7, 104, 109; socialism *vs.* 143
cascading effect 58
caste inequalities **53**, 53–5
China: birth rates 28, *28*; female labour 34–9, **35, 36,** *37, 38,* **39**; foreign direct investment

17, 17–22, *20,* **20–1,** *21–2*; GDP and *16,* 16–17; globalization 15, 18, 25, 28, 31, 38–9; industrialization 22–5, *24, 25,* 28, 119; introduction 14–15; labour markets 25–32, **26–7,** *28,* **29,** *30, 31, 32*; provincial trade *19*; rapid growth 3; supply-demand analysis 25–31, **26–7,** *30, 31*; trade and investment flows 15–22; trade growth 15–17, *16,* **17**; unemployment 29–30, *31*; uneven distribution of labour *31,* 31–2, *32*; wages 32–4, *33*
Codes of Conduct (CoC) 104
collective bargaining agreement (CBA) 126
communism 4
communist economic bloc (CMEA) 144
Communist Party 34
crony capitalism 52
Cuaderno, Miguel 113
cutting/making/trimming (CMT) jobs 155

Dalit groups **53**, 53–5
deindustrialization: Malaysia 10, 77–9, 84, 86, 93, 95–6; manufacturing and 4, 8; Philippines **115,** 115–21
Democratic Republic of Vietnam (DRV) 144
Deng Xiaoping 15, 18
Denmark 6, 7
Department of Labor and Employment (DOLE; Philippines) 111, 122
Department of Trade and Industry (DTI; Philippines) 111–12
deregulation: automotive deregulation 60; of economic sectors 114; financial deregulation 42, 59; outcome of 53
Doi Moi (renovation) process 143, 144, 147, 150
Doing Business Survey (2008) 61
downstream industries 58, 119

economic growth and development 2–5, 100
egalitarian economic expansion 52
electoral politics 6, 7

165